Terminus

TERMINUS

Westward Expansion, China, and the
End of American Empire

Stuart Rollo

Johns Hopkins University Press
Baltimore

Johns Hopkins University Press
2715 North Charles Street
Baltimore, Maryland 21218
www.press.jhu.edu

Library of Congress Cataloging-in-Publication Data

Names: Rollo, Stuart, 1987– author.
Title: Terminus : westward expansion, China, and the end of American
empire / Stuart Rollo.
Description: Baltimore : Johns Hopkins University Press, 2023. |
Includes bibliographical references and index.
Identifiers: LCCN 2022059601 | ISBN 9781421447384 (hardcover) |
ISBN 9781421447391 (ebook)
Subjects: LCSH: United States—Foreign relations—China. | China—
Foreign relations—United States. | United States—Territorial expansion. |
Hegemony. | BISAC: HISTORY / United States / 20th Century |
POLITICAL SCIENCE / International Relations / General
Classification: LCC E183.8.C5 R564 2023 | DDC 327.73051—dc23
LC record available at https://lccn.loc.gov/2022059601

A catalog record for this book is available from the British Library.

Frontispiece: Broken Column, linocut, 2022. Courtesy of David Wells.

*Special discounts are available for bulk purchases of this book. For more
information, please contact Special Sales at specialsales@jh.edu.*

CONTENTS

ACKNOWLEDGMENTS

I wish to extend my warmest and most sincere thanks to Professor John Keane for his guidance, support, and friendship through all phases of the composition of this book. The conversations that I had with John over the course of several years of research and writing were one of the great pleasures of undertaking this work. The value of his thoughtful and enlightening reflections on my work, and the inspiration I took from his own scholarship, cannot be overstated.

Professor Roy MacLeod gave me some of my earliest and most formative instruction on the relationship between empire and resources, and the necessity of a deep historical foundation for understanding the present, and he was kind enough to read and comment on an early draft of this book. My work and collaborations with Professors Tess Lea, Ian Tyrrell, and James Der Derian instilled in me an appreciation for the value of crossing disciplinary boundaries, taking transnational and critical perspectives, and writing with a vigor that I hope is reflected somewhat in the pages that follow.

My peer reviewers from around the world have provided me with encouragement and constructive criticism at both the point of completion of the doctoral thesis upon which this book was built and at the stage of commissioning by the publisher, which have strengthened my work, and for which I am greatly appreciative.

Eva Shteinman and Eda Gunaydin kindly read, edited, and commented on various parts of this work and, along with Darius Sepehri and Seamus Barker, were some of my dearest friends and most frequent discussants of many of the themes that the book deals with over the time I was writing it. Vukasin Vujasinovic hosted me and provided excellent and memorable companionship on a bicoastal research trip to the United States. Other family, friends, and fellow faculty members at the University of Sydney who enlivened me with their conversation and friendship throughout the length of this writing project are too many to name, but I thank you all.

I would also like to thank George Lucas, my literary agent, as well as Laura Davulis and the rest of the editorial team at Johns Hopkins University Press, without whom this book would still be a manuscript.

Finally, I would like to thank all the scholars, living and departed, whose work I had the pleasure of immersing myself in during the composition of this book. The great privilege of scholarship lies in the time one is able to spend sitting with so much accumulated knowledge and wisdom. It is a humbling experience.

Terminus

Introduction

The shifting balance of power between the United States and China is the most pressing issue in world politics today. The world order is in a period of flux due to structural changes in global economic, political, technological, and military affairs. This state of affairs is, in some ways, a new iteration of the timeless story of the dynamics between declining and rising empires, one told repeatedly in the Western tradition since at least the time of Thucydides. Relying on such a sweeping overview, however, misses the economic, political, and geostrategic context that makes this situation so uniquely perilous for the world. The consequences arising from a possible war between the two states are profound. Open conflict between the two nuclear-armed superpowers, regardless of the intensity, would at the very least lead to a toxic and precarious international security environment for years to come and, at worst, result in the mass death and destruction that has characterized wars of hegemonic competition in the past. A new cold war, with the world divided into rival camps, would see an intensified arms race, proxy wars, perilous competition for markets and natural resources throughout the global periphery and in the bleeding zones between the two blocs, and the constant threat of degeneration into full-scale armed struggle. Avoiding such a future is the principal task of those concerned with issues of international security today.

This task cannot be completed through a simple tallying of strategic assets or a calculation of economic figures applied to the rival national powers of the United States and China. The United States has been the far more influential party in shaping this dynamic. From the earliest days of its existence as a republic, the United States has been engaged in near constant imperial expansion. First westward, traversing continental North America, then on across the Pacific into Asia, and finally as the founder of a globe-spanning liberal institutional order that sought to enshrine US-style capitalism and democracy as the standards of international affairs after the Second World War. Today, as China rises and reshapes the economic and geostrategic substructures of world power, it is becoming clear that American empire has already reached its limits.

This book was not written as a comprehensive study of American empire in totality, which would necessarily incorporate extensive investigations of the cultural, religious, and ideological interplay between the United States and other nations and people across six continents. Such a study would also require close attention to the personalities and priorities of particular American political leaders, their relationships with foreign leadership, and even the considerable role that chance and indeterminacy have played in the progression of American history. Rather, this book was written with the more specific purpose of undertaking a deep historical and structural investigation of important, unique, and often underappreciated facets of American empire: its westward expansion into the Asia-Pacific region, its interaction there with China, and the economic and geostrategic structures that underlie this dynamic. Major American and world historical events are consciously viewed and analyzed here through the lens of the US-China relationship.

The historical account is then used to inform a discussion of the signs of contemporary American imperial decline: military overstretch, interventionist follies, the ravages of neoliberal economics, and the intensifying manifestations of domestic social and cultural schisms as the frontier of American expansionism meets its limits. American decline is contrasted with China's rise, with a commentary on the sources of Chinese strength and on the early stages of the Chinese imperial outflanking of the United States in key economic and strategic areas. Understanding the historical process of the westward spread of American empire, and its economic and geostrategic underpinnings, is a necessary endeavor to inform discussion on the most important dynamic in global politics today: the US-China relationship.

Many contemporary writers on international relations and American foreign policy place singular emphasis on the dynamics between the United States and China, and many historians have already identified the role of market expansion and the pursuit of the "Open Door" in propelling American empire. However, a detailed explication of the place of China in American imperial destiny that grasps the relevant economic and geostrategic dynamics from the origins of America's imperial spread until today has not yet been published. This is the story told in this book. It traces the historical progression of US-China relations and interrogates China's position as the terminus of American empire: first as the envisioned economic prize at the endpoint of westward expansion and crowning imperial jewel; then as the major thorn in the side of American imperial management of the Cold War in Asia; and today, as the single superpower challenger to American imperial might. The ancient Romans revered the god Terminus for his protection of inviolable boundary markers; recognizing and respecting such boundaries was thought to bring peace and justice, their transgression violence and strife.[1] The degree to which the United States understands the limits of its own power, and mutually establishes and respects geopolitical boundaries with China, will be the major determinant of prospects for peace between the two superpowers in coming decades.

While the desire for national security, the spread of Christianity, and the cultural and political impulses generated by ideologies like manifest destiny and American exceptionalism have been considerable factors in the historical progression of American expansion, the pursuit of resources, prosperity, and access to foreign markets for trade and investment has been the primary driver. China, traditionally the largest economy in the world, has been the lodestar toward which American market-oriented expansionism has been directed for much of its history. The pursuit of a guaranteed "Open Door" to the China market, first enshrined by US Secretary of State John Hay in 1899, came to characterize the American approach to world affairs and the management of its foreign policy objectives in general. Ensuring constantly renewed access to new markets, new supplies of raw materials, and new opportunities for American investment and entrepreneurialism provided the basis for rapid and persistent economic growth, the improvement of the American standard of living, the maintenance of social stability, and the nurturing of the democratic qualities of American political institutions.[2]

The post-1945 American vision of global empire was to secure this model in perpetuity, and, according to liberal theorists, provide prosperity, stability, and democracy to the rest of the world as it was reshaped in America's image. Although never truly global in the sense of fully unfettered influence over world affairs, American empire was pan-continental, constantly seeking opportunities for further expansion, and almost limitless in its ambition for reshaping and reordering the world's political and economic systems. In the early years of this system's establishment, the United States enjoyed a historically unprecedented preponderance of economic and military power. By harnessing this power, the United States was initially largely successful in securing its primary imperial objectives in key geostrategic regions. In Asia, China played the pivotal role in American Cold War geopolitical calculations: first, as the major platform from which it was feared that expansionist communism would spread to Southeast Asia and destabilize the regional economy, centered around Japan, that the United States was then fostering; and later, as a crucial partner in balancing Soviet power in the region.

Subsequent decades delivered more volatility within the imperial model. Over the course of the Cold War, American empire faced power fluctuations, strategic setbacks, and economic restructuring, only to emerge victorious after the collapse of the Soviet Union. The post–Cold War era of the unipolar moment was characterized by American triumphalism, a new wave of institutional, economic, and military expansionism, and ultimately political hubris and imperial overstretch.

Today, after centuries of westward expansion and 75 years at the apex of global power, American empire is facing a potentially terminal challenge as China reclaims its historical place at the center of the international economy. China has now replaced the United States as the world's largest economy by purchasing power parity, as the world's largest manufacturer, as the world's largest trading nation, and as the world's largest financial creditor. It is constructing a new international framework of energy, transport, and logistics infrastructure, funded by Chinese and international capital, which is already reshaping global trade flows and the supply and distribution of raw materials. The United States is dramatically refashioning its approaches to international economic and strategic policy in response. A US-initiated attempt to decouple the American and Chinese economies is under way, with a particular focus on the high-tech digital communications and military-industrial sectors upon which the twenty-first-century global economy will be based. The United States seeks to establish supply chains, from mineral sourcing and refinement, through research and development, to industrial production and distribution, which operate independently from China.

In the twilight of empire, the United States faces choices of the upmost importance. There are several paths that can be taken in the face of China's structural challenge to US global supremacy. One involves an attempt at managing the reinvigoration of liberal empire. Under this scenario, the United States would continue supporting a rules-based international political, economic, and military order that secures the interests of the United States and its allies, with itself firmly at the helm, in coordination with, and with the support of, many of the world's other powerful states. This was the policy of the Obama administration and is being renewed under President Joe Biden. For structural economic and geopolitical reasons that will be explored in the final section of the book, it is almost certainly unviable.

Another path would see the ongoing degeneration of American empire into a fully fledged exploitative hegemony. This would involve the continued transition of American empire into a combined political, economic, and military system that decreasingly pays even lip-service to the ideals of an institutionalized Pax Americana. Instead the United States would strike out on its own, relying on its military superiority and coercive influence to monopolize as much of the world's resources as possible for an ever-shrinking group of beneficiaries in elite corporate and political positions, both domestically and within partner nations. This was the path along which the Trump administration propelled the American colossus.

A third path would involve the purposeful and considered dismantling of American empire, and the founding of a post-imperial American political, economic, and social order. This would require profound change in American domestic politics and foreign policy, catalyzed by the current reshaping of the economic conditions within the United States and its relationship to international systems of production, trade, and investment. It would be achieved through the formation of a broad-based political movement against American hegemony and for the socio-temporal reorganization of American political economy in such a way that prosperity, security, and social stability can be achieved without the necessity for constant market and strategic expansionism. Such a movement away from empire would see America's role on the world stage transition into one that seeks to anchor international cooperation on pressing issues of peace and survival like clean energy agreements, arms control, and sustainable and equitable international economic development.

The configuration of world order is certainly changing. How the United States responds to these changes, through a wiser and more humble approach to securing domestic well-being and international cooperation or through a self-serving and antagonistic "America first" exploitative hegemony, will be the decisive factor for the prospects for global peace as these shifts occur.

These pressing issues of imperial destiny are deeply enmeshed with the geostrategic architecture of the Asia-Pacific region. The Asia-Pacific will be the major arena within which the prospects for superpower peace will be determined in coming years. The strategic features of the geographical space where the United States and China most directly meet today is a legacy of the high-water mark of American empire. It is centered around three island chains of US allies and territory to China's east, extending from Japan, Taiwan, and the Philippines to Guam and the Marianas, to Singapore and Australia, and finally to Hawaii. Organized in the aftermath of the Second World War, they form the geographical basis of US military strategy in the region.

This security architecture has, in turn, determined China's own geostrategic vision of the region: an imperative to break through the first chain by militarizing the islands and reefs of the South China Sea and claiming exclusive access to their surrounding maritime environment within the nine-dash line. The ultimate goal is to push the American forces farther east and away from China's coastal territory and its vital trade and energy supply corridors. It is this strategic environment that has shaped China's pursuit of anti-access / area denial military arsenals, and the subsequent US adoption of the AirSea Battle, and later the Joint Concept for Access and Maneuver in the Global Commons doctrine, to secure continued dominance.

American and Chinese strategic objectives in the Western Pacific are mutually conflictual by design. They are, in their current form, doomed to exacerbate rather than deter conflict. The rapidly increasing militarization of the region has produced a system of highly calibrated offensive capabilities poised toward one another, a plethora of trip wires that could lead to military confrontation, and an opaque approach to conflict escalation and de-escalation on both sides. A new strategic compact between the two superpowers, one that is more resistant to the frictions and pressures that can trigger war, is urgently needed.

The principles upon which a more transparent and stable regional military balance can be constructed are complex. Contrary to the neorealist understanding of security dynamics, a historical investigation of American security policy in the Asia-Pacific region demonstrates that its purpose has never merely been to maximize American power relative to other regional states.[3] Rather, its origins and function are deeply enmeshed within, and indeed pivotal to, the empire-building program of the United States. Thus, any program for changing the security architecture must account for how it impacts and is shaped by broader American imperial interests.

Achieving regional peace and stability therefore involves fundamental questions of world order: What are American imperial interests in East Asia? How are they supported and promoted by the regional security architecture? As China's wealth and power increase relative to the United States, can the empire handle decline and reshape itself and the world order peacefully? Articulating responses to these questions is particularly pressing given the growing disjuncture between American regional leadership in military affairs and Chinese leadership in regional trade, investment, and institution building.

♟ ♟ ♟

This book is purposefully heterodox in its methodological and epistemological approach. It is a contribution to finding a language to help us rethink the origins, growth, and decline of American empire. The category of empire is retrieved and reconstructed. Both liberal and Marxist theories of imperialism are drawn upon and critiqued. A revisionist historical approach, drawing on the work of Charles Beard, William Appleman-Williams, Walter LaFeber, and others, is used to explain the development of a market-expansion-oriented American empire in Asia, with an emphasis on the relationship between the formation of dominant sectional interests within the US polity and the structure of world order. The book incorporates neoclassical realist and Marxist critiques of American empire, as well as realist approaches to geostrategic power balancing, restraint, and the avoidance of great power war. It shows how liberalism suffuses the history of American empire and has formed its major ideological basis of support.

The book should be viewed in part as a reaction to the separation of history and political economy from many contemporary accounts of strategy in international relations. American empire is a vast construct with myriad economic, strategic, political, and cultural components. The history behind this empire matters. The emphasis on history underscores the contingency of American power on economic and geostrategic factors that change over time. Amnesiacs in policy planning view the power structures that exist today as being of a category distinct from those of the past, and as a result these planners often overestimate the structures' permanence. Those that remain ignorant of the past invariably misunderstand the present and cannot conceive accurately of, or appropriately plan for, the future.

♟ ♟ ♟

The question of whether the United States is in fact an empire should be settled from the outset. John Darwin describes imperialism as "the attempt to impose one state's predominance over other societies by assimilating them to its political, cultural and economic system."[4] Proceeding from this simple and elegant definition, the United States is certainly imperial. Indeed it is an empire with a more globally dispersed and powerful military, a larger and more internationally networked economic and financial system, and a wider array of political institutions and diplomatic arrangements than any other empire in history.

Like all other imperial powers, the United States has legitimized and understated its imperial position at various times through various methods. That it was a democratic "empire of liberty," that it was anti-colonialist, and that it sought to create a liberal system of markets and political institutions that would spread stability and peace were all, at various points, justifications for its so-named exceptionalism. The reality has been that forces within the United States assiduously worked toward crafting an economic, political, and strategic world system with the United States at the apex, from which it enjoyed unprecedented levels of wealth accumulation and military power. Since the launching of the Global War on Terror in particular, there has been a notable increase in scholarship spanning the political spectrum, from Marxist, liberal, realist, and conservative authors, investigating the pernicious consequences of American empire.[5] At the same time, many scholars and commentators have stepped forward to sing its praises.[6] Among historians, the debate has long shifted from a question of American empire's existence to one of its relative value to the world.

This was not always the case. The belief that the modern, capitalist United States could not by definition be imperialistic because of its incongruity with the great premodern empires of world history was, during a critical period for the theorization of imperialism in the early twentieth century, surprisingly widespread. Joseph Schumpeter, an eminent professor of economics at Harvard University, viewed modern imperialism as an anachronism springing from the autocratic heritage of precapitalist Western society, which would not have emerged independently from the logic of capitalism itself.[7] He argued that economic expansionism, while often relevant, is not the sole driving force of imperialism. Rather, imperialism is a result of a deep and latent drive in human psychology and social structures, similar to the linkages described by realists like Thomas Hobbes on the origins of international conflict within human nature. Schumpeter called it "an atavism in the social structure, in individual, physiological habits of emotional reaction."[8]

This understanding of imperialism does not fit with the history or structure of modern empires, American included. Schumpeter defined imperialism very strictly as "objectless," stating that "no one calls it imperialism when a state, no matter how brutally and vigorously, pursues concrete interests of its own; and when it can be expected to abandon its aggressive attitude as soon as it has attained what it was after."[9] According to Schumpeter, imperialism was expansion for expansion's sake. By definition, imperialism could not then occur for the sake of economic benefit of certain classes or interests. He reached back to ancient Egyptian and Persian expansionism and the spread of Islam to support his definition of true "objectless" imperialism, while dismissing the self-defined British and French empires of modernity. Where imperialism was found in the twentieth century, it was but a throwback to the precapitalistic modes of social organization that were themselves inherently warlike.

Schumpeter believed that with the passage into the "rational" system of modern capitalism, "cases of imperialism should decline in intensity."[10] "A purely capitalist world . . . can offer no fertile soil to imperialist impulses" because of the type of entrepreneurial person that is produced by such a system.[11] The capitalist man was rational, unwarlike, individualistic, and would be fundamentally opposed to "war, expansion, cabinet diplomacy, armaments, and socially entrenched professional armies."[12] Because of its historical breakage with Europe, Schumpeter believed that, of the capitalist countries, the United States was the least likely to exhibit imperialist tendencies.

In arguing for the peaceful nature of the United States, Schumpeter stated that over the course of the nineteenth century, despite many opportunities, the nation demonstrated an aversion to war.[13] He raised the continued existence of an independent Mexico as an example against American imperialism, without acknowledging that in the preceding century of American "peace" the United States forcibly annexed around half of the territory of Mexico at the conclusion of a war of aggression, conquered the territories of dozens of Native American nations, and absorbed the colonial domain of the decaying Spanish empire.

Schumpeter's argument that imperialism, where it does occur, is an autocratic hangover rather than something that would have evolved through the "inner logic" of capitalism itself is historically false.[14] We will see in the discussion of American history that follows in this book that this is a near inversion of historical reality. Over the course of the nineteenth century, what began as a relatively under-armed United States was propelled toward empire by willful expansionist policies spearheaded by Schumpeterian entrepreneurs lobbying for the expansion of state security and diplomacy as their commercial interests waxed westward.

Other approaches to understanding imperialism that emerged in the early twentieth century provide more coherent theoretical frameworks that align more closely with the historical realities of American imperial development. In stark contrast to Schumpeter, J. A. Hobson, perhaps the most prominent liberal theorist of imperialism, viewed empire as the warped outgrowth of capitalist sectional interest in foreign investment and failed democratic institutions. He described this process succinctly: "The economic root of Imperialism is the desire of strong organized industrial and financial interests to secure and develop at the public expense and by the public force private markets for their surplus goods and their surplus capital. War, militarism, and a 'spirited foreign policy' are the necessary means to this end."[15]

Hobson viewed empire as a "perversion" of nationalism on the road to internationalism. The failings of liberal democracy were at the core of this perversion, rather than the rationality of the system of capitalism itself. The state is captured by sectional economic interests, particularly financial, and redistributive policies that would allow for the domestic market to consume the growing output of industrialized society are not implemented. As a result, expansionist policies are pursued to capture export markets for certain industries and investment opportunities for finance, and a large and influential military-industrial complex is produced.

Hobson demonstrated that it was investment income, rather than trade income, that was the main economic engine of imperialism.[16] He argued that imperialism was bad for business as a whole, in that "at enormous expense it has procured a small, bad, unsafe increase of markets, and has jeopardized the entire wealth of the nation in rousing the strong resentment of other nations," but that it was adopted as state policy as a result "of certain sectional interests that usurp control of the national resources and use them for their private gain."[17] An "intelligent laissez-fair democracy which gave duly proportionate weight in its policy to all economic interests alike" would soon abandon imperialism, but a democracy dominated by corrupting financial and sectional interests was bound to pursue it.[18]

Marxist-Leninist theories of empire observed the same phenomenon of the ascendance of finance capitalism; but these theories viewed it not as the cabalistic corruption of liberal democracy but as a necessary result of the process of monopolistic capital accumulation, the relentless search for higher profits, the necessity of colonial expansion in the face of competition for resources and markets from rival capitalist powers, and the precursor to socialist revolution. Lenin believed that "colonial possession alone gives complete guarantee of success to the monopolies against all the risks of the struggle with competitors, including the risk that the latter will defend themselves by means of a law establishing a state monopoly. The more capitalism is developed, the more the need for raw materials is felt, the more bitter competition becomes, and the more feverishly the hunt for raw materials proceeds throughout the whole world, the more desperate becomes the struggle for the acquisition of colonies."[19]

The Leninist understanding of empire drew heavily from Hobson, the difference being that Lenin viewed imperialism as the highest stage of capitalism, rather than one of its possible historical evolutions. The key development of imperialism according to Lenin lay in the fusion of industrial and financial monopolies behind the protection of tariff barriers in developed capitalist states. These centralized monopolies become entwined with the economic and political institutions of society and push for imperial expansion to secure raw materials, markets, and, most importantly, outlets for capital investment as the rate of return in the developed industrial home economy falls. Another historical-material development had only just begun to be felt at the time of Lenin's publication of *Imperialism* in 1917: the emergence of a much more diversified pool of strategic raw materials as fundamental to industrial production and national security. These resources, essential for the production of modern manufactures and armaments, were often geologically concentrated in very few areas on the planet. Their integral role in modern industrial production added another layer to the relationship between geopolitics and empire-building.

More recently, David Harvey has added further layers of context in his analysis of capitalist imperialism. He describes the process of recurrent crises of overaccumulation and concentration of capital which receives diminishing prospects of profit in a saturated domestic economy of limited spatial and temporal dimensions.[20] Imperialism is described by Harvey as the "spatial fix" to this problem, whereby capital is exported as investment to the virgin fields of less market-developed regions of the world.[21] The pursuit of this economic practice is dependent on the mobilization of the state's military capacity to guarantee the security of these investments and to break down any local resistance to the disruption of local economies. The imperial spatial fix, Harvey argues, is preferred by ruling elites to a "temporal fix," which would involve redistribution, social reforms, and an enhanced role of the state in managing the domestic economy.[22]

Like Schumpeter, Lenin's theory of empire also runs into counterfactual examples from American history. The propulsion of westward empire before the introduction of monopoly capitalism, with strong continuities with American foreign policy afterward, challenges the qualitatively unique position Lenin gives to finance capitalism in imperialism. The clear differentiation in economic interests that led to the Civil War is another area in which the dependency on finance capital of the imperial project becomes questionable. Despite going to war to resist the sort of protectionist barriers that Lenin viewed as an essential aspect of the formation of imperialism, the Southern states were as expansionist as their Northern neighbors, sometimes, as in the case with the annexation of Texas and the Mexican-American War, notably more so. Southern imperialism was comparable in its advocacy for territorial expansion, the prizing open of the China market, and the creation of a strong navy, but from a different political-economic viewpoint to that of the North, which more closely aligns with Lenin's description of capitalist-imperialist development.

The historical work of William Appleman Williams bears this out. In *The Roots of Modern American Empire*, Williams demonstrated that the major force behind American expansionism was, in its origins, organized agricultural, rather than industrial or financial, interests. Williams saw the internal political and economic dynamics of American capitalism as ultimately directing imperialist expansion. The functioning of American democracy is important here. The American demos was predominantly rural and engaged in agriculture well into the twentieth century. The agrarian (Democratic) party held power extensively, both before and after the Civil War, and was engaged in aggressive imperialism, as was the party of industry and finance (Whig and later Republican). While Williams acknowledged that industrial and financial interests came to dominate the American political and economic system, the path to imperialism was paved by agriculturalists, who embraced economic expansionism as a means to increase export profits and to further their own sectional position in American politics.[23] Further to their economic and political pressure for expansion, Southern agriculturalists and slave-holders were instrumental in the development of a large standing navy, the primary military tool of westward market penetration, and the ideological linking of American empire with freedom and democracy.

Hobson's thoughts on the future of China, published over a century ago, are particularly illuminating today. He viewed China as the grand prize of global empire, so rich that, if opened, it could absorb surplus Western capital and enterprise for generations. The scale of China's wealth was such that,

Hobson believed, the Western states could transcend the competitive system of rival empires and ascend to a form of international imperialism, the development of which would bind together Western leaders in business and politics and secure a relaxation of militarism among Western states.[24] The ultimate outcome of this international imperialism would be manifested in the political and social structures of the West. Unchecked oligarchy in politics and a parasitism of industry would result in the greater part of the Western world resembling the lifestyle of the dividend-drawing class of nineteenth-century southern England, and "all the main arterial industries would have disappeared, the staple foods and manufactures flowing in as tribute from Asia and Africa."[25]

Although he thought it unlikely that China could reassert nationalist control of its territory through the military defeat of imperialism, Hobson did envisage a potential rise of China that, in many ways, resembles the political and economic dynamics that are emerging today:

> It is at least conceivable that China might so turn the tables upon the Western industrial nations, and, either by adopting their capital and organizers or, as is more probable, by substituting her own, might flood their markets with her cheaper manufactures, and refusing their imports in exchange might take her payment in liens upon their capital, reversing the earlier process of investment until she gradually obtained financial control over her quondam patrons and civilizers. This is no idle speculation. If China in very truth possesses those industrial and business capacities with which she is commonly accredited, and the Western Powers are able to have their will in developing her upon Western lines, it seems extremely likely that this reaction will result.[26]

Hobson's views on imperialism in the United States and China make his work particularly relevant to this book. In stark contrast to Schumpeter, Hobson viewed the United States as particularly disposed toward imperial expansion because of the rapid accumulation of capital and the stronger and more direct control over government by business interests.[27] His account, however, of "the sudden break in conservative policy, strongly held by both political parties, bound up with every popular instinct and tradition" against imperialism at the turn of the twentieth century is revealed to be inaccurate through the historical investigation undertaken in the first section of this book.[28] Rather, the period of formal American imperialism in the Asia-Pacific is a historical extension of the process of westward expansion that had been occurring for the entire history of the United States. Hobson correctly identified China as the principal target for American imperialism but missed the historical linkages of the China market to American expansion since at least the Jefferson presidency, predating the period of industrial capital accumulation by over half a century. Rather than being the initial driver of imperialism, finance capitalism is the economic system that comes to predominate at imperialism's more developed stage.

While economic forces propel empire, imperialism is most visible, and most commonly measured, in terms of military power. The structure of American empire allows for the exercise of pressure through various institutional mechanisms to encourage or enforce consent, without necessitating the deployment of military force. However, the threat of the unsheathing of the imperial sword is omnipresent. Max Weber described the consolidation of the monopoly to use violence as the defining characteristic of the modern state, without which the very concept of the state would disappear.[29] Empires have a similar relationship to violence. Violence is not the only, or even the most common, way that power is exercised, but the ability to project overwhelming military force underlies the entire imperial project.

This capacity to project overwhelming force is experienced differently depending on where one falls within the imperial order. For many states in the Asia-Pacific region, the armed forces of the United States are experienced as a shield; for others it is the saber. China has been the ultimate focus of American empire in the Asia-Pacific for most of US history: as a market ripe for commercial penetration, as a source of strategic raw materials, as an ally in war against a rival regional hegemonic threat in Japan, and as an enemy, and later key informal ally, in the Cold War against the Soviet Union. Today, China stands as the sole global imperial competitor and main focus of the American military apparatus. For the Chinese, American military might most certainly represents an acute threat to national security. Underlying this oppositional strategic disposition are the extensive commercial, organizational, and normative structures of American empire. Understanding and articulating the historical development of these structures, and the implications of their current entanglement with the brewing strategic rivalry between the United States and China, is the primary goal of this book.

PART I

WESTWARD EXPANSION
AND THE
COMMERCIAL ORIGINS
OF EMPIRE

CHAPTER ONE

The Long March Westward
and Native Dispossession

The history of American policy formation, state intervention in foreign commercial affairs, the construction of international diplomatic and economic agreements and institutions, and the conceptualization of strategy and deployment of military force supports Karl Polanyi's assertion that in a market society—of which the United States was perhaps the first and most pure by virtue of its history—social and political systems are shaped to facilitate the functions of the economy rather than the inverse.[1] The political economy of colonial North America, while internally differentiated, revolved around mercantilist connections to the British Empire.[2]

The impetus for American independence was greatly influenced by the gradual process of the development of a local American system of capital accumulation and the emergence of an independent American commercial class, with different interests to those of the business and political elites in Great Britain. It was the sense of an independent economic and political destiny that drove the leaders of the American Revolution. In the decades that followed, the vision of this destiny would solidify around the notion that the United States not only would independently develop the resources of the North American continent but would be an American empire that would come to fully harness and develop the resources of Asia, and particularly the fabled China market.

Many of the characteristics of American empire, including its commercial orientation, its expansionism, and its peculiar pattern of institution building, have their origins in the earliest years of the formation of the American state and the transition away from British economic dependency. In 1700 the Americas consumed only 12% of British exports; by the revolution, this figure had expanded to around 40%.[3] In 1700, 85% of these exports were wool products. By the revolutionary period, iron, cotton textiles, and other manufactured products were also prominent in the trade.[4] The balance of this trade favored Great Britain until the 1840s, when that balance shifted in favor of the United States.[5]

The North American colonies were absorbing a huge portion of British manufactures in the early stages of the first industrial revolution, at a time when mercantilist policies designed to enrich the mother country predominated. In 1750, British Parliament passed a law closing all of the iron mills in British colonies in order to protect British manufacturers.[6] Long-standing practices of illegal trade with French West Indian colonies, which accounted for around 50% of all of Boston's trade at the beginning of the eighteenth century, were clamped down upon by British officials around the same time.[7] Further impositions of taxation on tea and of the Stamp Act, which taxed newspapers and the mail, infuriated North American businessmen during the 1760s and 1770s.

The extension of the Canadian boundary to the Ohio River, which would limit American colonial expansion westward across the continent, along with the establishment of the Proclamation Line, which prevented expansion into the remaining Native American territories across the Appalachians, united northern land speculators and southern land barons against the "tyranny" of British imperial policy that limited their accumulation of wealth and power.[8] The famed destruction of a British East India Company shipment of Chinese tea in Boston harbor in December 1773, in reaction to the taxes levied under the British Tea Act, began a new stage of heightened resentment and militant action against British imperial economic policy in the North American colonies. The imposition of the Intolerable Acts, which punished the colonists of Massachusetts for their resistance to British economic and fiscal policies, lead to the formation of the First Continental Congress, the outbreak of the American Revolutionary War, and the Declaration of Independence.

The success of the American Revolution in 1783 was the originating point of the new increasingly unified national economy and society of the United States, pursuing its own material and geopolitical objectives, no longer those derived from a subordinate role within the British Empire. The American economy continued to be primarily agricultural for almost a century to follow, and the United States increased in importance as a British trading partner, but the imperial barriers to industrial development, including the legal restriction of various manufactures, trade, and transportation practices that subordinated the Americans within British trade and production networks, and the British imperial check on further territorial expansion, were re-moved.[9]

Tensions immediately emerged, however, around rival visions for the new republic. Hamiltonian Federalists advocated for a unified national economy and strong federal government along British lines, while Jeffersonian anti-federalists envisioned an agrarian society of gentleman farmers/enslavers, with most political power devolved to the states.[10] The Hamiltonian view of the nation held the day and lay the legislative foundations along which American domestic and foreign policy would develop. The tensions between agrarian free-trading and industrial-mercantilist interests within the American political economy would grow to define sectional and geographical rivalry within the United States until the Civil War. Although the Hamiltonian Federalists were more amenable to the protection of Native American rights than the Jeffersonian Republicans, the national visions of both groups led to expansionism of some kind: of markets for goods, labor, consumers, and capital; of territory; and of the national base of natural resources.

From the earliest days of the American republic, leading politicians and businessmen were conceptualizing this expansionism with a direct focus on the China market.[11] Victory over the British freed the Americans from the British East India Company's imperial monopoly on trade with China. The following year, the merchant ship *The Empress of China* departed New York Harbor for Canton. The successful exchange of American ginseng for Chinese tea, textiles, and porcelain on this voyage laid the foundations for the expansive China trade that would grow in the decades that followed. Commercial expansion in China became entwined with national security policy, as merchants demanded naval protection for their trade and American territorial expansionism, as continental ports, and later archipelagic coaling stations and naval outposts, were sought to provide the infrastructure required to fulfill American ambitions of becoming the colossus bestriding the trade of both the Pacific and Atlantic Oceans.

Thomas Jefferson wrote in 1785 that Americans' "decided taste for navigation and commerce" would likely preclude the young republic from ever enjoying a peaceful foreign policy.[12] His personal desire was for the United States to emulate the Chinese model of isolation from European commercial integration, but cognizant of the structural forces that propelled the United States toward commerce and keenly aware of the geopolitical competition the United States would face to secure its position in world trade, as president he pursued vigorously expansionist policies. The path that took the United

States from thirteen colonies straddling the east coast of North America to a continental empire in the course of the nineteenth century was certainly driven by the pressures of mass European immigration and the individualistic desire for wealth and land that imbue common perceptions of the American frontier, but, among statesmen, business leaders, and merchants, the path was directly linked to the extension of the marketplace across the Pacific.

Mustering state policy around this ambition, particularly in regard to national security, was a delicate process. While the ultimate commercial goal lay across the Pacific, US strategic policy from the revolutionary period up until 1891 manifested for the most part as continental expansion. The military apparatus that was established and operated in this period reflected this priority, entailing a small expeditionary naval force, coastal defenses, and a land army, supported by an extensive network of forts, capable of defeating both European and Indigenous rivals on the continent. The experience of British naval dominance during the Revolutionary War, and the reliance of the United States on its French ally for naval assistance, drove home the importance of maritime strategy to early American political leaders.[13] Concerns over defense from European seaborne invasion and the need to protect American shipping that emerged at the beginning of the federal period formed the foundation of American naval policy for the next century. This policy was based on the construction of coastal fortifications to protect cities, and a relatively small mobile naval force to conduct operations overseas.[14]

The continental military strategy, premised on the new post-revolutionary status of Native American land as open for expropriation, saw the development of a network of forts that would facilitate the settlement of formerly protected Native land and push the Indigenous people westward. The construction of forts in Native American territory began soon after the signing of the Paris Treaty in 1783, and within twenty years a chain of forts for the subjugation of Native American tribes, held by 2,500 soldiers, had been built stretching from the Great Lakes to New Orleans.[15] A pattern was established whereby the demands of civil society for economic opportunities, and often the extension of unauthorized and illegal settlements, alongside the expansionary geopolitical interests of the state were consolidated and pursued through the mustering of military power. Throughout the period, the United States assiduously navigated geopolitical tensions with and between rival European imperial powers and Mexico to extend its territorial holding across the entire North American continent, while also securing its economic interests through diplomatic and military cooperation with these powers, particularly Great Britain, in China.

For European Americans, victory in the War of Independence hailed a new era of political and economic autonomy. For the traditional owners of the land, the revolution was an unmitigated catastrophe. Historian Colin Calloway describes it at length: "Burned villages and crops, murdered chiefs, divided councils and civil wars, migrations, towns and forts choked with refugees, economic disruption, breaking of ancient traditions, losses in battle and to disease and hunger, betrayal to their enemies, all made the American Revolution one of the darkest periods in American Indian history. The emergence of the independent United States as the ultimate victor from a long contest of imperial powers reduced Indians to further dependence and pushed them into further Dark Ages."[16]

The Colonial Government in London had, for imperial and geostrategic reasons, often attempted to restrain the worst excesses of land and resource dispossession of the Native Americans. British efforts to curb colonial expansion after the Seven Years' War had been a major cause of the revolution among land-hungry settlers.[17] Seeing the British as the lesser evil, most Native tribes sided with them during the American War of Independence. After achieving victory, the new United States government let it be known that they would now treat the Natives as a conquered people, and an intense period of land seizures, ostensibly as compensation for war costs, was initiated.

The Continental Congress commissioned a report on Indian Affairs in 1783. The appointed committee considered the mass expulsion of all Native tribes from the northern and western territory of the United States but found that it would be too difficult to achieve; and if successful, it would strengthen the British position in Canada through alliances with Native tribes and cede to Britain a monopoly of the lucrative Native fur trade.[18] Instead the committee found that the most convenient process for taking Native American land would require the parceling of the territory, with some reserved for Native Americans while the rest would be disposed of by the new US federal government, which owed money to the foreign and domestic creditors who had funded the Revolutionary War.[19]

Most of the Native American tribes who fought on the American side of the war fared little better than those allied with the British. The Stockbridge Mohicans, who fought with the revolutionaries in several campaigns throughout the war, had lost all their land to settlers by 1783. Their appeals to the

United States government to secure their traditional homeland failed, and they moved westward from Massachusetts upon invitation and a grant of land from the Oneida Tribe, another American ally in the revolution, with most settling in Oneida territory in upstate New York by 1785.[20] Both the Stockbridge Mohicans and the Oneidas would be forced westward, to Wisconsin, in the 1830s, where they faced continued land pressure with advancing waves of settlers.[21]

With little foresight to their own pursuit of Native American allies during the Revolutionary War, the Declaration of Independence framed the victims of genocide and dispossession as "merciless Indian savages," threatening the destruction of the European settlers.[22] The characterization of Native American "savagery" was reinforced by the opinions and statements from leading American revolutionaries, like Washington, Adams, and Jefferson, on their bestial and vicious nature.[23] Popular representations of the violence and savagery of the Native Americans were used to legitimize the immeasurably greater violence and savagery committed against them by the United States government, as well as European settlers, for years to come. Amid the lofty discourse of the founding of a new empire of liberty and reason, the material realities of the violence of empire were already being enacted on its earliest victims.

The revolution had brought on a new spirit of development and destiny in the United States, and Native Americans, particularly through their occupation of the land, were seen as an impediment. In 1802, future president and early architect of American empire John Quincy Adams articulated this vision of American progress in an oration commemorating the arrival of the pilgrims at Plymouth, asking:

> Shall the liberal bounties of Providence to the race of man be monopolized by one of ten thousand for whom they were created? Shall the exuberant bosom of the common mother, amply adequate to the nourishment of millions, be claimed exclusively by a few hundreds of her offspring? . . . Have hundreds of commodious harbors, a thousand leagues of coast, and a boundless ocean, been spread in the front of this land, and shall every purpose of utility to which they could apply be prohibited by the tenant of the woods? No, generous philanthropists! Heaven has not been thus inconsistent in the works of its hands. Heaven has not thus placed at irreconcilable strife its moral laws with its physical creation.[24]

Nature's bounty awaited the citizens of the young and vital United States. Native America stood in their way. The Jeffersonian approach to the destruction of Native America through trading, entanglement, and "civilization," as opposed to mass killing, predominated in American public sentiment throughout the frontier era.[25] While the sentiment to simply eradicate Native Americans certainly existed, usually at the frontier, large-scale war was expensive and could result in disastrous reverses, as was discovered by General St. Clair in the Battle of the Wabash, when the Northwest Confederacy of Native tribes inflicted the largest proportional military defeat ever suffered by the United States Army.[26] The "more humane" approach of simply removing the material means of survival of the Natives, and watching them slowly fade into extinction, as was commonly anticipated by white observers, was more palatable and less risky. Under this system, the military's main role was to enforce the state's policy of land appropriation and to protect white settlers, operating from strongpoints and forts. When significant Native resistance developed, the military would be mobilized for head-on battle.

The interplay between economic expansion and geopolitics in the dispossession of Native Americans is demonstrated succinctly in a letter from President Thomas Jefferson to Governor William Washington in 1803. Just months before the Louisiana Purchase, when fears of facing an expansionist French Empire on the other side of the Mississippi animated American public life, Jefferson expounded on an idea for creating a government-run debt trap among the Native American tribes. Jefferson wrote that "to promote [the Indians'] disposition to exchange lands, which they have to spare and we want," government-run trading houses should flood the market with underpriced goods. When the Indians found themselves in unrepayable debt, they would become "willing to lop them off by a cession of lands." This was imperative, according to Jefferson, to confront the "powerful and enterprising" French by populating the eastern bank of the Mississippi with European settlers "from its mouth to its northern regions, that we may be able to present as strong a front on our western as on our eastern border, and plant on the Mississippi itself the means of its own defence."[27] The seizure of Indian land in the region was to be accompanied by the mustering of a force of 80,000 men and 15 gunboats, authorized by Congress, for an assault on French territory on the lower Mississippi.[28]

Napoleon's need to finance European wars and French concerns over the possibility of a United States–Great Britain axis being created as a result of French expansion in North America made these plans obsolete. Within months of Jefferson penning his letter to Governor Washington, the Louisiana Purchase had been negotiated with France. The treaty, signed on April 30, 1803, brought a gigantic territory west of the Mississippi under the control of the United States and eliminated the geostrategic threat posed by Napoleonic France on the North American continent. The wishes of the European inhabitants of Louisiana, to say nothing of the Native Americans, were of no concern in the negotiations or the execution of the purchase.[29] The acquisition of territory without any sort of democratic mandate was to become a theme in the extension of the empire of liberty. The idea that the geographical security of the United States must supersede the rights of self-determination of the land's inhabitants was a given in all future extensions of American territorial sovereignty, including the annexation of the Floridas and the extension of American territorial claims to the Pacific Northwest, formally agreed upon as part of the Transcontinental Treaty with Spain in 1819, under the express condition that the United States renounce all claims to Texas.[30]

The use of arms, land sales, money, and diplomacy to consolidate US control over the North American continent during this time paved the way for the declaration of the Monroe Doctrine in 1823. A pivotal moment in American ideological formation, the Monroe Doctrine stated that the entire Western Hemisphere was henceforth off limits to European colonialism.[31] Any European interference in political affairs, particularly in relation to the struggle for independence between Latin American states and the ailing Spanish Empire, would now be viewed as a threat to US security. A curious form of imperial anti-imperialism, the Monroe Doctrine was the beginning of the process by which the United States established hegemony over the Western Hemisphere and was intimately entwined with both manifest destiny, the belief that the United States was operating under a divine mandate to expand westward spreading capitalism and democracy, and American exceptionalism, the idea that the United States was, due to its inherent virtues, unique among nations in holding such a mandate. Not at the time a measure of the actual strength of the United States, the Monroe Doctrine nonetheless clearly articulated the hegemonic position to which it aspired. The security perimeter of the United States was thus radically expanded, rhetorically for the moment, but the military power to enforce this policy would soon develop.

ỉ ỉ ỉ

Harold Innis, while recognizing the economic drivers of imperialism, extended the study of its motive forces to account for the power of revolutions in technology, and particularly communications technologies, in imperial expansion. Communications, according to Innis, occupied a critical position in the organization and administration of empires.[32] The effective management of large areas depends to a large extent on the efficiency and reliability of communications. Crafting a cohesive American imperium that could be effectively managed and sustained, stretching from the Atlantic seaboard to the Western Pacific, from whence it could penetrate the China market, would require the extensive development of its interior lines of communication and logistics, as well as the further growth of American export industries.

The acceleration of the westward expansion of the United States was driven by several key technological and material developments of the nineteenth century. Successive and overlapping technological revolutions in industry, transport, and communications during this time had the combined effect of making the vast distances of the United States much more productive, transitable, and governable, allowing for the development of a more cohesive national economy and society. Eli Whitney's cotton gin and Oliver Evans's automatic flour mill, notable among a vast range of innovations, greatly increased efficiency in agriculture, by far the largest sector of the US economy at the time.

What had been in essence a cottage manufacturing industry was fundamentally transformed by the introduction of the machinery and methods of the first industrial revolution into American economic life. This process began around the turn of the nineteenth century, when Samuel Slater and his contemporaries began to replicate British textile production techniques.[33] Throughout the century, the production of machine tools, advances in metallurgy, particularly in the use of iron and steel, the mass adoption of steam power and railroads, and the use of coal as the major source of fuel, replacing wood, all played huge roles in creating the industrial economy that would reshape American society and its position in international affairs.[34]

The revolution in transportation and communications occurred along with the revolution of industry. The deplorable state of roads and transport infrastructure in the early United States meant that only the most valuable products were worth transporting, resulting in markets and production networks that were highly localized.[35] Despite anti-federalist tendencies, the Jefferson administration laid much of the groundwork for the physical unification of the states, investing millions of dollars on constructing canals and roads, improving the navigability of rivers, and connecting the frontier towns and cities to the eastern seaboard.[36] The states, the federal government, and charter companies spent much of the next century laying the infrastructural foundations of an economy interconnected by a diverse range of transport links. The roads and turnpikes that were being built from the immediate post-revolutionary years; the steamship, which began through a series of experiments in the 1790s before becoming established on the Hudson River in New York in 1807; the system of canals, the most famous of which connected the Hudson River to Lake Erie in 1825; and the vast network of railways, which began their spread across the continent in the 1820s, were all critical to the growth of an integrated American industrial and agricultural economy.

The impact of railroads was perhaps the most notable component of the transportation revolution, lowering transport costs and times, spreading economic activity throughout the sparsely populated hinterland, and in the process reshaping the political geography of the United States. Between 1840 and 1880 the United States' network of railways grew from 2,800 to over 100,000 miles.[37] The railroads became the arteries of American commerce, carrying both goods and communications, and they also became a model for the linkages between the state and the emerging dominant industrial capitalist class.[38]

The railroads were usually funded by public-private partnerships; private enterprise was protected by state-underwritten bond guarantees; federal and state law regarding property ownership and eminent domain were reconciled to support railroad expansion; limited liability was instituted; and huge parcels of land were granted to private companies to facilitate their construction of railroads. While massively increasing the economic potential of the United States as a whole, the effects of the transport revolution varied by locality. Many towns and rural centers were shrunk, as the local economies were integrated into larger networks.[39] Farming and manufacturing were made viable across vast swaths of the country that had previously been too remote from labor and markets. The ever-expanding territory was secured by peopling it with European Americans who were connected to the growing national economy, making both secession and invasion of foreign powers less likely.[40]

Morse's telegraph, which was conceived on the oceanic crossing from London to the United States in 1832, and Bell's subsequent improvements to the system completely revolutionized communications. The telegraph was widely adopted in the United States during the 1840s and often used in concert with the railways, allowing stationmasters to better coordinate movements on the railroads.[41] For the first time in human history, electricity was being harnessed in a way that tangibly affected people's lives. As a result of these technological and infrastructural developments, the means of communication and transportation became adequate to coordinate and distribute the rapidly expanding productive base of the American industrial economy. This complementary use of new communications technologies with new types of mass transport provided ideal conditions for the westward propulsion of American empire.

The provision and development of the raw materials these technologies depended on for construction, maintenance, and fuel played an enormous role in the American economy during this time. Coal and iron were the basic raw materials of early industrialism. Later, after more advanced industrial machinery and electrical and chemical technologies were developed, oil and a vast array of minerals became indispensable to the running of the American economy. Much of the iron used for the initial expansion of American railroads had come from Britain, and cotton, the cash crop of the first industrial revolution, was largely sold overseas. Oil was the first major resource within the industrial supply chain that was sourced, refined, sold, and used within the United States.[42] The oil industry, in partnership with the railroads that transported it, and the coal, iron, and steel combines that provided the raw materials for industrial machinery came to play the critical role in the industrial economy. The technological developments that heightened the importance of mineral extraction occurred around the same time that the western states were annexed to the Union. The mineral wealth of California, Colorado, Arizona, and other regions of the far west was the primary attraction to pioneers and settlers, whereas agriculture and grazing lands had been in the states to the east.[43]

The process of industrialization and the extensive development of interior lines of communication and transportation transformed the political-economic foundations of the United States and paved the way westward for empire. For many years after the American Revolution, the economy of the United States remained tethered to the British imperial system, most notably through the export orientation of the Southern cotton crop, the vast majority of which was destined for British looms.[44] As the nineteenth century progressed, economic patterns were reorganized. Agriculture, which had traditionally grown in value merely as a result of territorial expansion, began to become more intensively productive because of technological, organizational, and infrastructural advancements. At the same time, the focal point of economic activity began a long shift from the country to the cities. The opening of the St. Mary's River Canal in 1855 connected the largest iron-ore bodies of the United States in Michigan with the cheaply accessible and vast reserves of Pennsylvania coal and coke, resulting in the eventual development in that region of the world's largest steel industry.[45] The process of expansion and industrialization saw the United States transition into an independent leading force in the global economy.[46] While this shift in economic organization commenced in the late eighteenth century, not until the end of the nineteenth had it completely altered the internal structure of the US political economy, along with its foreign relations.

CHAPTER TWO

The China Focus in Westward Expansion

Jackal Diplomacy and the China Trade

The decades that saw the development of a national industrial economy in the United States were also boom years for foreign trade. In the three decades before the Civil War, America's presence in international commerce grew at a staggering pace. Total trade expanded from $134 million in 1829 to $687 million in 1860, an increase of 411%.[1] The tonnage carried by American merchant ships quadrupled during the same period.[2] While the majority of this trade continued to flow across the Atlantic between the United States and Europe, the vast potential of the China trade was what most captured America's mercantile imagination. The growing American commercial interests in the China trade spurred the beginnings of a formal state presence in the region during this period, with a permanent naval squadron and diplomatic representation in China and the Western Pacific established during the 1830s and 1840s.

The dramatic continental expansion of the 1840s was itself directly linked to the China trade. While conflicting sectional interests, geopolitical rivalry with European Great Powers, and the American pioneering spirit all contributed to shape and color the annexation and settlement of the continental United States, the pursuit of harbors and commercial opportunities as part of an American push to dominate the China market was the single greatest political propellant of the annexations west of Texas.[3]

American relations with China during the nineteenth century should only be viewed through the lens of transnational history. Particularly during the first half of the century, the United States played a more modest role in Chinese affairs than the major European powers. Great Britain acted as the prime mover in the opening of China to Western trade and capital, and the United

States was criticized by the British at the time as enacting "jackal diplomacy," in which they were unprepared to participate in the kill but eager to share in the feast. This is a common theme in historical scholarship of the period. John King Fairbank notably describes American involvement in China during this period as having "no vital decisions to make, no real issues of peace or war to face, except how and when to say 'Me, too.' "[4] On the scale of global power, this is a fair assessment. The importance of American policy toward China in these decades, however, lies in the development of a framework for geostrategic policy, continental expansionism, and the extension of the American security perimeter into the Western Pacific. All of which was integral in the formation of American empire.

Western "penetration" of the China market is referred to in such terms for the simple reason that the Chinese government was not a willing participant in, or an equal beneficiary of, the growing commercial linkages between China and the West during this period. China was economically self-sufficient. The Chinese Emperor Qianlong had rejected the advances of British King George III to send a permanent emissary to the emperor's court in 1793, saying that it could not possibly be entertained. The emperor, stressing his priority of performing good governance over the Celestial Kingdom, saw the entanglement of diplomatic and trade interests with foreigners as a threat. On the British wares he remarked that he "set no value on objects strange or ingenious, and [had] no use for your country's manufactures."[5] The Qianlong Emperor's concerns over the destabilizing effects of foreign penetration proved prescient.

Because of this self-sufficiency, American traders faced initial difficulties in selling their products on the Chinese market. In lieu of appealing American domestic products, a trans-oceanic network of trade sprang up, whereby American merchant ships would obtain spices, sandalwood, furs, bêche-de-mer, and various other exotic products throughout the Pacific en route to Canton to trade for Chinese silks, porcelain, and tea. This network, however, was incapable of furnishing exotic goods for the Chinese market on a scale that matched Western demand for Chinese tea and silks, and so silver was the main method by which Western traders purchased Chinese goods. With Western silver flowing into China, and Chinese goods flowing out, the Western countries faced a daunting fiscal imbalance. In the eighteenth century alone, over 150 million in Spanish silver dollars departed the West for China, exchanged mostly for tea.[6]

The trade of opium from British India, as well as the Turkish opium carried by Americans, provided a solution to this imbalance. While the trade in opium from India to China had begun as early as the 1760s, it increased rapidly in the early 1800s, growing from around 4,000 chests per year imported in the 1790s, to 40,000 by 1839.[7] Despite several imperial edicts banning its importation, by the 1830s opium eclipsed all other commodities in British trade with China. Silver began flowing in the opposite direction, as opium use among Chinese exploded. By 1840, an estimated 9 in 10 Chinese men living in the southeast coastal provinces were addicted to opium, with the habit siphoning off half of the income of the average peasant.[8]

The degrading effect of the boom in opium during the 1830s on the Chinese population, and on Chinese silver wealth, led the Qing government to action. In 1839 the opium trade was outlawed in China; any future opium smuggling would cause the cessation of all trade with the offending party. In response to the seizure of British opium and the threat of closing off foreign trade, British Parliament declared war on China. In the spring of 1840 16 British warships, carrying 540 guns and escorting 4,000 land troops arrived in Chinese waters. By 1842 Chinese forces had been defeated by the British, and a new era of foreign influence in Chinese affairs was inaugurated.

The Treaty of Nanking, which ended the conflict, set the general principles that would govern relations between China and the West for the next century. Five port cities were opened for foreign trade; Hong Kong was ceded to Great Britain in perpetuity; and Western merchants were allowed far more expansive trading opportunities. Diplomatic relations were established based around Westphalian principles and extraterritoriality, most-favored-nation rules for trading were adopted, and an indemnity of $21 million was levied upon China for war costs and the destruction of British opium.

In the aftermath of the First Opium War, propelled by concerns of impending British domination of the China trade, an American delegation led by Massachusetts lawyer Caleb Cushing was sent to negotiate American diplomatic and trade relations with China. The mission was crafted by three of the most prominent American politicians advocating continental and Pacific expansionism in pursuit of the China market. It was first proposed in a congressional report submitted by John Quincy Adams in 1843, planned within Daniel Webster's State Department, and executed under the presidency of John Tyler.

Adams, by this point in the twilight of his career, had played a major role in American expansionism in the preceding decades. He had supported the Louisiana Purchase under Jefferson, pushed strongly for US rights in North

American territorial disagreements with England and Spain, and, as President James Monroe's secretary of state, was the driving force behind the Monroe Doctrine.[9] Webster, who had been a key supporter of the Adams presidency decades earlier and a career proponent of northern mercantilist economic policies,[10] described Cushing's embassy to China as "a more important mission than ever proceeded from this Country, and more important mission than any other, likely to succeed it, in our day."[11] Tyler, a longtime advocate for Pacific expansionism, would extend the Monroe Doctrine to Hawaii during his presidency and set in motion the annexation of Texas that would be confirmed under his successor to the office, James Polk.

Cushing's instructions, penned by Webster, detailed the prerogative of securing an American presence in the ports of rich provinces newly opened to trade as a result of British aggression in the First Opium War. The instructions clearly frame the traditional Chinese systems of tribute and imperial hierarchy as obstacles to the free execution of American commerce and required Cushing to make all exertions to meet the emperor himself, foregoing any exchanges of gifts or tributes.[12] The main factor given by Webster for the likely "indulgence of a less suspicious and more friendly feeling than may have been entertained toward England" from the Qing dynasty was that, unlike England, the United States held no colonies in Asia.[13]

Without having yet developed the material capabilities to expand its empire into Asia, representatives of the United States government sought to present themselves as a well-intentioned friend, with no aggrandizing ambitions in the region. While Cushing was unable to secure a personal reception with the emperor, or even travel to northern China, negotiation with the Qing diplomat Kaying were successful, new Chinese ports were opened to American merchants, trade relations were to proceed under formal diplomatic relations, and the principle of extraterritoriality for American citizens in China was agreed upon.

British naval dominance during this period had a profound effect on American strategic planning. American trade with China was halved as a result of the British blockade during the First Opium War, and many American politicians viewed British designs on China warily.[14] British plans for expansion in Texas, Oregon, and California led Americans to fear for their security on the continent as well as worry about their foreign commercial interests. It was because of the British threat during this period that naval expansionism became a bipartisan priority within American politics. Traditionally, Southern politicians had been either hostile or indifferent to a peacetime navy. The

South was geographically insulated from maritime power due to a relative lack of large harbors or deep inland waterways, and the dominance of the North in merchant enterprise had framed the issue within the boundaries of rival sectional interest.[15] A perceived British threat to Texas, however, and her antislavery attitudes in general, led to a heightened sense of vulnerability to British maritime power in the South.

In 1840, reinforcements were sent to the East India Squadron, the first permanent US naval presence in the Western Pacific, established in 1835. In 1841, Secretary of the Navy Abel P. Upshur, a southerner who was instrumental in the later annexation of Texas as a slave state, advanced plans for the reform, enlargement, and modernization of the American fleet. Upshur believed that the proper size for the American navy was one-half that of the British fleet.[16] While this wasn't achieved during his tenure, a political consensus was being forged around the necessity for a strong, permanent naval force for American national security and the security of American commercial interests in the Pacific.

There were, even in this early phase of American expansionism, prominent politicians who held favorable views on British aggression during the First Opium War, focused not on the looming threat of growing British power to the United States but on the progress British imperialism represented in creating a world of open markets. John Quincy Adams offered a striking corollary to the Christian and Lockean justifications for the expropriation of Indigenous land in North America, in support of the aggressive war on China. He argued that the "right of commerce" necessarily followed the right of property: "If the state of nature between men is a state of peace, and the pursuit of happiness is a natural right of man's, it is the duty of man to contribute as much as is in his power to one another's happiness. This is emphatically joined by the Christian precept to love your neighbor as yourself—now there is no other way by which men can so much contribute to the comfort and well-being of one another as by commerce or mutual exchanges of equivalents. Commerce is then among the natural rights and duties of men."[17]

Adams argued that China, as a non-Christian state, had reverted to "the execrable principles of Hobbes," in which everyone has a right to buy, but nobody is compelled to sell. Foreshadowing the rise of the liberal, free-trading, and interventionist world empire to come, Adams denounced the "churlish and unsocial" Chinese system and declared that it was "time that this enormous outrage upon the rights of human nature, and upon the first principles of the rights of nations, should cease."[18] He described the opium issue and the

British invasion of Canton as "but incidents in that movement of mind on this globe of earth, of which the war between Great Britain and China is now the leading star."[19]

Adams's Christian fervor for a war on China to promote global free trade was discordant with his own time as president of the United States. It was during his administration, in 1828, that the "tariff of abominations" was created. It set a 38% tax on 92% of all imported goods and a 45% tax on raw materials such as tobacco and cotton—two of the South's strongest commodities—in the pursuit of blocking imports of European industrial goods for the development of northern manufacturing. The tariff brought on the nullification crisis of 1832–1833 that threatened to split the union over the imposition of barriers to trade within the United States and is widely viewed as an early driver of the tensions that ultimately led to the American Civil War.

Sectional Interests Unite for Expansion

American interests in the China trade, and the commerce of the Pacific more broadly, played a major role in the dramatic burst of expansionism that occurred on the North American continent during the same period. Since at least the presidency of Thomas Jefferson, American leaders had been eagerly anticipating the commercial bounty that a strong presence in the China trade would bring to the United States. This was always paired with an acute awareness of the threats that European colonial powers posed to its fulfillment. Much as the threat of British dominance of the China trade propelled the Cushing mission, so too did fear of British designs on Texas, California, and Oregon spur American expansionists to action on the continent. The increase in wealth that the acquisition of new land would generate and the imperative to avoid British control of strategic territory and markets united the increasingly divergent sectional interests within the United States around a program of westward territorial expansionism in the 1840s.

Empire building is always a contested process, and so it was in America. The vast annexations of this decade, which saw the United States grow to become a continental state, were influenced by both international competition with Great Britain and other European powers for global markets, as well as competing economic and social groups within the American polity, with different visions of American political-economy and society. Before the Civil War, the United States had not developed a single dominant interest group within society that could exercise hegemonic control over the state. Broadly speaking, control was split between the manufacturing, trading, and increasingly financial North and the cash-crop exporting, slaveholding South, with both competing to influence the newly emerging freeholding agricultural western states. As the first industrial revolution began to be felt in the United States, whose inhabitants were still at this point overwhelmingly rural, economic power began to consolidate in the north. Canals, steamships, and railways radically decreased transportation costs, created a more complex networked economy of production, distribution, and consumption, and stimulated overall commercial activity. The operational framework of this new national economy increasingly ran through the northeast; physically through infrastructure, financially through ownership and investment, and later politically through the ascendance of the Republican Party.

The separate economic models of the North and South manifested in intense political competition. Northern industry was firmly committed to a protectionist economic policy, seeking to limit competition of European manufactures in the American market. The Southern economy was dependent on access to European markets for its cotton exports, which at the dawn of the Civil War were responsible for around half of all American export earnings, and hoped to buy European manufactures cheaply in exchange for its cotton, grain, and tobacco.[20] The South, under leaders like John C. Calhoun, had long aimed to form an agricultural political bloc with the western states against the industrial North, based around lowering tariffs and protecting the institution of slavery.[21]

The lines of industrial development, however, negated the political efforts of the South in uniting with the West. The newly developed railway system that sprang up from the 1840s, connecting markets and lowering costs, ran east to west, without many southward linkages, as did the great canals that were constructed in the decades prior.[22] The economic benefits of this historical transformation flowed inordinately to the North, despite efforts by southerners to industrialize and create their own transportation networks.[23] This is perhaps most simply demonstrated by the lopsided rate of capital accumulation. The banks of the four major industrial states of Massachusetts, Connecticut, New York, and Pennsylvania had funds greater than the banks of all other states of the union combined in 1860.[24] Southern economist James Dunwoody Brownson De Bow noted these developments, lamenting that "the great cities of the North have severely penetrated the interior with artificial lines until they have taken from the open and untaxed current of the Mississippi the commerce produced on its borders."[25]

The North and the South competed to open up western regions and to establish them as either "free" or "slave" states, upon whose representatives in the federal government they could rely to forward their own sectional interests. The South pushed for the annexation of Texas out of a combination of fear and opportunism: fear that an independent Texas would fall under British influence and that its agricultural potential could challenge the South's dominance of global cotton markets; and opportunism in its aims to incorporate a new slaveholding state into the union and alter the political balance between free and slave states in the US Congress.[26] Cotton grown by enslaved people was by far the United States' largest foreign export. It was a clear priority among Southern politicians to protect the source of the South's wealth and political power. James Gadsden, the Southern diplomat, soldier, and businessman who would later oversee the purchase of southern Arizona and New Mexico from the Mexican government, wrote at the time that if the South failed to have Texas admitted to the union as a slave state, then they were doomed to remain "hewers of wood and drawers of water" for the North.[27]

Industrial and commercial leaders in the Northern states, meanwhile, were calling for the annexation of the Oregon Territory and California to establish American ports from which the penetration of Asian markets could be undertaken.[28] This was pursued out of a desire for both personal and national prosperity but also as a strategy for sectional dominance in domestic politics. Abolitionists and Northern industrialists believed that the key to winning the political support of western states against the South lay in opening Asian markets to their vast agricultural surpluses.[29] A sense of urgency propelled the movement for western annexation as Mexican governance in California seemed weak, and Britain appeared positioned to replace it. Both the North and the South made arguments for expansion grounded in economics and geopolitics, and both were successful in spurring the federal government to action.

Americans had begun to settle in Texas, the northeastern province of Mexico, in large numbers in the early 1820s. By 1836, white settlers had declared independence, enshrining the authorization of slavery into the Texan constitution. Texans petitioned the United States for annexation in 1837 but were rejected due to the disruptive effects it would have on the free-state and slave-state balance in Congress.[30] Great Britain had mustered the support of France to operate in concert with Mexico to block US annexation by supporting Texan independence. Mexican president Santa Anna was determined to reconquer what he viewed as a rebel territory, however, and British plans failed to prevent American annexation in 1845.[31] After the annexation of Texas, the

Polk administration offered to purchase California and New Mexico from the Mexican government and establish a new southern border on the Rio Grande. The offer was rebuffed.

The American push for war on Mexico to secure California and the Pacific coastline was also deeply entwined with geostrategic competition with Great Britain. The rising empire of liberty was deeply concerned that the reigning world imperial power would entrench itself on the California coast and cut the United States off from its westward path to the Pacific and China. The Royal Navy had dispatched several missions to survey the California coast in the 1820s and 1830s, and the potential annexation of California was discussed at the highest levels of British government. In 1841, demonstrating the confused and overlapping geopolitical fears that imbued international diplomacy in the era of rapid colonial expansion, the British minister to Mexico, Richard Pakenham, proposed a plan to Lord Palmerston, then British secretary of state for foreign affairs, to annex California, largely out of concerns that the French were intending on doing the same.[32] British conservatives, however, were at the time reluctant to burden their empire with more territory to govern and to extend geopolitical tension with its rivals to even farther-flung parts of the globe.[33]

By 1845, the British and French had both come to recognize that the United States was the only power truly poised to take and hold California. For the European powers too, the issue was viewed mainly through the lens of imperial competition and the China market. Advocating for further imperial expansion, the *London Times* editorialized that "England must think of her own interests, and secure the bay of San Francisco and Monterey . . . to prevent those noble ports from becoming ports of exportation for brother Jonathan for the Chinese market."[34] The influential French *Journal des débats* warned of the ominous implications of American expansionism in California for Europe. The old continent would soon find herself wedged "between the autocracy of Russia on the east, and the democracy of America, aggrandized by the conquest of Mexico, on the west . . . and suffer from their oppression."[35] As war with the United States appeared imminent in early 1846, the Mexican government offered to transfer California to Great Britain as security for a loan. The British, recognizing that Mexico's de facto capacity to enforce such a transfer on the ground in California was now questionable, declined.[36]

The solidification of the ideology of imperial expansionism that occurred during this period bears highlighting. It was in an 1845 article in the *Southern*

Democratic Review, demanding an end to all opposition to the annexation of Texas, that the phrase "manifest destiny" first appeared.[37] As has been discussed, ideology in the form of racial, religious, socioeconomic, and cultural bigotry had undergirded expansionism and the expropriation of Indigenous land since the earliest days of colonialism in North America. The 1840s were notable, however, for the apparent dissipation of significant resistance to the ideological discourses of manifest destiny that came to predominate. Fears that the incorporation of other races into the United States would degrade and dissolve the institutions of American democracy remained, as indeed they have throughout American history up to the present day, but much of their role in informing opposition to expansionism was rebuffed. In his inaugural address, James Polk directly responded to these fears of overextension and provided a mandate for the full continental expansion that he would oversee during his presidency:

> These objections were earnestly urged when we acquired Louisiana. Experience has shown that they were not well founded. The title of numerous Indian tribes to vast tracts of country has been extinguished; new States have been admitted into the Union; new Territories have been created and our jurisdiction and laws extended over them. As our population has expanded, the Union has been cemented and strengthened. As our boundaries have been enlarged and our agricultural population has been spread over a large surface, our federative system has acquired additional strength and security. It may well be doubted whether it would not be in greater danger of overthrow if our present population were confined to the comparatively narrow limits of the original thirteen States than it is now that they are sparsely settled over a more expanded territory. It is confidently believed that our system may be safely extended to the utmost bounds of our territorial limits, and that as it shall be extended the bonds of our Union, so far from being weakened, will become stronger.[38]

Indeed, the fear of democratic decay through expansion was essentially inverted. Territorial and commercial expansionism was to be the vehicle through which democracy and capitalism were to radiate outward. President Tyler, years before he secured the annexation of Texas, declared that he had peered into the distant future, having beheld the greatness of a free America "walking the waves of the mighty deep, carrying along with her tidings of great joy to distant nations . . . overturning the strong places of despotism."[39] Historian Norman Graebner describes Americans in the 1840s as being under the spell of Jacksonian democracy, viewing their political system with a "messianic consciousness" and holding the conviction that the destiny of republican governance lay within their hands.[40] Carl Schurz, diplomat, senator, and secretary of the interior, locates the material foundations of the ideology of manifest destiny in the movement of slave states to spread their "peculiar institution" and strengthen their position in the federal government.[41] The centralization of the supposed superiority of Anglo-Saxon blood and the reduction of the natural abilities of other races in much of the discourse around manifest destiny certainly support this thesis. A popular ideology, buttressed by a self-assurance of racial superiority and divine providence, was just as useful for garnering public support for the North's expansionist projects in Oregon and California.

While the geostrategic approach to territorial expansion of excluding rival powers and securing key ports features prominently in the historical record, a more foundational approach to geography and manifest destiny, which recurs throughout American history, was commonly used as justification. The idea of a "natural boundary" for the United States had been conceptually important in American politics since John Jay presented the Mississippi River as the most precise and appropriate natural boundary of the new nation.[42] Once the Louisiana Purchase had brought vast territories on the western side of the Mississippi under American control, the Rocky Mountains had served for a time as the "natural" boundary of the United States for geography-minded politicians.[43] When the practical possibilities for further expansion presented themselves, the Pacific Ocean appeared to be the clearest God-given boundary for the westward expansion of the United States. Arnold Toynbee pithily described the concept of the natural boundary as "a euphemism for the momentary conquests of brute force."[44] Unlike Max Weber's modern territorial states, which administer governance and violence within clearly delineated geographical spaces, empires are constantly dissolving and reframing boundaries and extending their mandate for violence beyond previous spatial limits.[45]

Simplistic conceptions of natural boundaries do not account for the commercial and military requirements of a growing westward-facing empire. Coaling stations and ports connecting the west coast of the United States to the markets in Asia would be required, as would naval bases for the protection of shipping and commercial rights, and the extending of the security perimeter to a position of "forward defense." The fact that the extension to a natural boundary simply produced another was well observed by critics of American imperialism. Congressional debates over the annexation of Hawaii are peppered with references to the natural geographical place of the archipelago 2,000 miles from the California coast being within the American system.[46] As early as 1842, President Tyler was extending the Monroe Doctrine to Hawaii in a special message to Congress. His justification partially rested on the geographical proximity of Hawaii to the United States, "much nearer to this continent than the other. . . . Far remote from the dominions of European powers."[47] However, the focus of the policy was to ensure the security of America's China trade through the exclusion of the possibility of European dominance over the island group that served as the main stop on the route to Canton. The second half of the "Tyler Doctrine" speaks exclusively of the market potential of China for the United States and the need for the proactive engagement of the American government to secure it.[48]

Graebner unambiguously highlights the China market in his explanation of American expansionist policy on the West Coast, evidenced through its centrality in political speeches and congressional debates, but notes that the editorializing and political proclamations at the time were also consistently animated with themes of racial superiority, destiny, and, of course, "freedom" for the rest of the world.[49] The peculiar anti-imperial imperialism of the United States was again highlighted here, as the threat of "conservative" and "monarchist" European colonialism was to be confronted with the American "liberal" and "democratic" kind. The globe-spanning scale of the American imperium to come also begins to take precedence over the modest aims of the North American continent that once satisfied expansionists. In an editorial anticipating the decline of British imperial power due to structural economic factors and the role the United States would have in "regenerating" a decadent Europe, the *New York Herald* called on President Polk to plan for the widened range of American ambitions: "No longer bound by the limits of the confederacy, it looks abroad upon the whole earth, and into the mind of the republic daily sinks deeper and deeper the conviction that the civilization of the earth—the reform of the governments of the ancient world—the emancipation of the whole race, are dependent, in a great degree, on the United States."[50]

Whig publications advocated for expansionism along more strictly economic and strategic lines than the Southern Democratic and popular presses. Henry Jarvis Raymond, founder of the *New York Times* and future Republican congressman for New York, warned that, if allowed to fall under British sway, California would grant her "absolute dominion of the Pacific Ocean, with all its islands, coasts and commerce, and place her in a position which might at any moment become infinitely dangerous to our safety and prosperity."[51] If held by the United States, however, California was destined to be the highway to Asia, the avenue to the unbounded wealth of the "glorious East."[52]

The same ideas were prominent in Congress. Advocating the annexation of Oregon primarily for its position completing the commercial pathway to Asia, which he had been pushing for since at least 1819, Senator Thomas Hart Benton combined the strategic, geographical, and commercial benefits of annexation with the patronizing racial bigotry that was typical of the time.[53] America's place on the Pacific, the future highway of world commerce, would secure valuable ports, both for trading and naval vessels. Its value as agricultural and mineral-laden land was promising. But its position connecting American commerce to Asian markets was his primary concern: "The trade of the East has always been the richest jewel in the diadem of commerce. All nations, in all ages, have sought-it; and those which obtained it, or even a share of it, attained the highest degree of opulence, refinement, and power."[54] Benton describes the entire history of the discovery, settlement, and exploration of the North American continent as that of connecting the western and eastern markets. Providing the new connection of these markets would not just rain wealth upon the American people but would benefit the 400 million Asian people on the other side of the Pacific, who would "receive an impression from the superior race whenever they came into contact."[55]

⚱ ⚱ ⚱

The dynamics involved in the clear expression of material interests in expansionist policy paired with the spread and discursive power of the ideology of manifest destiny during this period is a clear demonstration of the complementary melding of the economic, military, and ideological thrusts of American empire. While economic interests provided the impetus for these movements, and the basis of elite support, the ideology that sprang up to justify and explain it assumes a cultural power of its own that cannot be understood as economic determinism alone.

Just as Graebner points to the inadequacy of the ideology of manifest destiny to explain the carefully crafted expansionist policy, directed toward key geographical assets for their utility in the penetration of Asian markets, so too does economic determinism alone fail to explain the mass support for expansion.[56] In his exhaustive study of the phenomenon of manifest destiny, Alfred Weinberg unravels the complexity of this case of imperial expansionism and the desire for domination. A key point here is that the very charge made by French economist Francis Delaisi that "the bright cloak of Intellectual Imperialism serves to cover the sordid calculations of Economic Imperialism" testifies to a forceful public consciousness, and set of moral and discursive practices and standards, from which such economic interests require concealment.[57]

With a critical mass having now been built behind war and expansion, the United States extended its borders unilaterally, and war was declared on Mexico in April 1846. The recently enhanced US Navy played an important role in the conflict. In what was the first display of American naval power with major international ramifications in the Pacific, the US fleet captured Monterey, San Francisco, Los Angeles, and San Diego. Some or all of present-day Arizona, California, Colorado, Nevada, New Mexico, Utah, and Wyoming were ceded from Mexico to the United States at the conclusion of the war in 1848, under the treaty of Guadalupe. The United States emerged from the conflict as a continental power. Mexico lost half of its territory. The first federal senator for California, William McKendree Gwin, predicted on the Senate floor that, through the opening of the China trade, "California will soon in every respect be the New York of the Pacific, standing as a rival of the great commercial capital of the empire State of the Atlantic, each striving which shall confer the greater blessings on the other, and upon their common country-a rivalry which will give to each new elements of wealth and refinement, and whilst diffusing them all over the surface of our blessed land, will confer new strength, dignity and power upon the whole American Union."[58]

William Henry Seward, the future secretary of state, had similar visions for the impact of the newly annexed state on American imperial power. In a speech to the Senate titled "California, Union, and Freedom," Seward declared that, with California now in the union, "the world contains no seat of empire so magnificent as this." The United States, which now "offers supplies on the Atlantic shores to the overcrowded nations of Europe, while on the Pacific coast it intercepts the commerce of the Indies . . . must command the empire of the seas, which alone is real empire."[59] He would later entreat the United States Senate to "open up a highway through your country, from New York to San Francisco. Put your domain under cultivation, and your ten thousand wheels of manufacture in motion. Multiply your ships and, send them forth to the East. The nation that draws most materials and provisions from the earth, and fabricates the most, and sells the most of productions and fabrics to foreign nations, must be, and will be, the great Power of the earth."[60]

Civil Wars in the United States and China, and the Formation of the "Asia Threat" Discourse

Before 1848, foreign threats to American security had always been European or Native American. With the addition of vast and sparsely populated new territories on the Pacific Ocean, an "Asia threat" began to be conceptualized for the first time. The Asia threat has taken two distinct but interrelated forms in American history. The migration threat, which immediately followed the annexation of California, framed Chinese migrants as an existential threat to the civic and democratic norms and institutions of American society and government. The expansion threat, which would emerge into American consciousness later in the century, cemented the conception of the Pacific as a sphere of geostrategic competition from which an Asian power could project military force to threaten the continental United States should control of the ocean ever be ceded.

The issue of American prosperity was deeply embedded within both threats. Chinese migration led to the explicit race-based delineation of exactly who was to benefit, and who was to be excluded, from the bounty of the newly annexed territory. The reaction to Chinese migration in California from the middle of the nineteenth century also threatened the treaties under which the ongoing commercial penetration of China was being conducted. The Asian expansion threat would, in the twentieth century, come to challenge the entire system of American commercial empire in the Pacific itself.

In the United States, Asian migration was conceived of as economic, civic, and racial threats to the fabric of the empire of liberty itself. The economic aspect rested on the observation that Chinese laborers were willing to work for less than their American counterparts, which debased wage standards, the quality of life, and the industrial bargaining power of the working class. The civic threat lay in the conception of an arcane Chinese social and political system at odds with Western democracy and incapable of assimilation. The racial aspect lay in ethno-imperialist fears that the overwhelmingly male Chinese migrant population would either despoil white womanhood and "dilute" white blood or simply outbreed the white population and take the continent for the "Asian race."

The California gold rush began in the same year that the territory was annexed by the United States. With it came large waves of migration, a significant driver of which were the wars and destruction of the traditional southern Chinese agrarian economy wrought by Western incursions.[61] The first US census to include California counted 660 Chinese residents in 1850; by the next census in 1860, there were around 35,000. By 1880 there were 75,000 Chinese residents in California, almost 10% of the state's total population.[62] Curbing Chinese migration was a high priority in California, but the enactment of policy was piecemeal. The first Californian state legislature passed the Foreign Miners' Tax Act in 1850, one of many state attempts to discourage, limit, or ban Chinese migration that predated the federal Chinese Exclusion Act of 1882. A strong sense of resentment toward the federal government emerged as class and region defined starkly contrasting interests regarding China policy. Eastern diplomats and businessmen were eagerly engaged in prizing open the China market to American goods and capital; to their minds this had been the purpose of the annexation of California to begin with. The exclusion and poor treatment of Chinese in California threatened to jeopardize this project.

On the other side of the Pacific, American businessmen and diplomats continued to press for further concessions from the Qing dynasty following the First Opium War and the success of the Cushing Mission. The impact of the First Opium War on the Chinese political order was profound and is marked in China as the beginning of the "century of humiliation," during which China was repeatedly defeated militarily, compelled to make economic and territorial concessions to foreign powers, invaded, dismembered, and forced to pay war debts. The traditional Chinese defensive strategy that focused on protecting against barbarian invasions from the hinterland became inverted as the sea took the place of the steppe.[63] The gravest ramification of the Qing's defeat to foreign powers was not the economic impact of the opening of the Chinese market to foreign commerce but the internal conflict that was tied to it. Banditry, piracy, and anti-government secret societies all spread in the years that followed the First Opium War.

In 1850, the most destructive conflict of the nineteenth century broke out when members of the God Worshipping Society in Guanxi took up arms against the Qing dynasty. The Taiping Rebellion, as the conflict came to be known, lasted until 1864 and cost an estimated 20–30 million lives. British and French actions in China during this period were far more actively interventionist than American behavior. While the most important impact of Western states on the conflict lay in the structural conditions for large-scale civil war that were generated by commercial expansionism, military aggression, and the consequent decline of the capacity to govern of the Qing, and later in outright partisanship with the imperial dynasty, individual Americans also played intriguing and prominent roles on both sides. Although still in a relatively early stage of its influence in China, the young westward-facing American empire was increasingly impacting the process of disintegration of the old Chinese imperial system.

The Taiping Rebellion is a fascinating exemplar of the mosaic of tensions produced by Western involvement in China. The leader of the rebellion, Hong Xiuquan, failed mandarin and self-proclaimed younger brother of Jesus Christ, sought to overthrow the Qing dynasty and break the entire social, moral, and political basis of the Chinese dynastic order. At its height, the Taiping Heavenly Kingdom controlled much of southern and eastern China and ruled over 30 million Chinese. The Taiping movement was Han nationalist, pseudo-Christian, and in many ways proto-communist. The explosion of the Chinese population over the preceding century and the concentration of land ownership within a small rentier class had caused a dramatic increase in rents. The corruption of ruling authorities and the over-taxation of Chinese peasants created a deep-seated hostility toward Manchu rule, particularly in the South. Hong's "God Worshipping Society" quickly attracted peasants, miners, members of the Hakka minority, and supporters of other secret societies when it was established in 1847. The first armed conflict between the Taiping and the Qing occurred in 1850. The revolution spread rapidly. Nanking was captured and established as the capital in 1853, by which point the Taiping controlled most of southern China.

The Christian theocracy, with Hong as the "Heavenly King" supported by several other "kings" and "princes," attempted revolutionary change in the Chinese social structure. Private property was abolished; land was redistributed to peasants; equality of the sexes was established, with women allowed to serve in the civil and military administration; opium, tobacco, alcohol, foot-binding, slavery, prostitution, gambling, and polygamy were all prohibited; and the burden of taxation, which had particularly afflicted the peasantry struggling under a landlord class, was lowered.[64] The weakening of the central government as a result of the First Opium War, the trade imbalances caused by opium addiction, and the necessity to divert the military toward the sporadic outbreak of riots against economic conditions as well as the rolling confrontations with Western forces left the Qing ill-equipped to deal with a full-scale rebellion. The breakdown of the Co-Hong system and the opening of several other Chinese regions to foreign trade meant that many of the southern Chinese who had worked in industries related to trade had become unemployed and radicalized.

These structural factors that led to civil war were accompanied by the extraordinary personal story of Hong Xiuquan. Hong became convinced of his fraternal links to Jesus after reading a Christian tract given to him by an American missionary on the streets of Canton, and he sought out the guidance of another American missionary, Issachar Roberts. Hong would study under Roberts in Canton for several months in 1847 before returning to Kwangsi province and founding the God Worshipping Society. Roberts himself was awarded a somewhat ambiguous post as a dignitary of the Taiping Heavenly Kingdom in 1860 and played a prominent role in expounding Taiping propaganda to attract missionary and broader American support for the cause, before turning against the Taiping in what was an incredibly strange, and apparently delusional, affair.[65]

At the same time, an American adventurer turned brigadier general of the Qing army, Frederick Townsend Ward, was commanding the first Chinese army trained and equipped to Western standards, the "Ever Victorious Army," which played a critical role in turning the tide of the war before the ultimate defeat of the Taiping in 1864.[66] Ward had initially traveled to China as a soldier of fortune hoping to take up arms with the rebels, but having faced too much difficulty in making contact with the Taiping, began working for wealthy Chinese businessmen protecting their wares from piracy.[67] Through a progression of successes, and some failures, Ward's responsibilities and commissions grew to the point that, at the time of his death in 1862, he commanded four infantry battalions and an artillery corps in China.

The involvement of Western governments in China during the Taiping affair was characteristically self-interested and mostly concerned with the upholding of commercial treaties. American intelligence dispatches and the correspondences of the American legation from the period reliably focus on the effects of the rebellion on Western capital and trade in China, as well as the prospect of rebellion spreading among the secret societies to the treaty ports.[68] British, French, and American representatives all made official trips to Nanking to ascertain the status of their commercial privileges and ultimately decide on whether the rebellion would be advantageous to their interests. Despite assurances from the Taiping that trade agreements would be respected, American officials decided that their interests would be best served through a policy of neutrality.

Having conducted a mission to Nanking, American commissioner to China Robert McLane wrote the secretary of state in Washington that, although the Taiping were "composed almost exclusively of the ignorant and unenlightened population of the interior . . . unworthy the respect of the civilised world, and perhaps incapable of consolidating civil government," the policy of "strict and impartial neutrality should be maintained until the one or the other of the contending parties should obtain an ascendancy."[69] In the meantime, the United States agents in China should "conduct our relations with the empire that we may be ready to take advantage of the present crisis to enlarge our commercial intercourse, and extend the lights and blessings of civilisation."[70] Western trade did continue to both the Qing and Taiping during the civil war; the "lights and blessings of civilisation" carried by Western merchant ships and smugglers often came in the form of plentiful supplies of arms and opium to both sides.[71]

The opportunity to extend commercial penetration would present itself to Western powers in 1856, when Chinese authorities boarded the British-licensed ship *The Arrow* in search of an accused pirate. The Chinese arrested 12 local crewmen and hauled down the British flag. British authorities demanded an apology. When it was not satisfactorily forthcoming, they seized the opportunity to assert British military dominance and press for treaty revisions that had been thus far denied by the Qing. The British declared war on the Qing, hampering the dynasty's efforts to quell the Taiping Rebellion, despite having decided that a Taiping victory could likely prove catastrophic for British commercial interests in China. France joined the war as an ally of Britain to further her own commercial interests, as well as in response to the execution of a French missionary by Chinese authorities. While officially neutral, American naval officers and merchants showed great enthusiasm for the war. During the Second Battle of Taku Forts, American Commodore Josiah Tattnall famously declared that "blood is thicker than water," and provided covering fire for the retreating British forces.

Important elements of the American press were also very pro-war, going as far as to protest at American complacency in prying open the China trade through military means where diplomacy had not sufficed.[72] When in 1858 an advantageous peace treaty secured by British and French arms appeared likely, editors at the *New York Times* complained that "it is humiliating to think that, in a matter of such great interest to us as our trade with China, we have allowed others to do the work and reap the honor, while we are content enough to pocket the profits."[73] The war ended in 1860, after Anglo-French forces captured Beijing and burned the imperial summer palaces. The resulting Treaty of Tianjin saw further ports opened to trade, large indemnities paid to Britain and France, freedom of religion, granting of diplomatic representation of Western powers including the United States in Beijing, and the legalization of opium in China.

With commercial rights enshrined through the Treaty of Tianjin, the Western powers could now focus on collaborating with the Qing to defeat the Taiping. Ansom Burlingame, who served as the US minister to China from 1862 to 1867, would become very close with the power behind the Qing throne, Prince Gong. Burlingame sympathized greatly with the Qing at a time when his own president, Abraham Lincoln, was himself embroiled in a civil war against a rebellious South. In 1861 a French offer to directly intervene on behalf of the Qing was rejected out of fear that it would lead to more demands for concessions.[74] British and French forces participated in the defense of imperial positions against the Taiping, however, most notably in Shanghai in 1862, as well as imperial attacks on Taiping positions, notably in Anqing in 1861 and Ningbo in 1862.[75] In 1862 the British government facilitated the sale of an entire war fleet to the Qing, although it was to be disbanded upon arrival over a dispute in how it would be commanded. Britain would return to a policy of neutrality in 1864, after a particularly outrageous massacre of Taiping leaders in the city of Suzhou, when the outcome of the war was already secured.

The Taiping Rebellion ended in a sort of Pyrrhic victory for the Qing. The dynasty would splutter along for another 50 years, but the toll of fighting the revolution, and the inroads that Western power were able to make as a result of Qing preoccupation and weakness, would ultimately lead to the dissolution of the ancient Chinese imperial system itself. Early in the conflict, Karl Marx had predicted that the Taiping Rebellion, and the commercial turmoil that it would create by disrupting European exports to China, would provide the spark for the impending global revolution against capitalism.[76] He was wrong. European trade with China increased even during the war years.[77] The project of American empire building continued. The concessions that were opened for Western commerce in China during the course of the war laid out an even greater field for spreading networks of investment and trade.

China's relationship with the United States would grow closer under Burlingame. His status among the imperial court was such that, upon resigning his position as US minister in 1867, the Qing successfully convinced him to head a Chinese diplomatic mission to both the United States and Europe. Burlingame's diplomatic mission back to the United States was a success, resulting in a treaty between the United States and China that reaffirmed American trade privileges and secured most-favored-nation status for China in terms of travel and residence in the United States.[78] The most impactful section of the Burlingame Treaty guaranteed the rights of free migration between the countries. This would complicate domestic politics in the United States where, particularly in California, Chinese migration was an inflammatory electoral issue.

The American Civil War and Political Consolidation for Expansionism

The history of the American Civil War itself is far too complex to be covered here. But the key observation for the purposes of the study of American imperial expansion that the war leaves us with is the emergence of a dominant sectional interest within American national politics. As a result of the war, the Northern industrial capitalist system established primacy within American political economy. The specific set of interests and ideas generated by this system, the institution of a protective tariff for industrial development, the search for foreign markets for surplus industrial and agricultural production and later capital in China, the necessity of a modern navy, a more involved and outwardly focused foreign policy, and much else would go on to characterize and propel American expansionism in the Asia-Pacific region. The course and result of the war itself is well described in a few lines by Eric Hobsbawm: "The Northern states, though notably inferior in military performance, eventually won because of their vast preponderance of manpower, productive capacity and technology. After all, they contained over 70 per cent of the total population of the United States, over 80 per cent of the men of military age, and over 90 per cent of its industrial production. Their triumph was also that of American capitalism and of the modern United States."[79]

Even under Northern ascendancy, the sectional interests that politically defined the Civil War continued to play an important role in American politics in the decades that followed its conclusion. In 1861, with the passing of the Morill Tariff, an era of industrial protectionism was inaugurated within the United States that lasted into the second decade of the twentieth century. Contestation of the tariff reflected very similar political-economic lines as those of the Civil War itself. Northern industrialists advocated strongly for the tariff to protect their dominance in the American domestic market, while American agricultural exporters, mostly in the South, pushed for a policy of free trade. The tariff acted to redistribute wealth from agriculture toward industry within the American economy. It did this by forcing the internationally competitive agriculture-exporting regions of the South and West to buy overpriced manufactured goods from domestic producers in the industrial North, while receiving prices for their own goods set by the competitive global market.[80]

Richard Bensel describes the political structure of American democracy during the late nineteenth century as being a result of the continuance of competition between the industrial and agricultural sectional interests within American society.[81] In his exhaustive study of American industrialization, Bensel makes the important point that this was not a case of protecting one particularly critical industry for the benefit of the entire economy. Rather, it was a case of a coalition of industrial interests exerting influence over individual congressmen, and over the Republican coalition in general, for the benefit of northern industry, at the direct expense of southern and western agriculture.[82]

The Civil War had threatened to delay the process of western development and stifle American prospects in Asia. Visions of the commercial bounty a transcontinental railroad would bring had filled the minds of American business and political leaders since even before the annexation of California. The governor of Ohio had put it in simple terms, describing how the railroad would "produce results in commercial, moral, and political points of view vast beyond our limited capacity of conception at this time."[83] During the war, Congress had insisted that funding for the construction of the transcontinental railroad continue to flow, lest the warnings of a Californian congressman at the time came to pass and England take the opportunity to construct a railroad through Canada to Vancouver, monopolize the China trade for herself, and perhaps even annex Hawaii in the process.[84]

Under the stewardship of Secretary of State William Henry Seward, American foreign policy remained firmly focused on expansion, both during and after the Civil War. The purchase of Alaska (popularly known as "Seward's Folly") in 1867 secured the northwestern flank of the continent from rival European powers. He supported the construction of an isthmian canal to provide a maritime link between the coasts of the United States and had visions of an American empire, facing westward toward the China market, that encompassed the entire North American continent. Months before the signing of the Alaska Purchase, Seward wrote: "Give me fifty, forty, thirty more years of life, and I will engage to give you possession of the American Continent and control of the world."[85]

With political consolidation and Union victory came more rapid progress in connecting the northeastern industrial and midwestern agricultural areas to the Pacific shores. Chinese laborers themselves played an indispensable role in constructing the infrastructural foundations for the penetration of the Chinese market. The first key component, the transcontinental railroad, was completed with the help of some 10,000 Chinese workers in 1869.[86] The second, the isthmian canal, had been under consideration in American halls of power since at least 1826, when Secretary of State Henry Clay sent American delegates to the Panama Congress to explore construction possibilities.[87] During the 1870s the canal was being championed in Congress for the "almost unlimited commerce" it would bring with China. [88] It would only come after the turn of the century. With the diplomatic work spearheaded by Cushing and Burlingame on the other side of the Pacific, coupled with continental expansionism and infrastructural development in the United States, the consolidated American continental empire now stood to bridge the eastern and western markets—the feat that had so animated American commercial imagination for decades.

The boom in agricultural exports in the recovery from the depression of the 1870s solidified a consensus among many American politicians and businessmen, even in the industrial and finance-focused urban centers, toward overseas export markets as the focus of American economic growth during this time.[89] In the five years from 1875 to 1880, exports of American crude foodstuffs more than tripled in value from $79 million to $266 million.[90] This rapid expansion in overseas market presence was followed by a decline, as the European markets that were the major destination of American agricultural products began to increase their own domestic supply. The European states viewed the growing American market dominance as a strategic threat and instituted their own policies to spur domestic growth, ban American imports, and diversify their sources of supply.

This fluctuation served to reinforce the idea in American minds that US prosperity could only be ensured through secure and reliable access to foreign markets, enshrined in treaties but guaranteed by force and supported politically by a more robust sense of confidence in American imperial destiny. Simultaneous movements gained momentum to both regain footing in the European markets, but more importantly for world history, to penetrate and dominate the vast potential markets in Asia, with a particular focus on China.[91] During the 1880s and 1890s, agriculture, industry, and capital, traditionally divided in their visions of national economic policy, were firmly consolidated around overseas expansionism. Southern cotton exporters, midwestern grain and meat producers, railwaymen, who would benefit from the increased freight and investment opportunities in Asia, oil producers, and of course financial interests who saw the potential for greatly heightened returns on investment in less-developed regions of the world all supported expansionism as the foundation of American foreign policy.[92]

The delicate dynamics of the American relationship with China, still the key to the market while American naval power in the Western Pacific was relatively weak, were threatened by domestic political upheaval over Chinese migration. In 1876, in response to pressure from Californian politicians, media, and workers' groups, Congress commissioned a report to investigate the social, economic, and political impacts of Chinese immigration. The report, published the following year, documents a diversity of opinion on the matter. The business owners and investors, who drew profit from cheap Chinese labor, were against immigration restriction, while the white workers were "almost without exception" in favor of it.[93] The professionals, doctors, lawyers, small-business owners, and the like, who were purportedly less biased by their economic position in relation to Chinese labor, generally held that the negative social effects of Chinese immigration outweighed the positive economic ones.[94] The report concluded that it was "painfully evident that the Pacific coast must in time become either American or Mongolian" and that there was "a vast hive from which Chinese immigrants may swarm, and that circumstances may send them in enormous numbers to this country."[95]

It was a combination of cheap labor for the rapid development of the newly conquered west and the sense that free movement of people from China to the United States was part of a broader quid pro quo with the Qing dynasty, which also involved the free movement of goods and capital into China, that attracted the eastern merchant and emerging financial classes to Chinese migration. Underlying all of this was a continued consciousness that the fate of American empire lay in Asia and that the development of the western portion of the continent, with significant assistance from Chinese labor, was a crucial step in seizing it. Correspondence between Daniel Cleveland, a former New York lawyer and San Diego luminary, and John Ross Browne, Burlingame's replacement as US minister to China, exemplifies these considerations. Cleveland, having been consulted by Brown as an expert on the matter of Chinese migration, explained what was at stake: "A Chinaman will live where a white man would starve; and for this reason, he will labor for a small sum which, perhaps, will only provide him with the commonest necessities of life, while the white man, stickling for what he considers a principle, will not consent to receive less than the full value of his services. It is this fact, among other things, that renders Chinese labor particularly valuable to our State. It is cheap, reliable, and persevering. Their employees are not fearful of strikes and sudden suspensions of work, to their great injury." He added:

> Hitherto England has been the great power in China, but it is a fact well known to residents of that country that our nation is fast gaining the ascendancy, and we have reason to hope and believe that it will not be many years before we will exert a preponderating influence with that government. There are already many indications that this is taking place. The time will come when most of its trade will be monopolised by our commerce, and thus greatly increase this branch of our national industry and wealth. The government of China naturally feels a keener sympathy and a higher consideration for a nation which gives a home and employment to 75,000 of its people. . . . In failing to make a proper use of the opportunities and means afforded us by the residence of the Chinese here, we neglect our duty and interest in not using all honourable means to establish and maintain our ascendancy in Asia. The prize is within our grasp if we will only stretch out our hands to obtain it.[96]

Similar views are evidenced extensively throughout the historical record. The congressional debates over the passing of revisions to the Burlingame Treaty in 1880 and the passing of the Chinese Exclusion Act of 1882 center around the conceptualization of a "Chinese threat" to democracy, racial purity, social harmony, Christian values, and white control of the Pacific Slope, on the one side. On the other, fears of less-rapid development, unaided by cheap Chinese labor, and the abrogation of all commercial privileges to Americans in China.[97] An excerpt from a speech given in San Francisco, read to Congress during the hearing on the Chinese Restriction Act in 1882, sheds light on the level of hysteria reached in some quarters of those opposing Chinese migration:

> It is said that in Great Britain there will be put afloat this year at least one million tons register of iron ships and steamers; more probably, twelve hundred thousand tons or twelve hundred vessels of a thousand tons each. If occasion required, China could buy one-half of this fleet and with her own and such as she could get together she could start a thousand vessels on short notice bringing two thousand men each and hurl, almost before we know it, two million people on the coast. This could be readily multiplied, so that five, ten, or even twenty

millions could be hers in a comparatively short time. What would become of us in such a contingency? It is appalling to contemplate. And yet unfortunately it is all within the bounds of possibility. Survey the strategical and political situation and you will see that from Europe we have little to fear—from China everything.[98]

Opposed to the ethno-nationalists were those with broader visions of empire, many of whom had been the most active proponents of western expansionism in the first place. Congressman William W. Rice, arguing against Chinese immigration restriction, framed the imperial perspective most clearly during the congressional debates and is worth quoting at length:

Mr. Speaker, I protest against the passage of this bill: I protest against it in the first place for economical and commercial reasons. This Republic has fought and bought its way from the Atlantic to the Pacific. The faces of its people have ever been turned toward the west. This Republic has sought and has acquired this vast territory, and it has built railroads from the Atlantic to the Pacific, not merely to improve and possess the territory that lies between the two oceans, but that it might find its way to the Pacific and there indulge that craving which is more strongly characteristic of the Anglo-Saxon than of any other race, for commerce and adventure on the seas.

These great railroads, extending from the East to the West, are not merely transcontinental; they have commenced the circuit of the globe. Bills of lading are to-day made from European cities through Boston, New York, and Philadelphia to Chicago, Saint Louis, and San Francisco. Shall they stop upon the Pacific coast? That is not the purpose for which those railroads were built.

More than a generation ago Thomas H. Benton, statesman and prophet, standing in the city of Saint Louis and advocating the building of Pacific railroads, stretching his arm westward said: "There lies the road to Asia." He portrayed the prosperity and the wealth that would come to this country when over the iron track of those railroads the oldest empires should pour their riches into the lap of the youngest.

Now, when we have built our railroads girdling the entire continent, when we have reached the Pacific coast, we are told that we must stop; we are told that we must not reach our hands further and gather in the wealth of Pacific and Asiatic commerce. I have read in the papers that already merchants in California have lost large sums from the withdrawal of Chinese commerce. That but forebodes what will happen universally in California. The gentleman from Indiana [Mr. CALKINS] yesterday read from the opinions of a certain Mr. King—I know not who he is—that it would not affect our commerce and trade with China if we should pass this bill.

Sir, the Chinese are shrewd, they are human; they know well enough who are their friends, and they know well enough who are their enemies.

. . . Mr. Speaker, the adoption of this bill would shut the doors of China to American influence and American trade. It would prevent the surplus products which now crowd our warehouses, and which the 400,000,000 of the Chinese people need, from finding that market which would be so advantageous to us.[99]

Despite a presidential veto of the first bill in 1879 and the renegotiation of the Burlingame Treaty by James B. Angell in 1880, the movement to restrict Chinese immigration to the United States prevailed in 1882. The fears that it would curtail American business in China proved unfounded. The Chinese government was beset by European aggression in Asia at the time, particularly the French in Indochina, and despite official protests to the United States, it could not afford another enemy. With the rights to the free movement of goods in one direction secured and the free movement of labor in the other blocked, the issue of capital investment and the security of American commercial access to China, both in terms of naval strength and freedom from European domination of the China market, began to take on a singular importance in the US-China relationship and the American imperial project in Asia.

CHAPTER THREE

A Colonial Empire

Trade, Capital Investment, and Imperialism

China's value to American empire was not to materialize through the exchange of goods alone. The China market also represented a field for investment and a future engine for further production. Although American capital investment in China ultimately fell short of its perceived potential, thanks in no small part to contingencies of history like the Communist victory in the Chinese Civil War, to many American political and commercial leaders of the nineteenth century, investment promised to occupy American enterprise for generations and to furnish the table of the new American empire. In his early twentieth-century analysis of the process of Western domination over the Chinese economy, J. A. Hobson identified three stages: regular commercial trade of surplus products; capital investment and the development of infrastructure; and the establishment of a fully equipped modern industrial economy.[1]

Marxist theorists of imperialism agreed with Hobson on the importance of the distinction between the two earlier phases. Lenin wrote that "typical of the old capitalism, when free competition held undivided sway, was the export of goods. Typical of the latest stage of capitalism, when monopolies rule, is the export of capital."[2] Rosa Luxemburg described imperialism as "the political expression of the accumulation of capital in its competitive struggle for what remains still open of the non-capitalist environment."[3] China contained the largest and most promising single section of the world's economy ripe for opening and reorganization along capitalist lines. In China, the first stage was entered through the gradual increase in commercial intercourse of the eighteenth and nineteenth centuries, formalized through the Opium Wars and the fixing of treaties already described, and institutionalized through the Open Door policy established by the United States at the turn of the century. The impact of the period of commercial exchange was profound, heralding the most dramatic and tumultuous changes to Chinese society in millennia. The potential for the social upheavals of the financial phase was greater still.

It is important to note that the impact of Western-driven industrialization and capital investment in the Chinese economy was well divined by Chinese leaders ahead of time, and vigorous effort was expended to prevent it entirely or mediate the worst excesses of its breadth and rapidity. In 1868 the US legation in Peking obtained a secret memorandum addressed to the imperial court composed by Zeng Guofan, the commander of Qing forces during the Taiping Rebellion and one of the most politically influential Chinese leaders of the nineteenth century. In it, Zeng opposes foreign investment on the grounds that it would reduce Chinese trade and enterprise to naught, and cause the unemployment and beggary of the incalculable number of Chinese employed in the "inefficient" modes of pre-industrial manufacturing and transport.[4] Zeng wrote that "in regards to the two proposals of steamers going up all our rivers, and of building railroads, if foreigners are allowed to carry them on, the profits and advantages of our own country will gradually be carried off to other lands; and even if our own subjects join such enterprises, and get foreigners to conduct them, the rich and the strong will then engross the labour of the poor."[5]

In striking anticipation of the Boxer Rebellion that would occur three decades hence, Zeng continued:

> If, however, the foreigners press for their adoption unceasingly, it will be desirable to let them know that even if they should be able to force the authorities at Peking to consent, the provincial rulers, like myself and others, would still resist their introduction with all our strength; and if, by some means, we too should be compelled to give our consent, there would still remain the myriads of common people, who, in the extremity of their poverty, would see how they could better themselves, and rise to oppose the foreigners in a manner that all the authorities in China could not curb or repress.[6]

The upheaval of the Taiping Rebellion and resistance of the Chinese people, anticipated by Zeng, to the Western-led industrialization of Chinese society, which would later come to fruition in the Boxer Rebellion, exemplified the kind of turmoil Karl Polanyi describes as "the catastrophe of the native community" resulting from the "violent disruptions of the[ir] basic institutions" by the forced implementation of a new type of industrial market economy, championed by American imperialism.[7]

Foreign investment developed alongside trade in China. Factories began to be set up in the treaty ports after the Treaty of Nanking in 1842, using Chinese labor and raw materials. Their manufactures were initially ancillary to trade, in shipbuilding and repairs, and the processing of raw materials (like tea and silk) for export. By the 1880s this had expanded to the production of consumer goods, like matches, soaps, paper, and pharmaceuticals, which had previously been imported.[8] This was conducted extensively, but illegally, until 1895 when, as part of the conditions of the Treaty of Shimonoseki after defeat in the Sino-Japanese War, China permitted manufacturing in the open ports.[9]

The value of US trade with China was around $20 million annually in 1880.[10] By the turn of the century, American trade in China was worth around $30 million, accounting for approximately 10% of China's total foreign trade, with a notable increase in exports from the United States relative to imports from China.[11] The rate of growth in investment during this period was much higher still. American investment in China grew from approximately $8 million in 1875 to almost $25 million in 1900.[12] The characteristics of foreign investment in China during this period were changing too. After China's defeat at the hands of the Japanese in 1895, its attitude to foreign investment underwent a dramatic shift. The perception that China would have to modernize or lose its dominant position within Asia itself, not just at the hands of Western powers, became ascendant among Qing officials. This period saw a rapid increase in foreign investment in railroads, mining, and banking that had long been sought by Western businessmen.[13] During this time, American kerosene was processed at American plants in Shanghai, and American enterprises operated in rice milling, pulp and paper production, cigarette manufacture, textiles, and a variety of other fields within China.[14]

While trade remained the primary consideration of American political leaders at the time, the trajectory of capital investment was clear. The very nature of maximizing trade potential led inevitably to investment. The vast Qing empire required colossal capital investment in infrastructure, railways, ports, and sources of energy for transportation before the dream of American market dominance could ever be actualized. As investment poured into China, and as Japan rose as the first modern independent Asian great power, with the US economy continuing to produce a vast surplus of goods and capital demanding foreign market outlets, American political and business leaders began pushing for more military force in the region to back American commercial interests. These forces would require secure bases and coaling stations, and the capacity to defend American commercial rights if confronted by aggressive rival colonial powers. Brooks Adams, historian, political scientist, and scion of both the Adams political dynasty and the Brooks family of Boston mercantile financiers, described the geopolitical fate of the United States and Asia as it was seen by many influential Americans during the late nineteenth and early twentieth century:

> Our geographical position, our wealth, and our energy preeminently fit us to enter upon the development of Eastern Asia, and to reduce it to a part of our economic system. And, moreover, the laws of nature are immutable. Money will flow where it earns most return, and investments once made are always protected. Evidently Americans cannot be excluded from China without a struggle, and they may not, perhaps, be welcomed by those who have hitherto shown most anxiety to obtain a foothold there. The Chinese question must, therefore, be accepted as the great problem of the future, as a problem from which there can be no escape.[15]

From 1865 to 1898, the period between the end of the Civil War and the beginning of the Spanish-American War, the total US export trade grew fourfold.[16] Industrial products like iron, steel, and oil began to challenge the traditional export market leaders, cotton and wheat. Businessmen clamored for foreign markets for their surplus products, and politicians were increasingly responsive. Toward the end of the nineteenth century, with the growth and increasing global competitiveness of the industrial sector, the accumulation of capital reserves, and the shrinking of the internal frontier, the drive for imperial expansion in the United States reached new heights.

The American ardor for expansion was growing at the same time as European imperial power crescendoed. Hannah Arendt described the period between 1884 and 1914 as that in which the European bourgeoisie, long economically preeminent, began to aspire to political rule too. She recounts the internal political tensions this created in the state: "National institutions resisted throughout the brutality and megalomania of imperialist aspirations, and bourgeois attempts to use the state and its instruments of violence for its own economic purposes were always only half successful."[17] Statesmen and scholars critical of imperialism during this time recognized instinctively that a system in which patriotism was best expressed through profiteering, and the national flag used as a commercial asset, would, if left unabated, result in the destruction of the national body politic itself.[18] Imperialism was, by Arendt's reasoning, the first stage in the political rule of the bourgeoisie, not the last stage of capitalism, as Lenin had argued.[19]

The United States, although late to the imperial table in Asia, was, in this sense, more coherently politically structured toward empire than the European states, having undergone a pro-market and expansionist political revolution at its origin and having fought a civil war that cemented the supremacy of industrial interests within the state. American business, as has been demonstrated, was long accustomed to shaping American foreign policy. Alexis De Tocqueville had already described the necessity of going to America to properly understand the power of material prosperity over political behavior in 1835.[20] He observed that the typical American citizen has "always seen order and prosperity marching in step; it never strikes him that they could be separate; consequently he has nothing to forget and has no need to unlearn, as Europeans must, the lessons of his early education."[21] By the last decade of the nineteenth century, American order and prosperity had completed their march across the North American continent. Continued westward momentum led across the Pacific to Asia. The economic imperative for this was set; what remained to be constructed was a navy capable of protecting the commercial interests that lay at the heart of the nascent American empire.

The Enclosure of the Continent and the Importance of Sea Power on the New Frontier

American imperialists forcefully argued that, rather than ultimately leading toward the national decay that sceptics foresaw, expansionism would produce constant national renewal. Congressman Samuel S. Cox put the objection to the house: "When a State, which is commercial by situation, forgets the work of outbuilding its empire, it loses its inner vitality. The day that marks its failure to meet every rising opportunity of advancement abroad, marks its sure decline at home."[22] By the last decade of the nineteenth century, all such prospects for growth within the North American continent had already been seized. The US Census Bureau declared the closing of the internal frontier in 1890.[23] The continental period of American westward expansion, which involved the annexation of vast tracts of North America and its incorporation into the US political union, had come to a close. The next phase would be oceanic and colonial in nature.

Three years later, historian Frederick Jackson Turner penned the seminal work tying American political and economic structures with westward expansion, "The Significance of the Frontier in American History." In it, he claimed that the United States in the 1890s stood at the end of a historical epoch stretching back to the founding of the original European colonies.[24] The era of continuous expansion into bountiful "free" western lands was over. This, Jackson argued, not only raised questions about the continuance of the economic model of the United States but of its very political essence, which had to this point been shaped and influenced by its constant contact with an unruly frontier. In Jackson's words: "This perennial rebirth, this fluidity of American life, this expansion westward with its new opportunities, its continuous touch with the simplicity of primitive society, furnish the forces dominating American character."[25] These characteristics—economic dynamism, tendency to violence, egalitarianism, and a vibrant democracy—were made possible by the constant breaking of the links with past institutions, hierarchies, and customs at the frontier.

The conditions generated by constant frontier expansionism were relied upon to secure the American interests of prosperity, democracy, and domestic stability.[26] Turner correctly identified this and predicted, a few short years before the American assumption of a colonial empire through war with Spain, that the United States would continue to expand and demand an even wider field for its enterprises: "With the settlement of the Pacific coast and the occupation of the free lands, this movement has come to a check. That these energies of expansion will no longer operate would be a rash prediction; and the demands for a vigorous foreign policy, for an interoceanic canal, for a revival of our power upon the seas, and for the extension of American influence to outlying islands and adjoining countries, are indications that the movement will continue."[27]

The new epoch, with clearly distinct material conditions and relations among nations and empires whose relative power was also in a period of flux, both necessitated and itself birthed a much-altered set of ideas about the direction of the United States and the perils it faced. American intellectual, political, and business leaders at the turn of the twentieth century were firmer than ever in conceptualizing the continuance of the American interest around economic expansion into the Pacific and prioritizing the military architecture required to keep it secure.

American activity conducted during the continental period, from the revolution until 1890, was characterized by three clear strategic goals: national defense from outside invasion; securing and expanding the continental territory of the United States; and preserving the Union itself.[28] The pursuit of these entangled goals resulted in both the eruption of acute and intensive military conflict, as with the War of 1812, the Mexican-American War, and the American Civil War, as well as the ongoing mobilization of the United States Army against Native Americans throughout the entire period.

The strategic architecture of military bases within the North American continent during this period most reflected the military prerogative of defeating the Native American tribes in the interior and defending the Atlantic coastline against European aggressors.[29] The coastal defenses were located within the major urban ports, such as New York, Philadelphia, Baltimore, and Charleston, but the forts of the interior were located either at the frontier or often within what was considered foreign, Native American, territory at the time.[30] Many major operational military bases within the United States today originally operated as nodes in the sprawling military architecture of frontier forts and garrisons in the war against the Native Americans, and there were 138 of these separate installations by the middle of the nineteenth century.[31]

The continental period was bookended by the two most important conflicts between the United States Army and Native American forces. The first, the Battle of the Wabash in 1791, was the greatest victory ever won by Native Americans and the largest proportional military disaster the United States has ever suffered.[32] Chief Little Turtle led a force of around 1,000 warriors of the Western Confederacy against an expedition of approximately 1,400 US soldiers and militiamen, resulting in their total route and the suffering of around 1,000 casualties.

The defeat exacerbated the divisions within the governing class that led to the creation of the first political parties in the United States, produced the first ever congressional investigation into executive affairs, changed how the United States raised and organized its armies, and caused a panic over the destruction of the US military at a time when Spanish and British forces were perceived to be waiting to carve up the young and vulnerable republic.[33] Almost a century later the Sioux, Cheyenne, and Arapaho defeated Lt. Col. George A. Custer's Seventh Cavalry Regiment at the Battle of Little Bighorn. By this time the American colossus was in full motion; although culturally impactful and historically significant, the Native American victory barely delayed the advance of American empire and the consolidation of the American interior under the full control of the government in Washington.

The resistance of the Plains Indians was crushed by the US Army over the years that followed Little Bighorn. The Nez Perce and the Apaches fought notable wars against the United States Army during the 1870s and 1880s, but the continental expansion of the United States continued apace. In 1889 a huge chunk of Indian Territory was opened up to white settlement in the Oklahoma Land Rush. One year later the US Census Bureau announced the closing of the American frontier.[34] In the final days of that year, the Seventh Cavalry massacred several hundred Lakota Sioux men, women, and children at Wounded Knee in South Dakota. The United States Army had militarily defeated the Native American tribes, permitting the full European settlement of the continental United States. Manifest Destiny, in its original conception, was achieved. But the process of persistent expansion westward did not halt. Within eight years of the closing of the frontier, the United States would take up the mantle of colonial empire, declaring war on the decaying Spanish empire and acquiring their Caribbean and Pacific possessions, adding several populous countries to their preexisting collection of island territories, including Midway, acquired under the Guano Islands Act of 1856.

The new oceanic phase of American imperial expansion required a wholly different military apparatus than that which had preceded it during the continental era. As early as 1785 Thomas Jefferson was already anticipating the "frequent wars" which the United States would fight in the future to secure new markets for its economic surplus.[35] Viewing it as an inevitability, Jefferson advocated the construction of a substantial naval force to avoid the "insult and injury" that would be provoked by American weakness.[36] While the United States began operating a modest navy by relative standards from the passing of the Naval Act in 1794, and established a permanent Pacific squadron in 1821, it did not operate a truly substantial permanent naval force until the last decade of the nineteenth century. Once national and economic consciousness had turned maritime, the progress was rapid. In 1886 the United States deployed the 12th largest navy in the world. By 1907 it was second only to the British fleet.[37]

The most widely influential new set of ideas in the strategic realm during this period is certainly to be found in Alfred Thayer Mahan's *The Influence of Sea Power upon History: 1660–1783*, published in 1890. Through this book, and a wide range of essays and articles, Mahan provided a detailed thesis linking America's future greatness and prosperity with the expansion of its commercial empire. A strong navy as the military foundation of the empire was paramount for its success and endurance, he argued. This would require vast increases in both naval and commercial tonnage for the United States, the acquisition of a string of bases connecting America to her markets, and an isthmian canal, well defended by American ships, to connect the European, American, and Asian markets, as well as give strategic depth to American naval operations between the two coasts.

Mahan's underscoring of the role of commerce in national power transcended economics and incorporated ideas of national, and racial, character. For Mahan, American greatness would follow on from, and amplify, the Anglo-Saxon imperial power spearheaded by the British. Mahan believed that it was an aptitude and character for commercial pursuits that provided the very basis for national sea power, and the ultimate capacity to maintain a functional and prosperous empire.

The importance of foreign markets for commerce was for him obvious. Bases, coaling stations, communications hubs, and outposts were needed along the maritime routes connecting producers with markets. While the United States had begun acquiring unoccupied islands in the Pacific and elsewhere during the 1860s, it would need to add several pieces of long-inhabited real estate to ensure the security of its commerce and deny their occupancy to potential rival powers. In this way, commerce begat American colonial expansion in the Pacific. Mahan was a strong advocate of the annexation of Hawaii and the Philippines, and his arguments for expansionism influenced many of the key decision makers in the United States to pursue a colonial empire at the end of the nineteenth century.

Theorizing Empire and the Splendid Little War
Territorial expansion in the Pacific during the late nineteenth century was primarily conceived of as the accumulation of stepping stones and strongpoints to secure American commercial interests in China. The lead up to the more robust expansion of American military power into the region involved the development of the framing of Asian countries, particularly China, and later Japan, as threats to the United States itself. The framing of Asian states as economic, civilizational, demographic, and strategic threats, not merely commercial opportunities, during this time laid the foundations for Asia threat perceptions that persist today. The material drivers of expansion that had been propelling the United States westward for the past century were, at the turn of the twentieth century, becoming entwined with a new manifestation of ideological and strategic justifications for empire.

While sociological ideas permeated Mahan's writing, he was first and foremost a strategist. Other influential writers of the time, like Brooks Adams and Charles Henry Pearson, emphasized economic, and ultimately civilizational, struggle as the most significant consequence of American empire. The entirely complementary approaches to empire of these three men were synthesized in the politics of President Theodore Roosevelt and his close political allies, like Henry Cabot Lodge. Roosevelt, highly active in political and intellectual circles well before his presidency, was a friend and confidant of both Mahan and Adams, and a correspondent and self-described admirer of Pearson's. An avid reader and prolific writer himself, Roosevelt reviewed all three men's most influential books, *The Influence of Sea Power upon History*, *The Law of Civilization and Decay*, and *National Life and Character: A Forecast*, in the pages of American journals.[38]

In 1903 W. E. B. Du Bois identified the problem of the coming century to be the drawing of the global "color-line," which would decide "the relation of the darker to the lighter races of men in Asia and Africa, in America and the islands of the sea."[39] In the decades before his observation, Mahan, Adams, Pearson, and Roosevelt were articulating a civilizational credo for drawing this line firmly in favor of the white man's empire. The greatest threat to white supremacy in the United States and its nascent Pacific empire was always seen as emanating from Asia. This was perhaps most famously articulated by Pearson in his hugely impactful *National Life and Character: A Forecast*. Writing at the zenith of European imperial influence, Pearson predicted that the end of white global dominance was near at hand and that white men would soon "wake to find ourselves elbowed and hustled, and perhaps even thrust aside by peoples whom we looked down upon as servile."[40]

Pearson wrote extensively on Chinese migration in California, viewing the situation there as a localized example of what would soon be a global phenomenon, as China, and Asia more generally, began to mobilize its own labor power, natural resources, and industry, displacing white leadership in these fields and achieving a much higher degree of world power.[41] Pearson viewed this development with a sort of depressed resignation and sense of inevitability, but many of his readers, including some of the most important political figures in the United States, interpreted it as a call to arms against the rising tide of the "colored" races.

Theodore Roosevelt found the sense of inevitability of the decline of the west in Pearson's work "unduly pessimistic."[42] He wrote a lengthy and glowing review of *National Life and Character*, which he described as "one of the most notable books of the century," and emphasized his conviction of the importance of keeping the North American continent for the white race and excluding the "ruinous presence" of the Chinese.[43] In a personal letter to

Pearson, Roosevelt wrote of the great interest that his book had stimulated in Washington DC, stating that only Mahan's *The Influence of Sea Power upon History* could compare with *National Life and Character* for its effect on reshaping the global perspective of concerned Americans.[44]

Brooks Adams was also wary of the growing power of Asia and its implications for the new American empire. But, like Roosevelt, he thought that the United States could prevail under wise management and turn Asian commercial power to its advantage. He viewed the movement of the focal point of global wealth and power from Great Britain to the United States as the great historical development of the era.[45] Whether this remained centered in North America or continued westward to Asia would be the result of both industrial developments in Asia itself and the building of American administrative machinery for world power coupled with the political will to continue expansion.[46] If successful in this enterprise, Adams envisioned a new Anglo-Saxon empire, dominating global affairs, "whose right wing would rest upon the British Isles, whose left would overhang the middle provinces of China, whose centre would approach the Pacific, and who would encompass the Indian Ocean as though it were a lake, much as the Romans encompassed the Mediterranean."[47] Adams was unequivocal in his conviction that "the greatest prize of modern times is northern China."[48]

The first component for the successful execution of empire was in laying the most advantageous geopolitical foundation across the Pacific. The Hawaiian Islands, which had been in the sights of American imperialists for decades, were the keystone for Pacific geostrategy. President Tyler had extended the Monroe Doctrine to Hawaii in 1842, with the express rationale being its position in relation to the China market. With the rapid expansion of European imperialism in Asia in the latter decades of the nineteenth century and the feared growth of Asian power itself, American politicians and strategists began to view Hawaiian independence as insufficient for guaranteeing American imperial interests across the Pacific. Mahan saw Hawaii as the key to American power in the Pacific in three ways: as the commercial focal point of the trade routes that would sprawl from Europe, the Americas, and Asia, particularly following the opening of an isthmian canal; as the most suitable location of harbors and strongpoints to ensure naval dominance of the Pacific; and as the location that must be denied any potential adversary for its position in relation to the American west coast.[49]

Precluding British annexation of the islands was a major and longstanding concern. But it was Mahan's evocation of a Chinese threat to Hawaii, and in turn the continental United States, that proved a more prescient observation of the strategic fault lines that would drive American security policy in the Pacific in the coming century: "It is a question for the whole civilized world and not for the United States only, whether the Sandwich Islands [Hawaii], with their geographical and military importance, unrivalled by that of any other position in the North Pacific, shall in the future be an outpost of European civilization, or of the comparative barbarism of China." He added: "China, however, may burst her barriers eastward as well as westward, toward the Pacific as well as toward the European Continent. In such a movement it would be impossible to exaggerate the momentous issues dependent upon a firm hold of the Sandwich Islands by a great, civilized, maritime power."[50]

In 1893 a successful American-backed revolution overthrew the Hawaiian monarchy. The ultimate goal of annexation was walked back, however, by the incoming presidential administration of Grover Cleveland. Democratic opposition to annexation and imperial expansion prevailed for a brief time, but with the 1897 election of Republican president William McKinley, expansionists again took the lead. That year, McKinley appointed Theodore Roosevelt as assistant secretary to the navy. Having defeated China in the First Sino-Japanese war in 1895, Japan now occupied the foremost position in the minds of American imperial planners as the Asian threat to the United States. Mahan wrote to Roosevelt in 1897, weeks after his appointment to the position of assistant secretary of the navy, warning him of the dangers posed by Japan to the United States' position in the Pacific, particularly in relation to Japanese control over Hawaii.[51]

With the powerful business community coalescing around the need to secure access to foreign markets, driven home by the severe economic depression of 1893–1897, and a newly developed imperial ideology, highly cognizant of an emerging "Asia threat," becoming increasingly influential in elite circles of government, the United States stood ready to leap into colonial imperialism. The prolonged conflict over Cuban independence from the ailing Spanish empire provided the necessary spark. Well aware of the implications Spanish decline held for American imperial ambitions in both the Caribbean and the Pacific, Roosevelt ordered the recently modernized US Navy to be ready for war with Spain, despite the reluctance of President McKinley himself.[52] It was under Roosevelt's orders that Commodore Dewey was prepared, provisioned, and positioned to destroy the Spanish Navy in Manila Bay when war was declared in April 1898.[53]

The war itself went off without a hitch, with naval power proving decisive, as predicted. Before a treaty was signed, John Hay, who would be made secretary of state later in 1898 and author the inestimably influential Open Door Note the year following, wrote to Roosevelt celebrating the "splendid little war" in which he had played such an important role, both in preparation as assistant secretary of the navy and in commanding the "Rough Riders" cavalry battalion that fought in several key battles in Cuba.[54] After less than four months of fighting, and only 385 combat deaths, the United States achieved an overwhelming victory in both the Caribbean and the Pacific. Puerto Rico, Guam, and the Philippines were ceded to the United States, and temporary control was taken over a nominally independent Cuba.

Hawaii had been annexed by the United States during the war, with much of the congressional debate focusing on the need to take Hawaii to support Admiral Dewey in Manila.[55] Even George F. Hoar, one of the most consistent opponents of American imperialism in the Senate, was convinced by the arguments for annexing Hawaii. On the floor of the Senate, Hoar noted:

> If this be the first step in the acquisition of dominion over barbarous archipelagos in distant seas; if we are to enter into competition with the great powers of Europe in the plundering of China, in the division of Africa; if we are to quit our own to stand on foreign lands; if our commerce is hereafter to be forced upon unwilling peoples at the cannon's mouth; if we ourselves are to be governed in part by peoples to whom the Declaration of Independence is a stranger; or, worse still, if we are to govern subject and vassal states, trampling as we do it on our own great charter which recognizes alike the liberty and the dignity of individual manhood, then let us resist this thing in the beginning, and let us resist it to the death.[56]

For the moment, Hoar judged that imperial aggrandizement was not the objective of taking the Philippines as a colony. Despite its status among advocates for empire as the much-desired key to the Pacific and the China market, Hoar viewed its acquisition as a necessary defensive precaution. As occurs so often in a system of competing imperial expansionism, empire was justified on the basis that it prevented the extension of a rival imperialism. According to Hoar, "the question is not whether we are to advance our flag into the Pacific for the first time, but whether it is, on the whole, best that the little scrap of territory and the little handful of people that dwell under the walls and at the gates of our great fortified place shall be under our lawful control or shall be under the control of some foreign country, perhaps a powerful country, perhaps a hostile country."[57] Congressional advocates for commercial expansion were under no illusions as to its place in the growing empire. It was the "halfway house to the great markets of the east" and a necessary crossroads for America's "rapidly increasing commerce with the mighty hordes with whom we shall trade . . . across the Pacific."[58]

While Hawaii was framed as the strategic "key" to the Pacific, it was Manila's position as the eastern archipelagic entrepôt to the China market that had inspired Roosevelt, various members of Congress, and the New York State Chamber of Commerce to lobby McKinley to take and retain the Philippines well before the war with Spain was declared.[59] Colonial imperialism of this nature was controversial among the public and in Congress. Democrats were particularly circumspect on the difficulties of extending the Constitution to the doorstep of Asia. McKinley rallied the public to his cause with speeches highlighting the bounty to be gained through annexation: "We want new markets, and as trade follows the flag, it looks very much as if we are going to have new markets."[60]

Although this lust for markets moved the business community as a whole, many individual businessmen, particularly in the northeast, opposed imperialism on the grounds that it would ultimately reduce the moral stature, and in turn national vigor, of the United States and lead the world to further conflict and wars. Andrew Carnegie, at the helm of some of the largest industrial concerns in the country and at one point the richest man in the United States, was a staunch opponent of the annexation of the Philippines and of America's turn toward this new phase of imperialism in general.

Under the banner of the American Anti-Imperialist League, Carnegie and other businessmen joined with American political, intellectual, and cultural luminaries such as Grover Cleveland, Samuel Gompers, Carl Schurz, John Dewey, and Mark Twain to oppose American imperialism in Asia and elsewhere. Nevertheless, its commercial significance, and the fear that an independent Philippines or one retained by a prostrated Spanish Empire would simply be swallowed up by a rival power, led the United States to take and retain the entire island group at the end of the war.

The fear was not entirely unfounded. Britain had secured the large settler colonies of Australia in 1788 and New Zealand in 1840, established Singapore in 1819, and took Fiji in 1872. France took Tahiti and New Caledonia in 1842 and 1843 respectively, followed by Vanuatu in 1887. Germany joined the race in the later decades of the nineteenth century, taking New Guinea and Micronesia, and splitting Samoa with the United States. These colonies were accompanied by myriad smaller territorial "concessions" across Asia and, of course, by large mainland and Southeast Asian colonies as well. By 1900, when the US-German partition of the Samoan Islands occurred, there were no independent island states left in the Pacific.

The new territory acquired by the United States at the turn of the century was different in several important senses from territory that had been conquered or purchased previously. With the exception of Hawaii, there was no significant white settler–colonialism. Instead territories of millions of Native inhabitants were to be governed by a small handful of civilian and military administrators, much as the British and other European imperial powers did. Further, again with the exception of Hawaii, the new territories were to remain " 'unincorporated" under the governing power of the United States Congress but not offered the full protection of the US Constitution. This governance structure, unencumbered by concerns for local democracy, well suited their purpose as strategic strongpoints on the road to the China market.

The Open Door: Foreign Policy for a New American Century

As Turner had predicted, the closing of the continental frontier had only brought forth the view of new conquests. The United States emerged from the Spanish-American War with a fully fledged Pacific empire. Skeptics like Hoar would soon recognize the implications of this historic development and come to bitterly oppose American colonialism in the Philippines, but they were overwhelmed by the structural forces that had relentlessly propelled American expansionism since the revolution and found themselves fighting against an imperial tide. Through the ascendance of Theodore Roosevelt to the presidency in 1901, the United States found itself its first truly imperial head of state. Roosevelt had outlined his arguments for a new Pax Americana in his article "Expansion and Peace," written in 1899 when he was governor of New York. Here he drew a direct analogy between the harsh treatment of Native American tribes during the continental phase of expansionism and the necessity to continue fighting expansionist wars against the "uncivilized barbarians" on America's new frontiers: "peace can only come through war" as "the growth of peacefulness between nations . . . has been confined strictly to those that are civilized."[61]

The mission to bring a "civilized peace" to Asia coincided with the formalization of American economic policy in China and the development of a naval capacity to enforce it. The concessions won in Taiwan and Korea by Japan as a result of the Sino-Japanese War in 1895 and the spread of European spheres of influence in China caused alarm in the United States. Russian and German encroachments in Manchuria and Shandong, regions which absorbed almost two-thirds of American exports to China, were of particular concern. An outcry led by Charles Denby, American minister in China, and taken up by a variety of American business groups caught the attention of the State Department.[62]

In 1899 Secretary of State John Hay issued the Open Door Note to Japan and the European powers operating in China. The note was a statement of principle that no exclusive spheres of influence would be pursued in China and that commerce would operate based on the most-favored-nation terms, established in the wake of the Opium Wars. The spread of spheres of influence threatened to turn China into an arena of great power conflict, with the distinct possibility that a large part of the vast market that had enchanted American business interests for generations could be shut off to their trade and investment. All of the countries involved agreed in principle, on the proviso that all others also acted in accordance with the Open Door.

The Open Door eschewed the traditional patterns of European colonialism, while betraying a confidence that American economic supremacy would secure a large share of global commerce in the absence of barriers. It was not merely a policy for ensuring free trade, for the United States was, as we have seen, committed to a program of protectionism since the victory of the industrialist North in the Civil War. Rather, the Open Door was a new formula for an empire with global aspirations.

By ensuring equal access to trade and capital around the world, American merchants, businessmen, and bankers were expected to come to dominate international commerce and undermine European colonial domains.[63] A *New York Times* editorial, written several months before Hay's note was issued, characterized what would be called the Open Door policy as one that would bring prosperity to both the United States and the rest of the world, and provide a material foundation for global peace. It was, therefore, for the United States "the true mission that we have to carry out as a world power."[64] Applied initially in China, the Open Door policy would come to characterize the American approach to world order as a whole.

It was, in a sense, a model for what W. M. Roger Louis and Ronald Robinson would later characterize as "the imperialism of decolonization," and Thomas J. McCormick as an "imperium in anti-imperio."[65] Rather than creating a vast and burdensome formal empire over a swath of China, the United States opted for a lighter-footprint imperialism over smaller and weaker island nations that would act as stepping stones and strongpoints across the Pacific and ensure the United States' capacity to exert military force where necessary to secure access to the China market. The United States and Great Britain (by far the largest investor and trader in China at the time, whose position would be threatened by the appearance of foreign exclusive economic spheres of influence) were interested in keeping a centralized Chinese state that could be used to balance expansionist Japan and Russia in the region. They also feared the expenditure of vast resources that would be required to man colonial borders between European powers in China. China was more useful as a unified but subaltern state, which could be mobilized against other powers if need be, exploited as a market and outlet for capital investment, and used as a buffer, than it was as another colony.

Within months of the issuance of the Open Door Note, the entire system of Western commercial dominance of China came under threat from the anti-imperialist Boxer Rebellion, which saw Qing forces join a popular rural uprising against foreign economic and religious incursion into China. The rebellion was suppressed by the Eight-Nation Alliance of European imperial powers, Japan, and the United States, ending in the capture of Beijing in August 1900, and concluded with the official signing of the peace treaty the following year. America's most decorated war hero, Marine Corps Major-General Smedley Butler, was wounded in the Battle of Tientsin during the Boxer Rebellion. His experience fighting and commanding troops in China and Latin America would lead Butler famously to conclude that "war is a racket," in which the common man was taxed for the privilege of dying in foreign lands so that bankers, industrialists, and speculators could make and protect profits outside of the United States.[66]

The Open Door policy had mixed results. The "rights" of Western commercial interests were challenged by the Chinese themselves, and large Russian and Japanese incursions, threatening to carve out exclusive spheres of influence, occurred during the early years of the twentieth century. Still, the wholesale dismemberment of China by colonial powers never came to pass, even with the collapse of the Qing dynasty. The most significant impact of the Open Door Note was the establishment of the core commercial principles of American foreign policy that would later be enshrined in the liberal international institutions of American empire after the Second World War.

This system was based around a rejection of traditional colonialism, while maintaining an insistence on global economic openness and integration. In such a field, the comparative economic advantages of the United States would result in her assuming the leading position in the global economy without having to fight wars of conquest. While aggregate commercial engagement remained highest with other industrialized economies, American products and investment flowed increasingly into undeveloped markets during the early twentieth century, mainly in Asia and Latin America.

This formalized approach to international economic affairs was complemented by a corresponding crystallization of policy on military intervention. The Roosevelt Corollary to the Monroe Doctrine, outlined in his annual presidential speech to Congress in 1904, assumed for the United States the role of an "international police power."[67] Initially conceived in the wake of the Venezuelan Crisis of 1902, which involved a European naval blockade of Venezuela over unpaid war debts, the corollary asserted the right of the United States to unilaterally intervene in the economic affairs of its southern neighbors to preclude Europeans from doing so themselves. On American interests, Roosevelt declared: "All that this country desires is to see the neighboring countries stable, orderly, and prosperous. . . . If a nation shows that it knows how to act with reasonable efficiency and decency in social and political matters, if it keeps order and pays its obligations, it need fear no interference from the United States."[68] He drew on the Open Door as a shining example of the American sense of impartiality and its tendency to act "in the interest of humanity at large" to legitimize the new interventionist policy.[69]

While its origins lay in Latin America, the liberal interventionism expounded in the corollary, paired with the assertion of an Open Door to the economies of the developing world, effectively established the political, economic, and strategic framework of the American Century that lay ahead. The assumption of the military might necessary to support the new robust and assertive American foreign-policy framework was demonstrated in the final years of the Roosevelt administration with the circumnavigation of the globe by his Great White Fleet of 16 battleships. The world tour of the Great White Fleet announced the arrival of the United States as a global naval power. In particular, it signified the American capacity and determination to assert its economic and strategic interests and defend its newly won Pacific empire.

Roosevelt had also set in motion the grand geopolitical project that had captivated American leaders since Jefferson: the cutting of an isthmian canal.[70] In his first State of the Union address as president, Roosevelt had stated that "no single great material work which remains to be undertaken on this continent is of such consequence to the American people as the building of a canal across the Isthmus connecting North and South America."[71] In 1903, after supporting a military coup which brought Panama independence from Colombia and de facto status as an American protectorate, the Roosevelt administration took control of the construction of the canal, which was completed by the US Army Corps of Engineers in 1914.

The canal had important commercial and strategic applications. By connecting the east and west coasts of the United States via a sea route, it became a centerpiece of national economic activity and strategic unity. As a geopolitical construction, it conferred upon the United States control over the focal point of interoceanic trade and sea lines of communication between the Atlantic and Pacific Oceans, of particular importance in connecting both the European and eastern United States commercial centers to the China market. American naval power, which was traditionally concentrated in the Eastern Seaboard and Caribbean, could now much more easily be brought to bear in the Pacific, where the United States was administering its new empire.

In the United States, the years preceding the First World War, the most destructive interimperial conflict the world had ever seen, were spent mustering national economic and military strength and formulating a consistent foreign policy based upon the principles of the Open Door. Woodrow Wilson, who would go on to lead the United States during the First World War and play an influential role in the crafting of the peace to follow, made his views on the linkages between trade, investment, the military, and American empire clear in a series of lectures delivered at Princeton University, where he served as a professor and president of the university. He declared: "Since trade ignores national boundaries and the manufacturer insists on having the world as a market, the flag of his nation must follow him, and the doors of the nations which are closed must be battered down. . . . Concessions obtained by financiers must be safeguarded by ministers of state, even if the sovereignty of unwilling nations be outraged in the process. Colonies must be obtained or planted, in order that no useful corner of the world may be overlooked or left unused. Peace itself becomes a matter of conference and international combinations."[72]

The political, economic, and social transformation that took place in the United States during the period from the establishment of the republic to the dawn of the First World War was of a scope rarely seen in world history. In thirteen decades, a marginal community of states with a relatively undeveloped economy, a weak military almost wiped out by a Native American force in its early history, and a population of approximately 2 million, around half of whom were enslaved, grew to a transcontinental, transoceanic empire of over 100 million souls with the largest industrial economy in the world and the foundations for what would soon become the world's most powerful military. This transition was premised on the process of westward expansion and its economic, social, political, and strategic effects.

The march westward marshaled the territory and resources necessary for the base of American empire and shaped its social and political characteristics. Without fully accounting for the vast and complex tapestry of American expansionism, the China market had been conceptualized as its ultimate goal since the earliest days of the republic. This China-oriented commercial impetus has been entwined with dynamic strategic and geopolitical concerns that have shifted depending on the characteristics of the international system, and frictions with other powerful states during particular times and within particular spaces. By the beginning of the twentieth century though, the commercial and strategic basis for American empire in the Pacific had stabilized around an Open Door to the China market and a network of Pacific-island bases acting as stepping stones across the Pacific, supported by a powerful navy.

PART II

ASCENDING POWER TO UNIPOLARITY, 1914–1991

CHAPTER FOUR

The 30 Years Crisis

The First World War was pivotal in several senses that would go on to shape the course of American empire in the Asia-Pacific during the twentieth century. It was the first international large-scale, mass-mobilized, industrial war—in a sense the first modern war. This meant that the organizational and administrative nexus between private industry and the state was greatly strengthened. The planning of the American economy during 1917–1918, a large and distinct change in the organization of American economic life, was a step toward the formation of the American-led world economy after the Second World War. The massive increase in organized and targeted industrial output was accompanied by a variety of technological revolutions in chemistry, physics, and metallurgy that reshaped demand for natural, and particularly mineral, resources, having a profound effect on the American vision of geopolitics, especially in Asia. The growing awareness of the importance of Asia for strategic minerals was accompanied by the growing influence of Japan during the interwar years, and the consolidation of American strategic threat perceptions centered on the Japanese empire.

The transition of the United States from the world's largest capital importer to a net creditor as a result of the war, and the rise of the American dollar to the status of a reserve currency to rival and eventually supersede the British pound, signified the beginning of the ascension of Wall Street to the apex of global finance. Much of the structure of American-led institutions of world governance in years to come would reflect the priorities of financial leadership. Finally, the abortive attempt at creating a Wilsonian liberal organ of multilateral and cooperative world governance, the League of Nations, sprang from the failure of the balance of power to prevent large-scale international war when issues of imperial competition were involved. The League was a model for the United Nations, and its failure demonstrated to liberal internationalists the necessity for the leadership of the United States in crafting and maintaining world order.

The First World War critically weakened all the European empires that had dominated world politics for the past century. While the victors maintained and in some cases expanded their imperial domains during and after the war, it was, in hindsight, the beginning of the end of the age of rival European imperialisms. The United States emerged vastly richer and more powerful as a result of the war.

The only other major power to come out of the war in an improved relative position was Japan. Royal naval dominance of the Asia-Pacific had been sacrificed to consolidate the British fleet in the North Sea. The British had negotiated an alliance with Japan to ensure the protection of British interests in the Pacific, while its naval and military focus was drawn back to the hegemonic challenge in Europe posed by imperial Germany. Japanese ascendance and expansion continued because of the war. It appeared to many observers in Washington that the trajectories of the two growing Pacific powers would meet and clash at some point in the years to come, particularly as Japan made further inroads into the great prize of the China market and indeed into the territory of China itself.

The interwar years are often spoken of as being characterized by isolationism and the American retreat from global affairs. Many historians and scholars of international relations, like William Appleman Williams and Bear Braumoeller, have come to regard this view as highly exaggerated, more a political myth or legend than an accurate accounting of historical reality.[1] While there was a clear divide in political opinion between the impulse for liberal internationalism and a more removed American position in international affairs, focusing on the spirited but only very partially and temporarily successful rear-guard action of a minority of committed isolationists in American political life at the time belies the extensive American involvement in international matters diplomatic, economic, and military that occurred throughout this period. Developments in these fields of American foreign and administrative policy during the interwar years culminated in the production of a broad and cohesive approach to the securing of American strategic and commercial interests, which would become embodied in the American-led world order that would follow.

For the United States in the Asia Pacific, the period of the 30 years crisis was one of consolidation, preparedness, and ultimately triumph. The outcome of the Pacific War (1941–1945) was full American military control of the entire region and the relegation of its erstwhile hegemonic rival, Japan, to the status of a dependency. A new emphasis on access to strategic raw materials emerged and was a crucial development in the dynamic between economic policy and strategy. While the Open Door to secure export markets for surplus goods and capital remained as the cornerstone of American foreign policy, during the decades following the First World War, there was a notable increase in the acknowledgment of the necessity to secure the supply of certain foreign imports to fuel and expand the American economy. Of particular importance were those raw materials and strategic minerals upon which the advanced manufacturing and defense industries were newly dependent.

Industrial Mobilization and Finance

The First World War provided a vast bonanza for American industry, even before the United States entered the fray. From 1915, the American economy boomed on the back of industrial exports to the Entente Powers. From 1917, when the United States entered the war on the side of the Entente, the impact on the American economy was of a higher degree of magnitude. It had by then become apparent that the First World War was of a new and different type to previous conflicts.

The extraordinary number of lives lost and war materials expended during the vicious battles of Verdun and the Somme in 1916 had established this as a total war, requiring the mobilization of entire societies and economies to support events on the battlefield. The conflict quickly expanded to include a "war of materials." The effects of total war on American governance and America's view of its place in the world were profound. The United States emerged from the First World War with a highly coordinated system of state planning which integrated its national industrial, financial, agricultural, mineral, and military resources. While it was not to come to fruition until years later, this systematic approach to social, economic, and strategic organization produced a movement for the reorganization of international affairs along similarly administratively efficient lines.

Germany, stifled by the British blockade, still managed to sustain an incredible output of war materials between 1914 and 1918, the highest of any single nation involved in the conflict.[2] The combined weight of Entente production, however, easily surpassed that of the Central Powers in almost all major areas of war materials.[3] The United Kingdom and France were, predictably, the largest armaments producers in the Entente. The United States however had, within twelve months of full war mobilization, begun to approach levels of production that took Germany four years to achieve.[4] American industry provided Britain, France, and Russia with huge amounts of war materials throughout the conflict, a dress rehearsal for the even more colossal role the United States would play as the "arsenal of democracy" during World War II.

The war of industrial production in the United States was coordinated by the new War Industries Board (WIB), formed in July 1917. Headed by Wall Street financier Bernard Baruch, it was staffed by, among others, "dollar-a-year" businessmen "volunteering" their expertise for the war effort. The WIB was a synthesis of corporate America and the state. Businessmen had come to Washington en masse to organize the new war economy. Joining Baruch were Charles Schwab, president of the Bethlehem Steel Corporation; Howard E. Coffin, vice president of the Hudson Motor Car Company; and Herbert Hoover, entrepreneur-engineer and future president; among hundreds of others. Businessmen organized other new economic war administration agencies too, including the Emergency Fleet Corporation, the Aircraft Board, and the Food Administration.[5]

Writing in March 1918, Secretary of the Interior Franklin K. Lane noted that it was "easier to find a great cattle king or automobile manufacturer or a railroad president or banker at the Shoreham or at the Willard Hotel than it is to find him in his own town."[6] Baruch described the objectives of the WIB and its affiliates from American business simply: "to supervise the industries of America that the energies of each should, as far as practicable, supplement those of all others, and that all should contribute to the limit of their combined ability to one common purpose—the winning of the war."[7]

Perhaps even more important than the flow of materials during the war was the flow of capital. This was truly immense, to the point that it reversed a century-long trend whereby the United States imported capital from Europe to fund industrial development. The billions of dollars in loans that US creditors, most prominently JP Morgan, extended to the Entente nations in the First World War effected a transition from the United States being the world's largest net borrower of the nineteenth century to a major creditor. In 1914 US overseas investments stood at $4.82 billion, and borrowing at around $5 billion; by 1919 the small deficit had swung to a massive surplus of over $10 billion.[8] By 1929 this surplus had grown to $35 billion, seeing the United States overtake Great Britain as the world's largest creditor.[9]

Questions had begun to emerge around the beginning of the century over how comfortably the interests of the United States as the world's largest economy could be accommodated by a global financial system centered in London.[10] The economic shifts of the First World War set the solution to this dilemma in place, as New York began to replace London as the center of global finance and the global economy more generally. The pathway to the US dollar replacing the British pound as the global reserve currency, the stated objective of President Wilson's treasury secretary, was greatly advanced by this shake-up of financial markets.[11] The shift in global financial power toward Wall Street and away from the City of London was enhanced by the fact that the vast majority of the $9 billion of US war credits was owed by the comparably financially stable Britain and France, while over three-quarters of Britain's $3.3 billion of war credits was owed by the bankrupt and revolutionarily overthrown Russian empire, most of which had to be written off as a loss.[12]

The postwar American economy had undergone a transformation not just in administration, scale, and global influence but also in type. Prewar industrial capitalism had faced the central problem of production; now, after the boom of the war years, the new system of "consumer capitalism" faced the problem of maintaining aggregate demand.[13] Manufacturers and export-oriented agriculturalists had pushed the state toward a policy of empire over the preceding century in anticipation of the capture of the world's markets by American goods. With the wartime ascension of the United States to the heights of finance and industrial production, it seemed that the hopes that had so driven American expansionism were coming to fruition.

Director of the United States Council of National Defense Grosvenor B. Clarkson described the transformation of the American economy during the war. "Through it the huge, unwieldy, easy-going, individualistic, careless Colossus of the North became an army from its coasts to its placid farms, and learned to put into its blow the whole weight of its incomparable strength."[14] The amassed strength of the colossus was not simply to dissipate at the end of the war. The greatly increased national capacity of the United States should now, according to Clarkson, be used "to open and hold the markets that our over-developed manufacturing industries need for full-time production."[15]

President Wilson was in agreement. Wilson had made the decreasing economic prospects for ordinary Americans a cornerstone of his political career. In his acceptance speech of the nomination to run as the Democratic presidential candidate in 1912, he had spoken of America as a nation of "neglected ideals and neglected duties" wherein "people find life very hard to sustain."[16] This, he believed, was due in large part to the negative effects of monopoly capitalism, particularly the morphing role of tariffs, which no longer protected nascent industries from foreign competition but now entrenched wealth, privilege, and monopoly with captive markets for big business, while degrading the conditions of working people.[17]

The relationship between big business and the state had to be reformed, but this alone would not be enough. In order to achieve prosperity as a nation, the United States also needed secure access to foreign markets. American producers, he argued, "have expanded to such a point that they will burst their jackets if they cannot find a free outlet to the markets of the world. . . . Our domestic markets no longer suffice. We need foreign markets."[18]

Wilson was cognizant of the historical role of the expanding frontier in generating prosperity for American society. In 1896 he had observed that, with the closing of the frontier, "the days of glad expansion are gone, our life grows tense and difficult."[19] The solution Wilson envisaged was international free trade and economic integration, undergirded by a formal and stable system of institutionalized international relations. The First World War demonstrated the failure of the European imperial system, and the postwar peace settlement was Wilson's great opportunity to see this vision for American prosperity and international stability through institutional democracy achieved. The Republican victory in the 1918 midterm congressional elections and the ascension of Henry Cabot Lodge to the Senate Foreign Relations Committee chair, however, ensured that Wilson would not enjoy a free hand in shaping America's newfound role.

Strategic Resources, Asia, and World Power

The war in Europe had major ramifications for the global order and America's economic, military, and political role therein. Regarding Asia, two specific developments, which were essentially the acceleration of preexisting trends by the war, would have a significant impact on American geopolitical interests. Japan's occupation of German colonial Pacific Island possessions, as well as its concession in Shantung, clarified it as the major threat to the longstanding American imperial goals in China. A more fundamental change to American geopolitical interests in Asia was affected by certain technological developments accelerated by the war. The introduction of ferroalloys like manganese, platinum, tungsten, and nickel into industry, and their crucial role in the production of armaments, meant that, for the first time in its existence, the United States was dependent upon foreign sources of minerals integral to its economy and national security.

Detailed studies produced by academics, industry, and government in the years following the war revealed that East Asia was the region of the globe most critical in the supply of these resources. From this point onward, Asia would play a dual role in United States imperial planning. China remained the projected grand prize of global markets, and Southeast Asia emerged as a major source of strategic raw materials, without which the American domestic economy would cease to function. The issue of strategic raw materials and its interplay with US-China relations would become increasingly important in the decades that followed.

While conflict over limited resources has featured throughout human history, and many of the interimperial struggles of the early capitalist period were fought over territories and colonies that furnished the main raw materials for the consumer goods and industrial products of the eighteenth and nineteenth centuries, the particular dynamics of strategic mineral geopolitics were relatively new. The wide array of minerals essential to the production of modern technology and armaments made it so that total self-sufficiency was essentially impossible after the scientific advances of the First World War.

This was a particularly dramatic change from the conditions of abundance that characterized American economic life up until that point. The industrial revolution made coal and iron the two most valuable mineral resources for a modern economy. Although initially an importer of British iron and steel, the United States, with its vast coal, iron (and later oil) resources, enjoyed an abundance of these minerals crucial to the development of a competitive industrial economy. By 1900 the United States had supplanted Great Britain as the world's largest producer of these resources.[20] This industrial might translated into national power. Rapid scientific progress around the turn of the twentieth century, however, particularly in the fields of chemistry, metallurgy, and physics, greatly diversified the pool of resources upon which the United States and the rest of the industrial world drew for commercial and military production.

The relatively free international commodities markets of the first era of globalization provided the United States with secure access to these newly critical minerals. But the implications that this complex web of minerals supplies held for national security were soon driven home by events of the First World War. The guarantee of a free global commodities market vanished at the outbreak of the war, and access to strategic minerals and the capacity to deal with shortages contributed greatly to its outcome. Germany's lack of nickel, copper, and tin as a result of the British blockade was particularly detrimental to its war effort.[21]

The chief advocate for a new type of planning to deal with resource supply was Charles Kenneth Leith, professor of geology at Wisconsin University, who was appointed as chairman of the newly created federal Committee on Mineral Imports and Exports in 1917, and adviser to Bernard Baruch, the chairman of the War Industries Board, in 1918. In the wake of the cataclysmic consequences of the first fully industrialized global war, and cognizant of the role competition for raw materials, colonies, and markets had played in its causes, Leith advocated a liberal-institutionalist policy for the internationalization of minerals supplies.

The fact that no single economy could enjoy complete mineral independence under modern industrial conditions was viewed by Leith as a tremendous opportunity for peace through international interdependence.[22] In recognizing the economic origins of war, Leith articulated two distinct pathways toward very different conceptions of mineral security. On the one hand, the United States could seek self-sufficiency by maximizing its control over the limited global supply of minerals critical to the modern industrial economy, a course of action which would only spur future international conflict over limited resources. On the other, the United States could use its hefty weight in mineral deposits as a reserve for an international organization that would fairly distribute minerals among nations and discourage the outbreak of future wars.[23]

Under the conditions of geographical distribution at the time, the United States and Great Britain controlled a combined 75% of global mineral resources.[24] The impetus for taking action on resource distribution for peace would fall primarily on these two states. Writing for the United States Geological Survey, Leith reasoned that "whether the time has come to establish a league of nations with economic control can be determined only by our individual and collective answers to the question whether we are willing to make the necessary economic sacrifices, individually and nationally, in the interest of world harmony."[25] In 1919 Leith was appointed as a minerals adviser to President Wilson during the Paris Peace Conference. Despite having convinced Baruch, now head of the Economic Section of the American Commission to Negotiate Peace, of the importance of equalizing access to raw materials, and despite proposals emphasizing the importance of equal access also being submitted by the British, French, and Italian representatives to the conference, no action was taken.[26]

The peace conference did, however, produce the framework for the League of Nations, which was instituted by Part I of the Treaty of Versailles. The main purpose of the League was to establish mechanisms for collective security through international cooperation and settle international disputes through arbitration. Under its organizational umbrella the league also established a wide variety of organs to forge international cooperation on issues of health, economics and finance, labor, refugees, narcotics, and a number of other areas. The League was the product of President Wilson's vision of a liberal world order. While it was doomed to failure, in no small part because of the eventual refusal of an influential minority of isolationists in the US Congress to join, the organizational structure and ideological underpinnings of the League were a preview for how American empire, under conditions of globalization, would look, feel, and operate after the events of World War II.

Haves, Have-Nots, and the Japan Threat in the Pacific

The push for international cooperation to ensure equal access to raw materials critical for industrial development continued in Europe throughout the 1920s. At the Brussels Financial Conference in 1920 and the Genoa Economic Conference of 1922, Italian delegates spoke out against international trusts and monopolies that could manipulate global commodities markets and urged for an equitable international distribution of the materials necessary for industrial life.[27] The great question for world peace that was to be managed during this period was German disarmament and the maintenance of a balance of power in Europe favorable to the victorious allies. The focus on political solutions to this problem, and the sidelining of economic and financial factors that were its root cause, established a conscious group of revisionist "have-not" states, dissatisfied with the global allocation of resources and increasingly convinced that the League of Nations and other international organizations were working toward entrenching the status and wealth of the dominant great powers, rather than toward a more equitable distribution of these resources for the purposes of a sustained peace.

Italy and Japan, both having fought on the victorious side of the First World War, were the first to take a decidedly nationalist and expansionist turn toward capturing a greater share of global markets and resources. In 1922 scholar of economics, politics, and commerce Abraham Berglund already anticipated the expansion of Japanese empire into China's coal- and iron-rich provinces for the securing of the industrial base of the Japanese military and economy.[28] These were the same provinces that Brooks Adams had identified decades earlier as those upon which world power and the fate of American empire would pivot during the twentieth century.[29] Germany, which had become even more import dependent on minerals after having lost around 80% of its iron ore production, and 30% of its coal and steel production as a result of the peace settlement, would soon follow Japan as a "have-not" in its quest for raw materials.[30]

The United States was both fully aware of its status as a "have" power and of the importance of securing this in perpetuity from the earliest stages of the interwar period. With the critical role of resource supply in the First World War engraved in their minds and lacking a meaningful international framework for critical mineral distribution, American policymakers and military planners took to the task of ensuring mineral "preparedness" in case of future conflicts. In 1921 Colonel Harbord, in his posting in the Office of the Undersecretary of the War Department, drafted the "Harbord list" of 28 essential materials that had presented supply difficulties during the First World War. Harbord divided these into those "strategic" materials that must be sourced from outside the United States and those "critical" for which domestic procurement would be difficult. Soon after, 1922 saw the establishment of the Joint Army and Navy Munitions Board, which was to plan industrial mobilization and the procurement of supplies and munitions for national security.

Japan was the only other major world power, along with the United States, to have emerged from the First World War in an improved economic and strategic position relative to 1914. Theodore Roosevelt had warned his cousin and future president Franklin of the danger Japan posed to the United States upon his appointment to the position of assistant secretary of the navy in 1913, saying that "there is one matter so vital that I want to call your attention to it. I do not anticipate trouble with Japan, but it may come, and if it does it will come suddenly. In that case we shall be in an unpardonable position if we permit ourselves to be caught with our fleet separated."[31]

The Japan threat was even more entrenched in the minds of American leaders after having fought the war on the same side. During the 1920s, both the long-held goal of protecting the Open Door to Chinese markets and the new awareness of reliance upon strategic resource supplies from Southeast Asia were deemed to be increasingly threatened by the ascendance of Japanese power. German colonial possessions in the region had been ceded to Japan in the peace settlement. During the negotiations, President Wilson had unsuccessfully opposed the Japanese mandate on the grounds that it disrupted American sea lines of communication between Hawaii and the Philippines.[32] But with the mandate confirmed, Japan's place as the major threat to American interests in the Pacific was cemented.

Japan's role as preeminent threat to American imperial interests during this period is strongly reflected in the correspondences and writings of American military planners at the time. On November 4, 1920, Admiral Albert Gleaves, commander in chief of the Asiatic Fleet, wrote a detailed letter to the secretary of the navy addressing the implications to the United States of Japan's increasing power. Gleaves, also a notable military historian, was convinced of the centrality of the Japanese threat to American interests in the Asia-Pacific and the imperial scope of the conflict to come:

> As England was the obstacle to Germany in realizing her ambition to dominate the world, so the United States stands across the path of Japan, for it is probable that we would not regard with unconcern her further advances upon the mainland of Asia, or her occupation of the islands of the Pacific. This hope of the mastery of the East, is I believe, the inspiration of all Japan's endeavors and is the real cause of her anti-American feeling. Racial and commercial differences are burning questions, but they are subsidiary, although ancillary to the great proposition of Far Eastern control—economic, political, and military.[33]

This "proposition of Far Eastern control," centering around China, had been the driving force behind American imperial expansion westward into the region during the century prior. The United States would not allow Japan's own ambitions in this sphere to derail the project.

Contingency plans for a future war with Japan, code-named War Plan Orange, had been under development in the United States since the formation of the Joint Army and Navy War Board in 1903. These plans centered around the vulnerability of US Pacific possessions to Japanese blockade and amphibious assault, and they anticipated the need to develop a stronger American naval capacity in the Pacific to deter or defeat the Japanese in the region. In 1921, the United States pressed for the termination of the Anglo-Japanese alliance on the grounds that it enhanced Japan's capacity to threaten American Pacific interests. A compromise was reached which led to the Four-Power Treaty between Great Britain, France, Japan, and the United States, which was to uphold the territorial status quo in the Pacific. The Washington Naval Treaty, reached the following year, set material limits on the capacity of the American, British, and Japanese navies to effect territorial revisionism in the Pacific. The overall ratio of 5:5:3 on capital ship tonnage was to maintain a rough parity between the powers in the Pacific, where Japan held the advantage of force concentration. Along with the Treaty of Locarno in Europe, Winston Churchill described the Washington Naval Treaty as one of the "twin pyramids of peace rising solid and unshakable."[34]

While the Washington Treaty was received as a roaring diplomatic success in political and media circles, naval men were skeptical of the benefits to the US strategic position in the Pacific. In a lecture delivered at the Army War College in 1923 and subsequently distributed across the War Department, Captain Frank Herman Schofield, who would later serve as admiral and commander in chief of the Pacific Battle Force, criticized the agreement from a geostrategic perspective: "Sea power is not made of ships, or of ships and men, but of ships and men and bases far and wide. Ships without outlying bases are almost helpless—will be helpless unless they conquer bases and yet the Treaty took from us every possibility of an outlying base in the Pacific except one; we gave our new capital ships and our right to build bases for a better international feeling—but no one gave us anything."[35]

This perception that the agreement to cease the further militarization of US possessions in the Western Pacific was a mistake came to dominate American attitudes during and after the outbreak of the Second World War. It was a major factor in the decision to keep much of the island territory captured from Japan under direct American military administration after the war. Nicholas Spykman, founder of the Yale Institute of International Studies, however, argued that their militarization would have likely only hastened Japanese aggression, faced with an existential threat to the Japanese home islands.[36]

Most Japanese war material was engaged in the long, bloody, and often overlooked conflict in China. Had the United States moved to militarize its own Pacific possessions earlier, imperial Japan would likely have itself begun its own southern push. A wing of Japanese strategic thought had been advocating southern expansion as preferable to involvement in China for decades. In fact, the fear of a southward turn toward British, Dutch, and French possessions, and the source of American strategic materials, enlivened advocacy for the appeasement of Japanese expansionism in Manchuria in some Western political circles.[37]

Japan's initial burst of interwar imperialist expansionism was focused toward Manchuria. Following the staged Mukden Incident on September 18,

1931, the Kwantung Army invaded the northern Chinese province. By February 1932 Chinese state resistance had ceased, and Japan began the process of settler-colonialism and massive industrial investment in their new vassal. "Manchukuo" was to be the first step in the creation of an autarkic regional empire, what would later be named the Greater East Asia Co-Prosperity Sphere. The United States presented firm diplomatic opposition to Japanese aggression in China. The Stimson Doctrine, established in diplomatic notes delivered to Japan and China in January 1932, stipulated that the United States would not recognize any changes to the territorial status quo in China that were established through the use of force. The United States also cooperated with the European powers to produce the Lytton Report, adopted by the League of Nations in October 1932, which recommended that Manchuria be returned to Chinese control. In response, the Japanese delegation walked out of the League, never to return. Diplomatic remonstrances proved ineffective at curtailing Japanese expansionism, and the 1930s saw a progressive increase in interimperial tensions over China and the broader Asia-Pacific region.

Japan's imperial ambitions were heavily influenced by the development of American empire. Japanese statesmen and political thinkers had articulated ambitions for their own Asian Monroe Doctrine since victory in the Russo-Japanese War.[38] In the aftermath of the annexation of Manchuria, Japanese leaders were now openly declaring such a policy as the new de facto status quo in East Asia. This was in direct contravention of American imperial goals in the region, and, if successfully executed, would mean the end of American ambitions for the leading role in developing and exploiting the China market.

Investment, Resources, and the Second World War

During the 1930s, the United States, in the throes of the Great Depression and its aftermath, was in an indecisive position for the crafting of its strategic and imperial policy in Asia. The massive returns on investment and explosion of trade that had been forecast for American involvement in China had not yet borne the promised fruit. While capital investment had grown substantially since the Open Door was established at the turn of the century, it remained a miniscule part of total American foreign investment at around 1.3%.[39] Japan, on the other hand, had plowed massive investment into China, particularly Manchuria, even before the annexation. In 1931 around 82% of all Japanese investments abroad were located in China.[40] In that year, the United

States held approximately $196 million in Chinese investment, substantially behind the Soviet Union at $273 million and well behind Japan and Great Britain, which each held over $1.1 billion.[41]

While the United States lagged in its aggregate Chinese investments, the growth trajectory remained impressive. Compared with 1914, the relative importance of China within all British foreign investments had nearly doubled. In the United States it had increased in prominence four times over; in Japan, five.[42] By 1929 China was the fourth largest national destination of foreign investment in total, and the largest outside of the industrially developed West.[43] Total US investment abroad grew thirtyfold from $500 million in 1900 to almost $15 billion in 1929.[44] The United States was heavily committed to global investments and thus to the maintenance of global stability to ensure their returns. The obvious question that arose in the United States as a result of Japanese aggression in China, however, was whether it made economic and strategic sense to go to war for these particular investments. Many thought not.

American investment in Japan was roughly equal in size to its investments in China at the time, while its trade with Japan was around twice the size.[45] But the impact on global order, and the fate of the principles of the Open Door, that would come with unchallenged Japanese preeminence in China would have far outweighed its immediate investment value to the United States. Allowing Japanese imperialism to proceed in China not only had the potential to effectively shut the United States out of the China market but would also likely lead to further encroachments southward, which would threaten American investments elsewhere. The growing power of unchecked Japanese militarism would soon threaten the United States itself: its Pacific possessions, its investments, its trade, and indeed perhaps its west coast. Most importantly to many strategic forecasters at the time, the growing Japanese empire would compete with the United States for strategic resources in Southeast Asia and potentially cut off supplies upon which the United States was dependent for its industrial production and the American standard of living.

The issue of strategic resources was becoming entrenched within the nascent field of geopolitics during the 1920s. So too was it being incorporated into broader visions of world power, economics, and empire by American strategists, military planners, economists, geologists, and other scholars. The issue of resources distribution became prominent as a result of broader trends toward economic protectionism and the creation of discrete trade blocs within spheres of imperial influence that arose during and after the Great Depression. The Smoot-Hawley Tariff Act of 1930, which raised US tariffs on tens of thousands of imported goods, the British abandonment of its longstanding commitment to free trade with the institution of an imperial preference system in coordination with the Commonwealth in 1932, the establishment of significant tariffs in France, Germany, and the Netherlands, among many other countries, and the separation of the world into different currency blocs with divergent policies on gold-convertibility and exchange controls were some of the most important examples of the sharp movement away from liberal international economic policies.

Historian and long-term economic and security advisor to Franklin Roosevelt, William Yandel Elliot, wrote in 1933 that "the whole world is in for the worst dose of economic nationalism that it has ever seen. Worst because it will be deliberate; because the tools are at hand to make it more absolute than ever before; and because the conditions are present that will probably make the resulting dislocation of existing national economics more painful than ever before."[46] Such a world flew in the face of the Open Door vision of American foreign policy. In the specific field of strategic resources, it could spell disaster for the American domestic economy and capacity to sustain its national defense. In 1934, in response to calls from scientific organizations for better resources planning, President Roosevelt created the Mineral Policy Committee.[47] The committee issued a report recommending the creation of a minerals stockpile to be used in case of disruptions to American supply lines during war, a proposal that was supported by the War Department, the Bureau of Mines, and the American Society for Metallurgical Engineers.[48]

Despite an ongoing awareness of the importance of strategic resources supply in the ominous geopolitical climate of the mid 1930s, and regular and explicit appeals to the intolerability of existent global resource allocation from the "have-not" powers, these recommendations would not be enacted in the United States until the months before the outbreak of the Second World War. On April 25, 1939, the United States Congress passed the Strategic and Critical Materials Stockpiling Act, earmarking $100 million to be spent acquiring those "certain strategic and critical materials being deficient or insufficiently developed to supply the industrial, military, and naval needs of the country."[49] Despite a concrete awareness of the need for mineral preparedness among military planners, scientists, and policymakers, political disagreements and conflict with sectional interests meant that it was not until the eve of America's entry into the war that strategic resources planning began being enacted at a level comparable to that which the experts had been advocating for the preceding two decades.

Japan's naval expansion during the 1930s threatened to tilt the balance of power in the Western Pacific away from the United States, at the same time as its Kwantung Army was busy conquering vast swaths of Chinese territory and using it as an exclusive zone of economic development, in violation of the Open Door principles that had been foundational to American diplomatic and economic policy in China for the past half-century. It was during this period that American strategists, geographers, and policymakers came to view East Asia in particular as the most crucial region in the world for American strategic resources supplies.

In 1940 Professor Robert Burnett Hall composed a study for the *Geographical Review* investigating US dependence on strategic minerals. Hall, a pioneer of geographical area studies who would serve as a colonel in the Office of Strategic Services (the progenitor to the CIA) during the Second World War, argued that, contrary to popular belief, American control of the entire Western Hemisphere would not furnish adequate supplies of the 17 strategic minerals upon which the United States was most import dependent at the time.[50] It was in East Asia that Hall identified the solution to the United States' strategic minerals dependency. He found that only 2 of the 17 strategic minerals identified by the Army and Navy Munitions Board could not be foreseeably furnished from East Asia.

Hall argued that American dependence on Southeast Asian resources was so important that its "entire foreign policy must be adjusted to that fact."[51] As a result, he believed that "the United States would be compelled, for its very existence as a major industrial state, to wage war against any power or powers that might threaten to sever our trade lines with this part of the world."[52] He concluded that "only on the lands west of the Pacific, and especially on Southeastern Asia, is our dependence so vital and complete that our very existence as a great industrial power, and perhaps even as an independent state, is threatened if the sources should be cut off."[53]

Professor Stanley Hornbeck, the highly influential special advisor to Secretary of State Cordell Hull, described Hall's work as "the most interesting, incisive and concise exposition that I have seen anywhere of the tremendous economic importance, especially to the United States, of the Far Eastern area," when he circulated the paper through State Department channels.[54]

The same year, during a congressional debate on naval appropriations, Congressman Charles Faddis made an emphatic and empirically rich argu-

ment for the incorporation of geological, commercial, and strategic industrial knowledge into the formulation of American strategic policy in the Asia-
Pacific. Faddis believed that the Japanese desire to secure raw materials and
commercial advantage would lead it to expand into those regions upon which
the United States was dependent for its strategic raw materials and that the
United States must reinforce its position in the Western Pacific militarily, or
else be prepared for resource dependence upon the Japanese empire.[55]

Professor Nicholas Spykman came to a similar conclusion in his opus on
American geostrategy, stating that "the Asiatic Mediterranean is perhaps the
most important single source of strategic raw materials for the United States,
and its control by a single power would endanger the basis of our military
strength."[56] He added:

> If the Japanese could realize their dream of empire, the position of the United
> States in the world would be seriously affected. It would involve the loss of the
> Philippines, Guam, and probably Samoa. It would end the "Open Door" in China
> and make us dependent on Japanese good will for strategic raw materials of the
> Asiatic Mediterranean such as tin, rubber, kapok, and manila hemp, which are
> very difficult to replace. A "Japanese Greater East Asia Co-Prosperity Sphere"
> would mean the final destruction of the balance of power in the transpacific
> zone which would have ultimate repercussions on our power position in the
> Western Hemisphere.[57]

The shift in American imperial economic imperatives was made clear by
strategic calculations made in the lead-up and prosecution of the Pacific War.
The loss of large swaths of China to Japan was acceptable. In fact, Japanese
management and development of Chinese resources could even prove bene-
ficial to American business in the long run, as long as an Open Door to trade
and investment persisted between the Japanese empire and the United States;
but the loss of control over necessary supplies of strategic resources to the
United States was not acceptable. The line was drawn in Southeast Asia. A
full embargo of war materials by the United States was only implemented
once Japan had invaded Indochina, years after it had commenced a full-scale
invasion of China, and only because Roosevelt now saw an invasion of Southeast Asia, and American tin, rubber, and manganese supplies, as imminent.[58]

Strategic resources played a major role in the conduct as well as the causes
of the Second World War. Like the First World War, the Second saw a much
wider variety of minerals and other resources applied for military purposes
than ever before. A list compiled by the Army and Navy Munitions Board of

materials necessary for the war that presented supply issues for the United States reached 298 items.[59] Control over raw materials had been a clearly identified cause of the war, not least by Hitler himself, and the ability to secure their supply would, to a large extent, determine its outcome.

The advances made by the Axis in this department in the early years of the war were quite breathtaking. Before the war, the "have-not" Axis powers controlled a meager 5% or so of the world's mineral resources. By 1942 Axis-controlled territory accounted for around one-third of the world's mineral wealth.[60] In 1938 Charles Leith had warned that if its critical mineral supplies were shut off, the United States would return to "the horse and buggy days."[61] He identified chromite, manganese, tin, and tungsten among the most important minerals for which the United States was import reliant. Between 1939 and 1942 the Axis went from controlling 2% of world manganese resources to 30%, from 3% of chrome to 30%, from 6% of tungsten to 60%, and from 1% of tin to 72%.[62]

The disconnect between awareness, planning, and policy execution that characterized the US approach to strategic resources during the 1930s was reversed by the outbreak of war. Resources planning was undertaken on a massive scale. For the duration of the war, the United States simultaneously implemented several policies for advancing its resources interests. Legislation was passed that allowed the Reconstruction Finance Corporation to purchase and store reserve supplies of critical minerals; the Combined Raw Materials Board was established, through which the United States and Britain pooled their resources and jointly overcame supply problems presented by Axis expansion; and the War Production Board, which conducted important research on substitution and the efficient use of raw materials, was brought into being. While strengthening their own resources supply situation, the US government also looked for every advantage to weaken their enemy's. The Board of Economic Warfare, which conducted preclusive purchases of neutral mineral supply to prevent it falling into the hands of the Axis, enjoyed some success in this field. The thorough organization of the allied resource base and the destruction of Axis industrial infrastructure through strategic bombing played critical roles in the eventual victory.

A Geopolitical Theory for American Empire

America's Pacific War in particular saw the imperial fusion of the geological and geographical aspects of strategic planning with military execution. Geopolitical considerations of global power distribution had risen to unprecedented prominence during the 30 years crisis. Mahan was certainly the sage of the geopolitics of American Pacific empire at its inception. Now theorists like Nicholas Spykman, Halford Mackinder, E. H. Carr, Rudolf Kjellen, C. K. Leith, and many others were shaping the way American empire would be perceived and planned. While the great foundational geopolitical works of Friedrich Ratzel (*Anthropogeographie*) and Mahan were completed during the nineteenth century, it was during the interwar period that the study of geopolitics became a truly mainstream, and in some cases dominant, political science.

Mackinder's conception of world power as being geographically determined by the relations of the "rimland" (referred to by Mackinder as the "inner" or "marginal" crescent) of the Eurasian continent to its "heartland" contradicted the Mahanian conception of global dominance through sea power.[63] It was the vast continental resources that the heartland, stretching from the Volga River to the Yangtse and the Himalayas to the Arctic, could muster that Mackinder believed would enable it to outproduce and outgun maritime powers in the long run, if ever politically unified. According to Mackinder, "Who rules East Europe commands the Heartland; who rules the Heartland commands the World-Island; who rules the World-Island commands the world."[64]

The geopolitical struggle of the European theater in the Second World War, and the Nazi vision of *lebensraum* in *Mitteleuropa*, sat within the heartland tradition. Karl Haushofer, the Nazi geopolitical theorist, presented a conception of world politics revolving around ethno-states in perpetual competition for power and global dominance.[65] While the ultimate test of dominance of the heartland was won on the eastern front during the war, where some 80% of European combat casualties occurred, it was Nicholas Spykman's inversion of the heartland/rimland relation described by Mackinder that provided the synthesis between the importance of airpower, sea power, land power, and Eurasian dominance that animated American strategic policy in the postwar world.

Spykman's geopolitical summary of world power ran thus: "Who controls the rimland rules Eurasia; who rules Eurasia controls the destinies of the world."[66] Of particular relevance was Spykman's understanding of how the geopolitics of the Pacific would be shaped by the defeat of Japan and how the postwar management of American geostrategy in the Asia-Pacific would be crucial to prevent the emergence of a rival hegemon in the heartland of Eurasia.

Spykman published two books during the Second World War: *America's Strategy in World Politics: The United States and the Balance of Power* (1942) and *The Geography of the Peace* (1944, posthumously). In these works, he made several observations on the strategic situation that would be faced by the United States in the postwar world that showed incredible foresight. *America's Strategy in World Politics* was both a popular bestseller and a prominent tome of reference for the political class at the time of its publication.[67] His prediction, just months after the bombing of Pearl Harbor, that, to secure essential strategic resources and the regional balance of power, the United States would soon need a strong rebuilt Japan as an ally against the far greater threat of a powerful and unified China was particularly prescient in light of postwar and contemporary issues of power and resource politics.[68]

Spykman put forward the argument that underlay the future Cold War strategy of the containment of the Soviet Union while the Second World War was still raging; if the land masses of the old world are brought under the control of a few empires and organized under conditions of industrial and military efficiency, then the United States will be politically and strategically encircled.[69] For Spykman, it did not matter whether this was done under Nazi Germany, Japan, the Soviet Union, China, or any other state or grouping; the threat to the United States remained the same. He argued that disorganization and infighting in the old world was the only reason that the United States was ever allowed to achieve its position of preeminence in the Western Hemisphere. With Eurasia united by a rival power, the United States could not rely on its hegemony in the Western Hemisphere for permanent security and prosperity.[70] If it were cut off from the markets, resources, and forward defensive positions in Asia and the Western Pacific, the American empire would wither.

His concerns over a United States that limited its influence to the Western Hemisphere, unable to procure strategic raw materials necessary for modern industry and national defense, cut off from the foreign markets that underlay American commercial prosperity, and encroached upon by the newly emerged hegemonic powers of Eurasia, held little enthusiasm for the prospect of an isolationist foreign policy. His geostrategic analysis concluded that, for the United States, "there is no safe defensive position on this side of the oceans."[71] This accorded with President Roosevelt's rationale for entering the Second World War: that an isolationist United States could not exist in a state of peace and prosperity, separated from the travails of the rest of the world, but would rather find isolation "the nightmare of a people lodged in prison, handcuffed, hungry, and fed through the bars from day to day by the contemptuous, unpitying masters of other continents."[72]

Spykman believed that, in the First World War, the United States "won the war, but lost the peace."[73] To avoid making this mistake a second time, the United States would have to recognize that power struggle continues uninterrupted, but by other means, during peacetime and commit itself to exercising a decisive role in the peace settlement and the creation and maintenance of the world order that was to follow. This was a vision of American empire without Wilsonian liberalism at its heart. It took for its core of analysis military power, resources, markets, and geography. Spykman's thesis was received with a certain measure of horror by many of the liberal architects of postwar American order, devout supporters of American exceptionalism, and the mission to promote capitalism, democracy, and human rights abroad. Despite the sinking popularity of the field of geopolitics in postwar Western academia, as it came to be strongly associated with Nazism, and the firm entrenchment of liberalism at the heart of the American postwar order, the realism embodied by Spykman's analysis of American strategic priorities remained influential in large sections of the policy-planning network.[74]

CHAPTER FIVE

American Hegemony

Planning the Postwar American Empire

The outcome of the Second World War was nothing less than a complete revolution in the structure of power in world politics. Paul Kennedy describes the interwar years as a period of crisis among declining empires, as Germany, Japan, Great Britain, and France vied to maintain or increase their respective grips on world power while the Soviet Union and the United States, now developed into the sole viable aspirants to hegemony, had not yet assumed positions of global leadership.[1] The framework for global power in the war's aftermath was unmistakable. Some perceptive scholars and political commentators had been predicting the separation of the world into two competing poles centered around the United States and Russia for over a century.[2] The outcome of the Second World War brought this distribution of world power into being.

Between the two superpowers, the overall economic, military, and diplomatic advantage was always held by the United States. American politicians, business leaders, state planners, and military strategists were well aware of the importance of shaping the immediate postwar environment to reflect the interests of the United States. The field of American imperial influence and activity was vastly broadened. The pursuit of commercial and strategic goals in East Asia now fit in with a more complex tapestry of global imperial interests.

The events of the Second World War had almost destroyed any vestiges of serious isolationist advocacy within American politics. The sense that the United States could exist unmolested in a Western Hemisphere imperium was shattered, both by events and by a new elite political consensus. The dominant question of American foreign policy changed from "whether" to "how" the United States should work to shape world affairs. Military and strategic affairs play the major role in popular conceptions of the lines along which the postwar environment was planned. They were certainly important. Economic questions, however, and the US imperative to construct a global economic order in its own image, were given by far the most attention. In his history of US foreign policy formation during the war, Gabriel Kolko observes that "there was a remarkable unanimity in Washington on this objective, and it was by far the most extensively discussed peace aim, surpassing any other in the level of planning and thought given to it. While the United States faltered for a time in regard to its postwar political objectives, it entered and left the war with a remarkably consistent and sophisticated set of economic peace aims."[3]

Those already convinced of American imperial destiny, and those who had the most to gain from it, had been busy laying out the blueprints for the zenith of American power well before the crisis of the war was settled. Media discourse during and immediately after the war is filled with ideas on how the United States should use the opportunity it had earned to reshape the world, with a strong emphasis on open global markets and the "freedom of individual enterprise."[4] In a series of extended editorials overseen by Henry Luce, publisher of *Life, Time,* and *Fortune* magazines, the argument was raised that American democracy itself could only survive under the conditions of an expanded new "great American century" following the war.[5] This world order was to be built upon the rocks of integrated global capitalism and American military supremacy, and undergirded by the unparalleled strength and vitality of the American economy as it emerged from the war.

The material position of the United States relative to the rest of the world at the end of the war was extraordinary. With 6% of the world's population, the United States held approximately half of the world's wealth in terms of gold, reserve currencies, and International Monetary Fund reserves.[6] Its gross national product was roughly equal to the rest of the world combined.[7] It was the largest producer of oil, owning or controlling 59% of the world's oil reserves, and would maintain that position into the 1970s.[8] In 1947 the United States held 70% of the world's gold reserves; this combined with the massive demand for US dollars gave it an unprecedented level of control over global financial liquidity.[9] The military gap between the United States and the rest of the world was also vast. The global network of overseas bases that the United States had developed during the war numbered over 2,000.[10] The USA held a nuclear monopoly until 1949; it had the largest and best-equipped air force in the world; and by 1947 US Admiral Chester Nimitz could credibly claim that the United States now enjoyed a "control of the sea more absolute than ever possessed by the British."[11]

The United States occupied an unprecedented position of global dominance. The unique scale of this preponderance of power brought with it a new type of empire for the United States. Postwar American leadership would not be along the lines of the American empire in the Pacific that had formed during the nineteenth century; it would not be one of many competing empires within the international system. Rather it would assert empire on a global scale, seeking to integrate the entire planet or, at the least, the entire non-communist planet into a single economic and political system, liberal in nature, in terms of open markets and nominally democratic institutions, but with the United States sitting indisputably at the head. For the first time in history, a single imperial power controlled both ends of the Eurasian land mass.[12] For the first time in history, an empire now enjoyed hegemonic control of several key regions of the world outside of its own neighborhood.[13] The implications of American imperium were not lost on prominent British politicians, who were themselves feeling the reins of empire slip from their hands, despite having just defeated their main imperial rival for the second time in 30 years. Harold Laski, chairman of the British Labour Party during the early years of the Atlee administration, wrote that

> America bestrides the world like a colossus; neither Rome at the height of its power nor Great Britain in the period of its economic supremacy enjoyed an influence so direct, so profound, or so pervasive. It has half the wealth of the world today in its hands, it has rather more than half of the world's productive capacity, and it exports more than twice as much as it imports. Today literally hundreds of millions of Europeans and Asiatics know that both the quality and the rhythm of their lives depend upon decisions made in Washington. On the wisdom of those decisions hangs the fate of the next generation.[14]

Britain's postwar foreign secretary, Ernest Bevin, assessed American power and influence as such that "the US was in the position today where Britain was at the end of the Napoleonic Wars."[15] The United States had attained the military, economic, and political power for world empire, but postwar American imperium did not spring fully formed out of these conditions alone. Rather, it was consciously shaped by the most powerful individuals and groups in American politics and business. These groups, referred to by George Domhoff as the "policy-planning network," consisted of a network of think tanks, foundations, lobbying groups, and policy-discussion forums through which corporate and political elites formulated and articulated their policy preferences to the government.[16]

Inputs for the formulation of American imperial policy during this period were numerous and varied, but the most concentrated, consistent, and effective effort to reshape US foreign policy around the anticipated realities of American empire was undertaken by the Council on Foreign Relations. The council's policy-shaping efforts had begun even before American entry into the war when, in 1939, Secretary of State Cordell Hull enthusiastically accepted a proposal from council leadership that it should take upon itself the task of postwar planning for the State Department. The collaboration, working under the title of the Advisory Committee in Problems of Foreign Relations until 1942 and the Advisory Committee on Postwar Foreign Policy thereafter, produced a total of 682 studies for the State Department and White House between 1939 and 1945.[17] The general parameters of the new world order that the State Department and the council sought to create were articulated by Hull in May 1941: the reduction of trade restrictions, non-discrimination in international commercial relations, and the availability of raw materials to a global market without discrimination.[18] The details were to be filled in by the State Department and its research groups from the council.

Walter H. Mallory, executive director of the council, described the collaboration as representing "a new departure in the history of our Government. It marked the first time, so far as I know, in which the services of private individuals, through a private organization, were put at the disposal of the Government systematically and which had a direct and continuing impact on the formulation of policy."[19]

The origins of the council, described in its own self-published history, were as a club of "high-ranking officers of banking, manufacturing, trading and finance companies, together with many lawyers," whose purpose was to liaise with distinguished foreign visitors in support of furthering international commerce.[20] An injection of internationalist scholars to the council during the early years after its founding in 1921 gave it heavyweight status in academic circles; indeed some of the best scholarship on American foreign policy was published in the council's masthead journal *Foreign Affairs*, both before and after the Second World War. Its raison d'être has always been to increase the synergy between American business interests and US foreign policy. Peter Grose, former executive editor of *Foreign Affairs*, described it as the place where "academic and government expertise meet[s] practical business interests."[21] It was, for all intents and purposes, the think tank of American empire, where corporate interests were fused with liberal internationalist scholarship.

The council's members list was and remains a who's who of the most powerful framers of American foreign and security policy, titans of industry and Wall Street, and leading media figures. Its founding chairman, Elihu Root, was one of the most influential American statesmen of the early twentieth century, serving as a US senator for New York, secretary of war, and secretary of state under the McKinley and Roosevelt administrations. It is testament to the influence of the council that it held too many extremely prominent members to list; around half of all top foreign-policy officials in the US government were council members during this period, but some of the most recognizable and relevant names of the early Cold War include David Rockefeller (chairman of the council and Chase Manhattan Bank), Allen Dulles (director of the CIA), John Foster Dulles (secretary of state), and Henry Kissinger (national security advisor and secretary of state).[22]

The core focus of the council's work for the federal government during the war concerned the implications for the United States of the division of the world into two competing economic and political power blocs. Council research established that the section of the world most necessary to United States interests, without the trade and resources of which the United States would face major threats to its national interest, lay in the "Grand Area" covering the entire Western Hemisphere, stretching eastward across the Atlantic to Great Britain and westward across the Pacific to Asia.[23]

The Asia-Pacific region was considered particularly important to the United States in this equation as a market for American manufactures, a destination for investment capital, a source of raw materials, and an area of geostrategic leverage. In 1945 Edwin A. Locke, President Truman's personal representative to China, had attempted to convince the Kuomintang government to temporarily transfer the administration of China's industrial and mining sectors to American experts and firms.[24] Despite a familiarity with the economic nationalist tendencies of the Kuomintang, American planners had hoped that China would open itself to development along American lines, using American capital, and serve as a bastion for capitalism in Asia. Indeed, the expectation in Washington since the undertaking of the Pacific War against Japan had been that China, under the leadership of the Kuomintang, would establish itself as the major Western-aligned regional power of the postwar order.

Even with $2.8 billion dollars' worth of American economic and military aid between 1945 and 1949, which contributed to their colossal material advantage over the Communists, the Kuomintang could not win the Chinese Civil War.[25] With the "loss" of China to the Communists in 1949, the Asia-Pacific took on newfound significance, with important conceptual and material implications for American global empire. The long-standing dream of securing the China market as the premier destination of American trade goods and capital investment was extinguished. Japan, the erstwhile enemy, now stood as America's major Asian ally and bulwark against the further spread of communism. To support Japan and keep a key part of the world within the capitalist camp, the United States made the conscious decision to prioritize its broader imperial interests in the region over its own short-term economic benefit.

The clearest departure of United States foreign policy during this period lay in the recognition that the United States now held responsibilities that would at times preclude the pursuit of immediate economic interests. Rather than working to ensure that its vast material superiority over Europe and Japan continue in perpetuity, American planners recognized that longer-term American interests in global stability, most importantly the stability of a global capitalist economic order with an open door for American trade and investment, lay in rapidly rebuilding the former colonial powers and integrating them into a new American-led international economy. A collaborative study between the Woodrow Wilson Foundation and the National Planning Association, a prominent business advocacy group with a large crossover membership with the Council on Foreign Relations and high-ranking federal government officials, described the new dynamics of American foreign economic policy during the early stages of the Cold War: "The United States must be willing at times to forego certain short term direct economic advantages in favor of the more substantial and enduring benefits to the United States, to the West, and to the rest of the non-Soviet world, which improvements in the functioning of the international economy can bring. . . . No nation can rise to the tasks of international leadership—such as those which history has thrust upon the United States today—unless it can summon the will to transcend in some degree a foreign policy based on prudent, short-run calculation of its national interest."[26]

The planning to maintain the resources and market access of the Grand Area drew heavily from the lessons of geopolitics. It would not be enough to set the terminus of American empire at Britain and Southeast Asia. A rival power dominating the Eurasian landmass would always represent an existential threat to the archipelagic markets and resources critical to the United States and indeed ultimately threaten the United States itself. The imperative to contain Soviet, and later Chinese, power by asserting American influence in Europe and Asia became the cornerstone of American foreign policy in 1947 and remained so for the duration of the Cold War.

While the principles of the policy of containment can be traced through the progression of American imperial scholarship and strategic planning, its single most influential inspiration was certainly the article "The Sources of Soviet Conduct," published in *Foreign Affairs*, anonymously attributed at the time but later revealed to have been written by influential national security advisor, council member, and future US ambassador to the Soviet Union George F. Kennan. Kennan had composed the "Long Telegram" to the State Department while chargé d'affaires in Moscow the previous year, which detailed his arguments for the concerted confrontation and containment of the Soviet Union. With this article, he brought his views to the general public. The essential message of the article was that the Communist Party had agglomerated massive authoritarian powers to itself for the purposes of dictatorial rule within the Soviet Union, under the false premise that the noncommunist world was bent on the destruction of socialism. As a result of this, Kennan argued, the Soviet state had developed along lines that hugely inflated those organs that dealt with security, internal and external, while those departments of administration concerned with the well-being of the citizenry were allowed to wither and die.[27]

Kennan articulated a vision of Soviet power that was primarily interested in maintaining its own position of leadership within the borders of the Soviet Union, and secondarily, patiently but persistently pursuing a policy of world revolution. Under such circumstances, Kennan believed that "the main element of any United States policy toward the Soviet Union must be that of a long-term, patient but firm and vigilant containment of Russian expansive tendencies."[28] Kennan's vision of the global balance of power and the necessity of American containment of the Soviet Union became the basis of American Cold War strategy.

Leading luminaries of American business and government argued that, to block Soviet expansion, the United States now had to orchestrate the entire "Western" community of nations in a permanent "politico-military coalition."[29] In Europe, this hinged on reconstruction and the reconstitution of Western states, including West Germany, as stable and prosperous capitalist bulwarks against the spread of communism. For Asia, this orchestration's primary manifestation lay in the revitalization of Japanese economic dominance over the region and the creation of a strategic architecture that would ensure American military hegemony. American military power in Asia would be used throughout the Cold War in conjunction with covert actions run by military intelligence and the CIA, described by political scientist and former CIA consultant Chalmers Johnson as "the President's private army," to overthrow "hostile" regimes and support American-aligned political leaders.[30]

The American Lake

While the military balance in Europe was heavily contested from the very beginning of the Cold War, in the Pacific the United States reigned supreme. Unlike in Europe, the United States did not need to consider the interests of its victorious allies to any great extent. During the war itself, British leaders had agreed that the Pacific would be treated as an exclusively American theater of operations, a concession that continued into the peace.[31] Japan, the United States' major strategic rival for the past four decades, was now reduced to vassalage. China, with the latent potential to dominate Asia in the period to come, was for the time being weak and disunited. The Soviet Union, the only viable opponent to American global empire, was, due to its relatively weaker military and economic position and the immense resources it was committing to reconstruction and the occupation and administration of much of Eastern Europe, limited in its capacity to influence Pacific geopolitics. The United States enjoyed a large degree of freedom to continue along its historical path of westward expansion and to further develop the Asiatic component of its new global empire.

The study and implementation of geopolitical principles during the period of the 30 years crisis bound together closer than ever imperialism as an economic and political practice with American grand strategy and military planning in the Asia-Pacific. The impetus to open and dominate markets in Asia now formed an integral part of a broader global project to integrate the world under an Open Door economic system. The objective here had shifted from the single-minded pursuit of American commercial interests to the more intricate imperial project of restructuring the region's economy around rebuilding Japan as a pillar of the global capitalist economy and safeguard against communist expansion.

In the immediate aftermath of the war, American planners had considered the partial deindustrialization of Japan and the financing of alternative poles of industrial development in Asia through Japanese war reparations.[32]

By early 1947, however, it was becoming clear that the nationalists would not achieve an outright victory in the Chinese Civil War. Initial American policy to fundamentally reshape Japanese society and economy through parliamentary restructure, demilitarization, land reforms, and the breakup of Japanese industrial conglomerates shifted in 1947 to firmly focus on rebuilding the Japanese economy. By the time of the victory of the Chinese Communists in 1949, the full-scale redevelopment of Japan as Asia's preeminent industrial power through massive American support was well under way.

For the United States itself, the importance of Asian markets had declined relative to the value of Asian strategic resources, upon which a huge portion of the United States' industrial economy and defense industry was now import dependent. Just as military conquest had propelled American empire into the Pacific during its search for markets, so too would the use of military power define the pursuit of American imperial interests in the Western Pacific throughout the Cold War. The power dynamics in the Asia-Pacific region were in many ways much simpler now, and the scope of American power and influence so dramatically heightened that the crafting of American policy was in essence the final say on the strategic architecture of the entire region. To secure the markets and resources of East Asia and to limit the viability of a hegemonic challenge from the Soviet Union or China, the United States set about establishing permanent military dominance of the entire region as the new strategic status quo.

The experience of the Second World War directly influenced the geographical logic of American strategy in the Western Pacific in a manner that has persisted until today. The United States had left its Pacific possessions unfortified in accordance with its obligations under the Washington Naval Treaty. The rapidity of Japan's advances through these territories in the early stages of the war and the difficulties the United States military encountered in reclaiming them left the lasting impression that limiting American military power had been a mistake. The "blood and treasure" expended by the United States in its Pacific Campaign was used to justify postwar ownership and control of Pacific Islands.[33]

President Roosevelt had desired a multilateral UN mandate over the islands. But the Joint Chiefs of Staff saw their sole possession by the United States as a necessity for prevailing in any future conflicts against an aspiring East Asian hegemon.[34] After the war, chief of naval operations, Admiral Chester Nimitz, argued against a UN mandate in conversation with President Truman: "The sovereignty of the ex-Japanese mandates should be taken by the United States. . . . The ultimate security of the United States depends in major part on our ability to control the Pacific Ocean, that these islands are . . . essential to that control and that the concept of trusteeship is inapplicable here because these islands do not represent any colonial problem nor is there economic advantage accruing to the United States through their ownership."[35]

The strategic argument held sway, and American control of large swaths of Pacific territory was instituted after the war. Under the title of a UN "strategic trusteeship," a concept created solely to meet the requirements of American military planners, including basing and fortification rights, and applying only to Pacific island territory, the United States established total military dominance of the Western Pacific. These small Pacific islands would soon be used for, among other things, the testing of nuclear weapons and ballistic missiles. The native inhabitants of one of the islands, Bikini Atoll, were evicted by the US military in 1946. Over the next 12 years, 23 nuclear devices were detonated on the island. It is still deemed uninhabitable due to nuclear fallout.

The lesson the United States took from its experience in the Pacific theater during the Second World War was to treat the Pacific Ocean as one "integrated strategic physical complex."[36] In essence, the ocean became an American lake. The United States took control of Japanese colonial territory, the Pacific being the only region in which the Atlantic Charter's position against territorial aggrandizement was explicitly ignored by a Western power. American hegemonic strategy called for the control of entire island chains. No longer willing to leave Pacific islands "unattended," even those islands not being used by the US military had to be denied to other powers.[37] This manifested as a shift away from what Michael Green describes as the possession of Pacific territory that would act as "stepping stones that would sustain American engagement laterally across the vast Pacific," provided by the possession of Hawaii, Midway, Wake, Guam, and the Philippines before the Second World War.[38] The strategic objective became the control, through alliances and territorial expansion, of the networks of islands stretching longitudinally along the Pacific, in anticipation of the future projection of force across the Pacific from a rising Eurasian power.

The United States, half a century after Mahan shook up the strategic outlook from Washington with *The Influence of Sea Power upon History*, established "sea command" in the Western Pacific as a core part of its national security policy. Broadly understood, this meant that, for the foreseeable future, the United States would enjoy the capacity to use the ocean as it pleased, while being capable of denying such use to any adversary.[39] General Douglas MacArthur, supreme commander of Allied forces in the southwest Pacific area during the war, stated that, as a result of these American military installations and alliances, "now the Pacific has become an Anglo-Saxon lake and our line of defense runs through the chain of islands fringing the coast of Asia. It starts from the Philippines and continues through the Ryukyu Archipelago which includes its broad main bastion, Okinawa."[40]

The emphasis of military planners on the Ryukyu islands is particularly telling as to the long-range strategic outlook of the United States in the Pacific. Okinawa is just shy of 2,000 kilometers from Vladivostok, which was the home port of the Soviet Pacific Fleet, separated by South Korean and Japanese territory and waters. Although the USSR was the main immediate threat to the United States, all of the postwar planning for American security architecture placed the Ryukyus in the highest category of importance for military control.[41] Their frontage upon mainland China and their key place in the chain of islands running longitudinally off mainland Asia make the islands critical real estate in dominating the maritime approaches to Asia and preventing a mainland Asian power from extending its naval reach into the Pacific.

The policy envisioned by Spykman during the war—of a system of balancing alliances featuring, but not exclusive to, Japan—to contain China was remarkably similar to the "Hub and Spokes" American-led security architecture that has been the main feature of regional security from the immediate postwar period until today, in which the United States acts as the "hub" in a network of bilateral alliances with numerous regional states ("spokes"). In an April 1947 study commissioned by the US Joint Chiefs of Staff, rebuilding Japan as a military and economic power was identified as critical for the security of American global empire for the reason that Japan was the "one nation which would contain large armed forces of our ideological opponents in the Far East while the United States and her allies in the West launched a major offensive in that area."[42]

The same year, a report from the State-War-Navy Coordinating Committee designated "top secret" described the risks to the "full accomplishment of world economic stability, the type of world trading system the US seeks, or US political objectives in several countries," should the flow of military equipment, military collaboration, and economic aid to strategic areas encompassing Asia, Europe, the Middle East, and Latin America decrease or subside.[43]

Japan was identified as the pivotal state in Asia for securing American interests in the region and preventing the spread of Soviet influence.

The strategic balance was, of course, the most tangible and visible aspect of American security policy during this period. But the underlying political and economic interests were, as always, the drivers of the policy. Rebuilding Japan would be the single most important American project in the Asia-Pacific, but the benefits of a re-industrialized and highly integrated Japanese economy would in turn support the grander ambitions of the United States.

A clear-eyed understanding of the connection between military power and economic interests is evident throughout the work of American strategists, policy planners, and state officials during the period. The bounty that several centuries of continental expansion and the two most destructive wars of human history had heaped upon the United States was not to be wasted through naive ideas of beneficence, global values, or peace. Instead, the United States should focus on consciously constructing a foreign policy that would cement for perpetuity all the relative military and economic advantages that it now enjoyed. George Kennan, in a policy-planning document for the State Department, wrote that

> We have about 50% of the world's wealth but only 6.3% of its population. This disparity is particularly great as between ourselves and the peoples of Asia. In this situation, we cannot fail to be the object of envy and resentment. Our real task in the coming period is to devise a pattern of relationships which will permit us to maintain this position of disparity without positive detriment to our national security. To do so, we will have to dispense with all sentimentality and day-dreaming; and our attention will have to be concentrated everywhere on our immediate national objectives. We need not deceive ourselves that we can afford today the luxury of altruism and world-benefaction.[44]

He went on to acknowledge that communism held not only greater attraction but also "greater reality" for the people of Asia living under modern conditions of economic underdevelopment. To maintain American economic supremacy under these conditions, the United States would have to do away with "unreal objectives such as human rights, the raising of the living standards, and democratization," and instead recognize that "our influence in the Far Eastern area in the coming period is going to be primarily military and economic."[45]

In light of this, Kennan argued, the United States should focus on identifying those territories that were indispensable to American interests in the region and work toward their militarization and control. The First Island Chain, from Japan to the Philippines, was the preferred geostrategic anchor for the United States in Asia according to Kennan[46]—a role that the islands continue to play in American regional strategy to this day.

In his famous "Speech on the Far East," Dean Acheson, secretary of state under President Truman, laid out the vision for an American "defensive" infrastructure along the offshore islands of Asia: "The defensive perimeter runs along the Aleutians to Japan and then goes to the Ryukyus. We hold important defense positions in the Ryukyu Islands. . . . They are essential parts of the defensive perimeter of the Pacific, and they must and will be held. . . . The defensive perimeter runs from the Ryukyus to the Philippine Islands."[47]

In Asia and across the rest of the world, the United States would draw military lines from which it could project power in support of its global imperial vision. This would require the maintenance, and in many cases vast expansion, of the network of bases that had begun to be developed during the Second World War. In 1938 the United States had a relatively modest defense budget, no military alliances, and no troops stationed on territory that it did not control.[48] Of the over 2,000 overseas bases created during the war, around half were retained by the United States after its conclusion, in anticipation of their usefulness in a forthcoming global confrontation with communism.[49] By 1955 the defense budget had ballooned over 50 times compared to prewar levels.[50] By the mid-1960s, the United States was committed to over 43 nations by treaty and agreement; it had approximately 375 major foreign military bases and 3,000 minor military facilities spread across the globe as a network designed to contain the Soviet Union and China by surrounding them with overwhelming military force.[51]

The Island Chain strategy was paired with the Hub and Spokes system of regional alliances established through agreements made around the Treaty of San Francisco in 1951. Attempts would be made to integrate the region into a multilateral alliance like the North Atlantic Treaty Organization with the launch in 1954 of the poorly named Southeast Asia Treaty Organization, whose membership consisted of France, the United Kingdom, Pakistan, the United States, Australia, New Zealand, Thailand, and the Philippines. But underfunding, lack of military integration, and no shared strategic or ideological vision outside of an anti-communist orientation condemned the alliance to languish almost from inception until its disbanding in 1977. The real military power in Asia revolved around the United States and its major regional allies Japan,

South Korea, and Taiwan, which were the bilateral relationships of the Hub and Spokes system; a mutual defense treaty with the Philippines; and its southern anchor in a 1951 treaty with Australia and New Zealand.

In the light of Chinese artillery attacks on Taiwan during the mid-1950s, Secretary of State John Foster Dulles reflected on the pivotal role of the United States military in the region and expressed fears for what the expanded power of China would mean for the American security perimeter:

> There is no cohesion among these various [Asian] states. Only one thing bolsters the whole of the line—the will and the strength of the United States. If this cracks, the whole line will crack.
>
> We cannot cede the offshore islands to the Communists without disaster. That would enable them to begin their objective of driving us out of the Western Pacific, right back to Hawaii, and even to the United States! If an earthquake were to swallow up Quemoy and we lost it that way, that would not be so bad as losing it by having to turn it over to the Communists.[52]

For Dulles, the Island Chain strategy was the "formidable deterrent to the domination of the Pacific by Communist imperialism."[53]

The structure of the new global capitalist economy was a major determining factor in the vast spread of American military bases during the Cold War. As capital began to flow seamlessly across borders, the prerogative of the United States military became to ensure that the largest possible portion of the global marketplace was open to capital investment, that labor markets would be at the disposal of multinational corporations, and that the strategic resources of the third world would be available to be used by the Western bloc as insurance against a potential Soviet-led minerals embargo. During the earlier stage of American empire, the strategic network of bases and colonies cut across the Pacific to ensure equal access of American commerce in Asia, and the prevention of the emergence of rival spheres of imperial exclusivity in China. The new global Open Door entailed preventing communist or socialist governments emerging where possible and intervening, openly or clandestinely, to overthrow them when prevention failed, to ensure that Western commercial interests faced minimal resistance from local populations. This required a much vaster network of bases but also allowed a higher level of flexibility. American empire during this period often goes unrecognized, or called by other names, because it functioned differently to classical European imperialism of the nineteenth century.

American imperium was itself, somewhat ironically, heavily dependent on the old European colonial empires for the development of its military infrastructure. The American commitment to exploiting European colonial possessions as geostrategic assets after the Second World War was pervasive around the globe. Christopher T. Sandars refers to the American military apparatus during the Cold War as a "leasehold empire" by virtue of the preponderance of bases located in European colonial territory.[54] American support for European colonial regimes during the Cold War was heavily premised on the continuance of American military access to colonial territories. Of the vast network of bases that the United States held during the 1950s, close to 70% were situated in territories colonized directly by either the United States or, as was more often the case, by European powers.[55]

When formal European decolonization did later occur, it was undertaken in such a way as to preserve the economic relations of core and periphery, with a particular emphasis on natural-resource extraction.[56] This was the process referred to by historian W. M. Roger Louis as "the imperialism of decolonization."[57] The French through the "French Community" program, initiated under de Gaulle, saw "self-governance" offered to French African colonies, while financial, military, economic, foreign, and resource policy continued to be dictated from Paris.

British plans for decolonization were much the same. Prime Minister Clement Atlee was conscientiously informed by his cabinet secretary that his government's directives on the matter "could be said to fall within the ordinary definition of imperialism."[58] When ties to European colonial powers were firmly severed, the United States and the Central Intelligence Agency took an active interest in ensuring that those groups most aligned with American imperial goals, usually made up of a nexus between businessmen and the upper echelons of the military, would retain power. Dozens of direct and covert interventions were undertaken by the US military and the CIA to support their chosen ruling cliques across the third world during the Cold War.[59]

The American security architecture in Asia that was consolidated during the early years of the Cold War played a pivotal role in the major political and economic developments in the region for its duration. Viewed in isolation, this architecture can appear as a clear-cut example of American containment of the USSR and China. This is an accurate but limited appraisal. To more fully understand the impetus behind this vast military architecture, one must place it within the broader context of the global political and economic order that the United States established during the same period.

Global Market, Global Order, and Asia

The new regional order being established in Asia by the United States was a central pillar of the broader global imperial project. The term "global" is used here to describe American empire in the totalizing sense of its material scope, ambitions, and international expansion over time. The American imperial project was never global in the sense of total and pervasive influence over world affairs. Rather it was international and pan-continental in the spread of its integrated network of markets, allies, clients, military bases, and proxies while being global in its ambitions, although restrained by the power realities of the Cold War and by multitudinous areas of resistance within the third world and the Western bloc itself.

It is necessary to understand the institutions of this global political and economic regime in order to make sense of American strategic policy in Asia. For the United States, Asian geopolitics were now, more than ever before, enmeshed with broader concerns over the global balance of power, empire, and commercial interests. American global empire was, in its essence, a project of integrating the resources and markets of the world into a unified capitalist framework. This was the embodiment of what William Appleman Williams described as the Open Door principles as applied to China in 1899–1900 becoming "the central feature of American foreign policy in the Twentieth Century."[60] This process was of course conceptualized, designed, and executed by the United States but coordinated and administered by a vast array of new international organizations.

For matters of security, the major institutions were the UN security council; the North Atlantic Treaty Organization (NATO); the Southeast Asia Treaty Organization (SEATO); the Australia, New Zealand, and United States mutual defense pact (ANZUS); and the Organization of American States (OAS). The recently demonstrated nuclear capabilities of the United States provided the ominous backdrop for the parameters within which security competition of the coming Cold War would be fought. For economic and financial affairs, the major global organizations included the Bretton Woods institutions the International Monetary Fund (IMF) and the International Bank for Reconstruction and Development (World Bank), as well as the General Agreement on Tariffs and Trade (GATT) and later the World Trade Organization (WTO). With their vast administrative portfolios extending across the spectrum of organized international activity, the one thing in common was that the threads of power and influence running through them would all converge in the United States. These organizations worked toward a common goal, establishing the physical, political, and economic security and stability of governments across the globe that were positively inclined toward national economic development along lines that complemented and strengthened American empire.

The overarching economic goal of this system was not merely nationalist or mercantilist, working toward the enrichment of American elites at the expense of all others. Rather it was the creation of a stable global economic system, with benefits sufficiently attractive to other centers of global power that they would be willing participants, particularly in Western Europe and Japan. Great Britain, with her vast colonial network of trade and raw materials, was of particular importance to the project, which would ultimately decide the balance between socialist and capitalist organization of the global economy.

In large part, this system represented an "empire by invitation," wherein large segments of the international community, particularly in the developed West, actively encouraged the United States to take up the mantle of world leadership, and provided it with the territorial assets and institutional-administrative capacity to do so.[61] Security and stability were major factors in the eagerness of large sections of the Western world for American global leadership—the 30 years crisis had demonstrated the worst possible outcomes of multipolarity and contested hegemony—but so too was the fact that the United States promised to institute an international economic regime that would continue to well serve the wealthiest and most powerful sections of other Western societies.

President Truman was emphatic in his insistence that the world must not devolve back into the system of oppositional autarkic spheres that had developed during the 30 years crisis. He saw an American-led system of global capitalism, with sufficient incentives for buy-in from other international powers, as the path away from this. The new system was by design an economic, not just political, system of global integration. He described the system and its goals as such:

> We, in America, are unanimous in our determination to prevent another war. But some among us do not fully realize what we must do to carry out this policy. There still are those who seem to believe that we can confine our cooperation with other countries to political relationships; that we need not cooperate where economic questions are involved. This attitude has sometimes led to the asser-

tion that there should be bipartisan support for the foreign policy of the United States, but that there need not be bipartisan support for the foreign economic policy of the United States. Such a statement simply does not make sense. Our foreign relations, political and economic, are indivisible. We cannot say that we are willing to cooperate in the one field and are unwilling to cooperate in the other. I am glad to note that the leaders in both parties have recognized that fact. . . . We are the giant of the economic world. Whether we like it or not, the future pattern of economic relations depends upon us. The world is waiting and watching to see what we shall do. The choice is ours.[62]

This global economic integration and resulting political cooperation between states were to occur strictly on the terms of free market capitalism: "Freedom has flourished where power has been dispersed. . . . The pattern of international trade that is most conducive to freedom of enterprise is one in which the major decisions are made, not by governments, but by private buyers and sellers, under conditions of active competition, and with proper safeguards against the establishment of monopolies and cartels."[63] These sentiments reflected those offered by Secretary of the Treasury Henry Morgenthau, when describing the purpose of the Bretton Woods institutions, to create "a world in which international trade and international investment can be carried on by businessmen on business principles."[64]

The macro-economic concerns that would define the new era of American-led global capitalism were the avoidance of another "Great Slump," as had occurred after the First World War, and the avoidance of the breakdown of world trade into competing autarkic spheres, as had occurred after the Great Depression. The Depression had shrunk American international trade in both relative and aggregate terms. The massive boom in American agricultural and manufacturing capacity provided by its position as the "arsenal of democracy" during the Second World War needed now to be shored up in the peace. By the end of the war, US trade had increased to over four times its 1939 levels.[65] Avoiding a slump in trade, production, and employment required the crafting of a global economic system that would keep the world's markets open to the United States.[66] The British pound had proven unable to underwrite a global economic system during the interwar years, so now the US dollar, and American power more broadly, would step into this role.

These economic interests were paired with social and political considerations. Unregulated capitalism would produce crises that would destabilize societies and provide fertile ground for communist expansion. The continuance of a global system that produced "have" and "have-not" nations in terms of market access and resource distribution would repeatedly lead to international conflict. Rampant economic inequality, market disruption, mass unemployment, and inequity in resource distribution were established as the limits at which the market would be bound by regulation from the state and the newly developed institutions of economic management. The institutionalization of the mediation between the objectives of social stability, international order, and global markets is the defining characteristic of the American-led postwar economic order described as "embedded liberalism" by John Ruggie.[67] In practice this entailed a system that moderated the negative social effects of the free market through the provision of welfare and the management of economies to reduce unemployment. From the 1970s, this grand bargain would begin to unravel as neoclassical and neoliberal economic policies saw the global market become disembedded from the broader goals of a functional and humane society, spearheaded by an inflated and unregulated financial sector.

The new American empire was thus not revolutionary in scope; rather it institutionalized, reasserted, and regulated the dominant modes of capital accumulation that had existed in the West for the past two centuries. The deepest and thickest institutional connections of the new American world order ran between the United States and other wealthy capitalist states rather than between the various metropoles and colonies, as they had done before.[68] Through this thick network of financial, trade, military, and political connections, the United States formed a new apex that overshadowed, but in many cases also supported, existing colonial relationships.

This global capitalist economic order was to be underwritten and expanded by American military power. Six days after outlining his plans for the new economic order, President Truman delivered his special message to Congress on Greece and Turkey, which defined the "Truman Doctrine," one of the foundational building blocks for the Cold War security policy of the United States. In the speech, Truman drew a sharp line between the democratic and capitalist "free world" and the authoritarian and communist Soviet bloc. He asked Congress to grant $400 million in military and economic aid to Greece and Turkey to oppose the growing influence of communism. Truman framed the complex national political struggles as a simple choice between freedom and oppression, and established the United States as the champion of freedom around the world: "The free peoples of the world look to us for support in maintaining their freedoms. If we falter in our leadership, we may endanger the peace of the world—and we shall surely endanger the welfare of this Nation."[69]

The Truman Doctrine announced the confrontation of the spread of communism by the United States, militarily and economically, throughout the globe. In a sense this was the extension of the Monroe Doctrine to the entire world. The effect of all global political events upon the United States, its economic system, and its "national interests," were to be considered, and direct intervention was to occur when these effects were judged to be detrimental. The US State Department had judged that the likelihood of a communist Greece falling into the Russian orbit was slight; more likely it would resemble non-aligned Yugoslavia. But under the new American system of global capitalism, states dropping out of the American system and pursuing independent nationalist development was almost an equal threat to world order as an expanding Soviet empire.[70]

To achieve its objectives in Europe, the United States implemented the European Recovery Program (ERP). Better known as the Marshall Plan, this committed the United States to spend $17 billion over four years (1948–1952) with the aim of rebuilding the European economies that were shattered by the war. The economic goal of the program was to move Europe away from autarky, nationalism, and the possibility of a slide into communism, but toward a common market, internationalism, free currency convertibility, and free trade.[71] In a similar manner to the way the IMF and World Bank would influence economic, social, and developmental policy of borrower countries, the Marshall Plan forced left-wing governments in Britain, France, and Italy to reduce foreign debts, balance budgets, and place downward pressure on wage growth, with the goal of placing deflationary pressure on European finances and making them more competitive in global trading markets.[72]

The Asian equivalent to the Marshall Plan, the Dodge Plan, was focused on rebuilding the Japanese economy and establishing Japan as the Asian anchor of American world order. Named after its architect, prominent banker and financial advisor to General Douglas MacArthur, Joseph Dodge, the Dodge Plan revitalized the massive Japanese industrial cartels that had existed before the war and instituted sweeping programs of austerity to keep wages and state services low, while structuring an export-oriented economy running off underpriced labor for competitive advantage.

The insistence on export-oriented growth, rather than the stimulation of domestic demand through wage growth and spending on social services and civilian infrastructure, centered around the need to keep the yen valued at a stable rate of 360 to the US dollar. Japan ran a huge trade deficit to the United States during this period, and the only way to keep the American economy growing and avoid the economic slumps and mass unemployment of the 30 years crisis was to keep Japan and Europe financially solvent and capable of absorbing American surpluses. The dependence of Japan on export markets in Asia would play an important role in American military and political intervention in the region during the Cold War, particularly in Vietnam. If Japan's traditional markets and resource suppliers became communist, as China and North Korea had by the end of the 1940s, it may be forced to integrate itself with a communist Asian system, which would be a huge blow to American empire, slam shut the Open Door, and undermine the very reason the United States had fought the Second World War.

An American-Led Asian Co-Prosperity Sphere

The dominance of the American economy in the wake of the war produced problems of its own. The reconstruction of the other centers of industrial power in Europe and Japan required large imports of food, raw materials, capital goods, and technology. The United States was the only source of most of these, but Europe and Japan were unable to pay for them. Before the war, American trade deficits were financed by raw materials sold to the United States by colonial dependencies, whose enterprises were owned by Europeans, or financed by European investments in the United States itself. Decolonization threatened this system. Asian colonies had been particularly profitable for Europe; now India, Sri Lanka, Burma, Malaysia, Cambodia, Vietnam, Laos, and Indonesia were gaining or moving toward independence. In the wake of the Second World War, the Europeans and Japanese were running gigantic trade deficits with the United States ($12 billion in 1947)[73] without the ability to acquire American dollars to pay for them, a problem that came to be known as the "dollar gap."

If the United States could not create a world system in which Europe and Japan were able to rebuild and prosper, then US exports to the other developed economies of the world would suffer. America, having enjoyed an unprecedented decade of economic boom, would be liable to a severe bust as its export markets disappeared, and the economic misery and social and political instability of the Depression years could return. It was feared that this would ultimately result in the second-tier industrial powers of the world seeking economic partnerships with the Soviet Union.

Having identified Japan's major vulnerability to the communist world as its dependence on foreign resources and markets, a Joint Chiefs of Staff committee reported in January 1950 that the security interests of the United States hinged on "finding and securing an area to complement Japan as did Manchuria and Korea prior to World War II."[74] The first priority for the United States was then "stabilizing and securing Southeast Asia for its food and raw materials," for the use of Japan immediately, and the world system of American capitalism more broadly.[75] John Foster Dulles agreed, writing that if Japan was to be kept outside of the communist sphere, it would need open access to the agricultural products, raw materials, and markets of Southeast Asia.[76]

During the Second World War, State Department plans had placed China as the key ally that would anchor American economic and strategic interests in Asia.[77] It was anticipated that, under the leadership of Chiang Kai-Shek, China could be incorporated into the international-market and regional-security order being underwritten by Washington. But, as a result of communist ascendancy, Japan now took center stage as the bulwark for American empire in Asia. The Stars and Stripes had replaced the Rising Sun; however, most of the economic goals of the East Asian Co-Prosperity Sphere were now enshrined as pillars of American foreign and security policy in Asia.

The model for a new Asian economic order enjoyed bipartisan support. Eisenhower's Republican administration was arguably even more enthusiastic in pursuing these policies than its originators in Truman's Democratic White House. In 1955, responding to a question from Republican senator from Vermont, Ralph Flanders, that highlighted the long-run threat that restored Japanese industrial capacity posed to American manufacturers, Secretary of State Dulles confirmed his belief that "the future of Japan lies primarily in an exchange of its industrial products for the food and raw materials of the countries of southeast Asia and south Asia."[78] Dulles had just returned from Vietnam, where dollar aid was being distributed to the Vietnamese government. In the past the Vietnamese had received financing in French francs, which would be spent in France. Now that the aid was in US dollars, it was anticipated that the aid money would flow back to the United States via Vietnamese purchases of Japanese manufactures.

War with Asia, Recession, and Resurgence

War on the Mainland

The "loss" of China to communism dramatically reshaped its position in relation to American empire. Long envisaged as the grand commercial prize of westward imperial expansion, China was now cast as the central threat to the new regional economic order that the United States was creating around Japan. The most consequential conflicts of the Cold War for the United States, in Korea and Vietnam, were conducted in large part as a response to the perceived threat of China. This threat was conceptualized in several different ways: as the grand existential threat that expansionist communism posed to global capitalism; as a classical geostrategic threat that China, along with the USSR, posed through the extension of their power and influence into neighboring countries; and as a threat to the US capacity to keep the region's natural resources and markets within the American imperial system.

In January 1950 Secretary of State Dean Acheson announced that the era of paternalistic and exploitative relations between West and East had ended and that a new day had dawned, wherein Asian people would decide their political destinies for themselves.[1] With the delivery of the National Security Council (NSC) policy paper "United States Objectives and Programs for National Security," better known as NSC-68, to Truman in April of the same year, any hope that Acheson could be taken at his word and that Asian nations would be left to determine their own future was dashed. The escalation of the Cold War with the Soviet Union during this period was dramatic. Kennan, the original architect of containment, had been marginalized by Acheson for his "soft" approach to the Soviets. Kennan resigned from the NSC and was replaced by Paul Nitze, an anti-Soviet hawk who oversaw the creation of the new American strategic policy for fighting the Cold War.

Prepared in collaboration with the Departments of State and Defense, with Acheson himself a key member of the research group, NSC-68 dramatically elevated the threat perception of the Soviet Union to the United States and planned for the militarization of American society in response. NSC-68 characterized the objectives of the Soviet Union as "the complete subversion or forcible destruction of the machinery of government and structure of society in the countries of the non-Soviet world and their replacement by an apparatus and structure subservient to and controlled from the Kremlin."[2] As a result, the Soviet Union threatened the "destruction not only of this republic but of civilization itself."[3] Combatting such an existential threat, the NSC argued, would necessitate a huge boost in military spending, including conventional and nuclear arms increases, a reduction in social welfare programs and non-military state services, civil-military cooperation, particularly in tech and weapons production, media and cultural messaging and propaganda, psychological warfare, and the encouragement of popular uprisings in the Soviet sphere. The effort was costed at around $50 billion per year, triple the amount requested by the Pentagon in 1950.[4]

NSC-68 also set the tone for American attitudes toward Communist China. While the Soviet Union was always the primary global competitor during the Cold War, China was here already being framed as the "springboard" from which communism was likely to spread to Southeast Asia, threaten the economic viability of Japan, and potentially shift the entire region outside of the American world order.[5] The outbreak of the Korean War two months later and the opening of direct conflict between the US military and the People's Liberation Army further centered China as the main threat to American empire in Asia. The same year, the State Department instructed American embassies around the world that French success in Indochina was crucial to prevent "Chinese imperialism" in Asia, the same justification offered for American intervention in Vietnam in the official Joint Chiefs of Staff history of the conflict.[6] The impetus to contain Chinese and Soviet influence, as well the spread of socialism or any nationalist political movements deemed "anti-Western" and a threat to the US-led world order, pushed the American security perimeter into the mainland of Asia itself during the first half of the Cold War.

Korea and Vietnam

The Korean War began in August 1950 when DPRK (North Korea) forces crossed south of the 38th parallel in an attempt to forcefully reunify the country under Northern rule. A US-led counteroffensive pushed the North Koreans back past the 38th by late September. Hoping to use Northern aggression as a pretext for unifying the country under the leadership of the South, a US-led counteroffensive was ratified by presidential order on September 27. It was an abject failure and an early warning of the risks of the transition from a "containment" to a "rollback" strategy, which would be, for a time, advocated by Truman, Acheson, Eisenhower, and his Secretary of State John Foster Dulles. Some voices in American strategic planning were already wary of the implications of imperial overstretch. George Kennan, having been recalled from Princeton to the State Department, had warned against a risky counter-invasion of the North.[7] His advice went unheeded but proved prescient when American encroachments on the border of North Korea and China brought the People's Liberation Army into the conflict, leading to a destructive war of attrition, which saw the deaths of up to 5 million people, over half of whom were Korean civilians.

The end of active hostilities in July 1953 resulted in a stalemate along the 38th parallel that continues to this day. For Maoist China, it represented a victory against the "paper tiger" of US imperialism in Asia. In the United States, it entailed a long victory for the crafters of NSC-68 and the militarization of American foreign policy. By the end of the war, the annual defense budget was $52 billion, sitting in the $30–$40 billion range for the rest of the decade, with even the smallest budget of the period two and a half times the size of pre–Korean War military allocations.[8] It would also provide a significant and long-term market for the industrial production of Japan, one of the most important pillars of American regional policy during the early Cold War period. Through the Offshore Procurement Program, the Korean War was a huge boon to the Japanese economy, particularly in the auto- and truck-manufacturing sectors, which would characterize Japanese manufacturing leadership during its years of rapid growth.[9] At the outbreak of the war, Japan's industrial output was only one-third of its 1931 level.[10] From the years 1950 to 1953 the United States spent over $2.3 billion on defense procurements from Japan, a level of foreign spending that would have been intolerable to Congress during peacetime but was seen as necessary and justified during war.[11] Almost three-quarters of Japanese industrial output was geared toward arms production for the United States during this period.[12]

In fact, the massive rearmament effort spurred by the Korean War and NSC-68 solved the US dollar liquidity problems that had threatened to hamper global postwar reconstruction. American military aid to foreign governments and the buildup of its own military capabilities expanded with little interruption between 1950 and 1973, providing the world economy with the high levels of guaranteed spending, loans, and investment that undergirded what many refer to as the "golden years" of postwar capitalist expansion.[13]

NSC-68, the Truman Doctrine, and the Korean War inaugurated a period of the Cold War in which competition took a much more militarized tone. Lasting until the 1973 withdrawal from Vietnam and rapprochement with China, this period was characterized by the United States effectively waging a series of wars contesting control of the eastern Eurasian rimland, in a policy drawing heavily from Spykman's conception of geostrategic world power. The overarching objective of this policy was to ensure the integration of the most productive areas of the third world into the system of American global capitalism and to secure natural resources for capitalist industrial and defense production.

This objective would bolster Japan's position as the industrial, trading, and capital accumulation center of Asia and as the regional pole of the capitalist world system. The Mahanian emphasis on sea control, and the fortification of strongpoints in the Pacific, had given way to a far more all-encompassing and imperial view of a global security order that would, by its very definition, find and face threats anywhere in the world that offered opposition to American empire and its position of economic and strategic dominance. The geostrategic conception of the island chain articulated by Kennan, Acheson, and MacArthur was expanded under Dulles to incorporate two land anchors on the mainland, Korea in the north and Indochina in the south.[14] It would take the death and destruction wrought by the Vietnam War to arrest this hubris and finally place a high-water mark for the centuries-long process of the persistent extension of the American security perimeter farther and farther westward.

American involvement in Vietnam began before even the outbreak of the Korean War. On May 1, 1950, President Truman announced that the United States would arm and fund French military efforts to suppress independence struggles in Indochina, and the Joint Chiefs of Staff had already been instructed to begin organizing military support for the French the year prior.[15] The visions of the People's Liberation Army sweeping through Southeast Asia in coordination with domestic communist revolutions that animated American fears for the region as a whole were tied to specific economic functions of the region within American empire. Control of Southeast Asia and the ability to maintain bases and friendly harbors for American ships there were necessary to secure the sea lines of communication along which Gulf oil transited to the Japanese market. More importantly, Southeast Asia was itself the major supplier of raw materials and market for Japanese manufactured products as designated under American plans for the integrated global economy.

In 1953 President Eisenhower was advocating for American military intervention in Southeast Asia on the grounds of securing its mineral resources for American empire. Speaking to assembled state governors just days after the armistice agreements concluded the Korean War, Eisenhower drew their attention to the interdependence of the global economy, US prosperity, and its military strength. He raised the First Indochina War to illustrate this, telling the governors that "you don't know, really, why we are so concerned with the far-off southeast corner of Asia."[16] The truth lay, according to the president, in a domino theory of Asian minerals and raw materials, and a cascading threat to the global Open Door:

> If Indochina goes, several things happen right away. The Malayan peninsula, the last little bit of the end hanging on down there, would be scarcely defensible— and tin and tungsten that we so greatly value from that area would cease coming. But all India would be outflanked. Burma would certainly, in its weakened condition, be no defense. Now, India is surrounded on that side by the Communist empire. Iran on its left is in a weakened condition. . . . All of that weakening position around there is very ominous for the United States, because finally if we lost all that, how would the free world hold the rich empire of Indonesia?

He concluded: "So, when the United States votes $400 million to help that war, we are not voting for a giveaway program. We are voting for the cheapest way that we can to prevent the occurrence of something that would be of the most terrible significance for the United States of America—our security, our power and ability to get certain things we need from the riches of the Indonesian territory, and from Southeast Asia."[17]

In the famous address in which he first outlined the domino theory of the spread of communism in Southeast Asia, President Eisenhower emphasized Japan as the endpoint in the chain. If Southeast Asia were to fall to communism, "it takes away, in its economic aspects, that region that Japan must have as a trading area or Japan, in turn, will have only one place in the world to go—that is, toward the Communist areas in order to live. So, the possible consequences of the loss are just incalculable to the free world."[18] Richard Nixon would echo these views at the height of the Vietnam War, stating that the American intervention in Vietnam had provided a shield for Indonesia, "containing the region's richest hoard of natural resources, . . . by far the greatest prize in the Southeast Asian area."[19]

To Southeast Asian nationalists, the proposition that they should retain their subordinate colonized role as a provider of raw materials and agricultural products to a group of industrialized capitalist core states under the umbrella of American empire was understandably unappealing. French Indochina suffered 4 million deaths during the Second World War, and the violence and indignity of French colonialism was a continued reality of daily existence. The Việt Minh, a nationalist independence coalition that had resisted Japanese occupation during the Second World War, continued their struggle against imperialism when the French sought to recolonize Vietnam after the war.

The First Indochina War simmered between French forces and Vietnamese nationalists between 1946 and 1954. The United States bore up to half of the total cost of the French war effort, doing so in the hope that a French victory in Southeast Asia would both secure the region from communism and reassert French authority in Europe as a leading power.[20] The decisive Vietnamese victory at Dien Bien Phu on May 7, 1954, broke the French will to continue the fight and scuppered American hopes of a triumph for the capitalist world order. The subsequent French withdrawal left Vietnam divided along the 17th parallel, with the north supported by China and the Soviet Union, and the south a functional dependency of the United States. A communist insurgency in the south developed almost immediately. By 1963 a combination of the successes of Viet Cong guerrillas and popular discontent at the corrupt and nepotistic leaders made the situation in South Vietnam appear critical in Washington. After a CIA-assisted military coup in November 1963, the Pentagon became increasingly involved in military planning and operations in South Vietnam.[21]

The Vietnam War is commonly conceived of as a folly in which the United States, with the best intentions, intervened for political reasons in support of liberty and to stop the spread of totalitarian communism. For the actual planners of the war, the material considerations were of far greater importance. The war was a symptom of broader American imperial objectives in Asia. These were to create an integrated economic region in which Southeast Asia was to supply food and raw materials to industrial Japan, and strategic resources like tin, oil, and tungsten to the United States and its allies, and to contain China in order to prevent its interference in this economic arrangement.

In the minds of American politicians and strategic planners, China, not the Soviet Union, was the primary security threat in Vietnam. In fact, in a memorandum to President Johnson written in 1965, Secretary of Defense Robert McNamara conceived of the American strategic objective of the Vietnam War as providing a southern bulwark which would work in concert with the preexisting Soviet "containment" of China to the north.[22] McNamara viewed the prospect of expanding Chinese influence in Southeast Asia as another iteration of emerging imperial challenges to the Open Door and American global security and economic interests. In advocating for the expansion of war in Vietnam to the president, McNamara wrote that "China—like Germany in 1917, like Germany in the West and Japan in the East in the late 30's, and like the USSR in 1947—looms as a major power threatening to undercut our importance and effectiveness in the world and, more remotely but more menacingly, to organize all of Asia against us."[23] Under such an arrangement, McNamara feared that the resources of Asia would be mobilized to support a rival economic and military bloc, led by China, that would divest the United States of its markets, threaten American positions in the Pacific, and most importantly, through its opposition to free-market capitalism, challenge America's ability to "move the world, as best we can, in the direction we prefer."[24]

A decisive American victory in Vietnam would, it was hoped, produce a different region and a different world. Japan would provide Asia with skilled industrial labor, manufactures, and capital investment. Asia would remain within the American global capitalist order, and China would eventually be coaxed into reengaging with the capitalist world. Internal communications and policy documents from the State Department, the National Security Council, the Council of Economic Advisers, the Pentagon, the Joint Chiefs of Staff, and the White House composed during this period testify to the belief that the fate of Japan between communism and capitalism, and thus Asia at large, would be determined by access to markets and materials in Southeast Asia.[25]

The United States was willing to sacrifice 60,000 lives, and inflict far larger suffering and destruction upon the Vietnamese people, to check what it believed was Chinese expansion and keep Southeast Asia as a market, resource supplier, and strategic geographical location for American military forces. This is an important development in understanding the structure of American empire after the Second World War. Certainly, Southeast Asia was seen as a vital source of strategic resources that would have a direct bearing on the United States, but more importantly it was conceived as the region upon which Japanese prosperity and stability hinged. The implications for the global system of capitalism and American power as a whole were the primary concern. United States strategic policy had become globally imperial, abstracted from the immediate national defense or economic interests of the United States and its citizens.

The Vietnam War ended in failure, and over its course the United States receded from its unprecedented pinnacle in world political, economic, and military power. Scholarly dissent persists over John F. Kennedy's commitment to the escalation of tensions in Vietnam. Historian, and longtime friend and confidant of Kennedy, Arthur Schlesinger Jr. argues that Kennedy was drawn reluctantly into Vietnam, mostly through the path dependence of Eisenhower's policies, a claim supported by Kennedy's longstanding skepticism of American military involvement in the region from as early as 1951.[26] Revisionist historians have painted Kennedy as a staunch Cold Warrior in his own right, committed to large-scale and persistent counterinsurgency operations in the region in pursuit of containment.[27] His assassination in 1963, when American intervention in the conflict remained comparatively modest, precludes any definitive statement on the matter.

Kennedy's successor, Lyndon Johnson, who had himself questioned Eisenhower's policy in Indochina, demonstrated a hawkish attitude toward Vietnam as early as 1961 when, having returned from a vice-presidential trip to South Vietnam, he warned that it was too important to lose to communism. He foresaw that the failure to act decisively in Southeast Asia could lead the United States to adopt a "fortress America" mindset, pull back its defense perimeter to the West Coast, and leave "the vast Pacific . . . a Red Sea."[28] Under such circumstances, the global order that the United States had built over the past two decades would effectively cease to exist.

The full-scale direct American war on Vietnam began during Johnson's presidency after the staged Gulf of Tonkin Incident, when, on August 4, 1964, his administration, with the notable involvement of Secretary of Defense Robert McNamara, claimed that the USS *Maddox* had come under torpedo attack from North Vietnamese forces. These "attacks" were later proven to have never occurred.[29] The administration passed legislation that would allow the president to commit US forces to the defense of any nation in Southeast Asia threatened by communist aggression or subversion, with executive discretion granted to both define the "threat" and prescribe the "countermeasures." Upon learning of the passage of the legislation through both congressional houses with minimal opposition, President Johnson joked that the resolution "was like Grandma's nightshirt. It covers everything."[30]

This legislation would be used to initiate the Rolling Thunder air-bombardment campaign over North Vietnam in February 1965. The next month saw the first large-scale deployment of American ground troops in Vietnam. American troop presence peaked in 1967 at 535,000. Over the course of the war, 6.2 million tons of bombs, missiles, and napalm were used by the United States in Vietnam, Laos, and Cambodia, almost three times the tonnage of air munitions that were used by the United States across the entire Pacific theater during the Second World War.[31] An estimated 1.7 million people were killed during the eight years of direct American involvement between 1965 and 1973.[32] The United States lost the war. In the face of stiff resistance in Southeast Asia and flagging congressional and public support for the war at home, the Nixon administration withdrew all US forces by March 1973, under the guise of the "Vietnamization" of the conflict. Despite a massive material advantage, courtesy of American munificence, the South Vietnamese forces were completely overrun by the North by April 1975. The Vietnam War was the first time that the United States had been thoroughly routed on its centuries-long path of westward expansion. The effects on morale and public faith in the American imperial project would color the entire decade.

Rapprochement and a Multipolar Region

Despite acute crisis points like the Berlin Blockade and the Cuban Missile Crisis, the Cold War was characterized by a general commitment between both superpowers to avoid direct military conflict. Until the 1970s, China was deemed the major threat in Asia: it was with China that the United States engaged in open warfare in Korea; fears of Chinese forces penetrating Southeast Asia and stripping Japan of its economic subordinates were what drove the Vietnam War; and it was the Chinese military threat to the Western Pacific toward which American strategic planning and military forces were poised. The emphasis on China's role in challenging American empire was enshrined in the National Security Council plans for "combating the Chinese communist infiltration of Southeast Asia," endorsed by President Eisenhower and continued by Kennedy and Johnson.[33]

Even at the height of the Cold War in 1966, Hans J. Morgenthau, one of the most important realist scholars of the twentieth century, argued that confronting the China threat in Asia actually offered a broad field for cooperation between the United States and the Soviet Union. Speaking to the US congressional subcommittee on the Far East and the Pacific, Morgenthau stated that China was in the process of becoming the dominant power in Asia and that the Soviet Union had the same interest in hedging against that eventuality as the United States did: "It is not only we who have an interest in creating a balance of power against China, it is first of all the Soviet Union which has such an interest. . . . Our interests run on parallel lines in all of Asia."[34]

The rapprochement with China under the Nixon administration and the dissipation of the period of détente with the Soviet Union as the 1970s drew on turned this strategic equation on its head. During this time the groundwork was laid for the later emergence of China—first as an independent pillar of world power, in coordination with which the United States aimed at balancing Soviet ambitions in Asia; later as a rival superpower and sole viable challenger to American global hegemony. The recalibration of the power balance in Asia and the world at large during this period involved, as always, highly interdependent economic and geostrategic factors.

By the 1970s, after years of failure, disillusionment, and mass slaughter in Southeast Asia, it was becoming recognized in Congress that the United States was not only losing the war but that the financial effects were deleterious on the United States and its position in the global economy. In April 1971, Senator Jacob Javits argued before the United States Senate Committee on Foreign Relations that "the Vietnam war has so weakened international confidence in the dollar that our world financial position is being jeopardized. It has so eroded the motivation of the American worker that our productive and technological superiority—our greatest strength—is threatened. . . . It has so strained our resources as to bring on a great inflation and a dangerous erosion of confidence in our economy resulting in serious unemployment."[35]

In 1969 President Nixon had articulated his "Guam Doctrine," which envisaged an "Asia for the Asians," and a more restrained American role in the region.[36] While emphasizing the importance of continued US engagement in the region that embodied both "the greatest threat to the peace of the world" and the "greatest hope," Nixon was emphatic that the responsibility for regional security would increasingly be shouldered by the Asian nations themselves.[37] The principle behind the Guam Doctrine, a withdrawal from the attempt at maintaining unilateral American hegemony, was also translated into global strategy. The "two-and-a-half wars" principle, under which the United States retained the capacity to fight and win simultaneous major wars in both Europe and Asia while also containing a third-world insurgency, had been Pentagon orthodoxy during the 1960s. The Nixon administration oversaw a revision of this strategic standard to a new baseline "one-and-a-half wars" capacity as part of its "new approach to foreign policy to match a new era of international relations," in 1970.[38] This amounted to the capacity to defend a full-scale attack in either the European or Asian theater, while deterring an attack in the other and responding to minor threats in a third region.[39] Critics of the policy described it as an attempt to maintain containment of communism without committing the resources required.[40]

The key to pulling this off lay in the flipping of China from "enemy" to "enemy of my enemy" with regard to the Soviet Union. The success of "Ping-Pong diplomacy" between China and the United States in 1971 and Nixon's visit to China in 1972, where the Shanghai Communiqué was jointly released, laid out the roadmap for the normalization of relations between the two countries. In 1967 Nixon had written in *Foreign Affairs* that China was the "common danger" that united the rest of Asia and that Asian countries now recognized the United States' presence in the region as "not an oppressor, but a protector."[41] In his account of the Asian balance of power, Nixon dismissed the Soviet Union's Asian territory, and its material and strategic interests there, as merely "an appendage of European Russia."[42] The focus, according to Nixon, should be on four regional giants: China, Japan, India, and the United States. He called for a new multilateral Asian regionalism and rightly perceived that Asia would never enjoy security and stability while China was locked out of the community of nations.

During his presidency, Nixon sought to engage China to create a new balance of power in Asia. One in which the United States could continue to play a predominant, but no longer unilateral, role in a stable regional order. Henry Kissinger, who served in a beefed-up role as national security advisor and secretary of state, held a complementary realist view of world politics to Nixon and played a leading role in America's strategic realignment during the 1970s. This realignment proceeded along three keys lines: the "Vietnamization" of the Vietnam War, which allowed US troops to withdraw from the mainland in Southeast Asia and recommit to a strategic position of offshore balancing; the shifting of a greater share of the load for mutual defense onto regional allies; and engaging China, which would isolate North Vietnam and serve as a useful counterweight to Soviet influence and power in the region.[43]

Having identified China as "the major world power which adopts a very aggressive attitude in its foreign policy" in his Guam Doctrine address, Nixon had, within four years, pivoted the United States toward an Asia policy that would recast the Soviet Union and its allies as the main rival in Asia. This major policy shift resulted from a confluence of conditions: a drastically altered strategic environment on the ground in Southeast Asia; a reduced appetite among the American public to pay the requisite price of American military preeminence in the region; the ascendance of a realist approach to fostering a balance of power in Asia that American policy planners hoped would see a friendlier China act as an embedded counterweight to the Soviet Union in the region; and Nixon's own personal vision for multipolarity and the reintegration of China into the international political community and global economy.

The Nixon years represented an acknowledgment of global systemic change and a recalibration of American imperial policy. The realism of the 1970s, wherein the United States would abandon the pursuit of unilateral global hegemony in favor of a position of first among equals, contrasts starkly with the approaches to foreign policy of the administrations that followed. In a seminal essay written the year he was appointed national security advisor to Nixon, Kissinger argued that the two-decades period since 1945, wherein the United States' foreign policy was organized around "the assumption that technology plus managerial skills gave us the ability to reshape the international system and to bring about domestic transformations in 'emerging countries,'" had now proven unworkable, given the shifting realities of international power.[44] According to Kissinger, this policy needed to be replaced with a stable international order based on international political multipolarity even while military bipolarity continued between the United States and the Soviet Union.[45] This new order would entail the development of independent political power in Europe and Japan, already the most important foreign partners and stakeholders in postwar American empire, but it would also necessitate the incorporation of Communist China into the community of nations.

Speaking to an assembled group of US ambassadors to Europe in 1975, Kissinger declared that "the problem of our age is how to manage the emergence of the Soviet Union as a superpower."[46] In a global institutional sense, this management was done through the implementation of agreements like the Nuclear Non-Proliferation Treaty, the Strategic Arms Limitation Talks, the Anti-Ballistic Missiles Treaty, and the Helsinki Final Act. In terms of regional power, geopolitics, and military strategy, Kissinger emphasized the role that China would play in balancing the Soviet Union in Asia.[47] Internal White House documents on strategic communications with China show that the United States was pushing China to more deeply engage economically and diplomatically with the West in order to form a united front against supposed Soviet hegemonic ambitions in the third world.[48]

Recession, Resources, and Reaganite Resurgence

Rapprochement with China and the tentative steps toward multipolarity were occurring at a time of deep social, economic, and political malaise in the United States. The development of "Vietnam Syndrome" after the loss of an unjust and brutal war saw the first mass challenge to widespread public conceptions of US global leadership as an unconditional force for good. At the same time, the Civil Rights Movement had effected a similar challenge to the naive understanding of the inherent good of American social, political, and cultural structures on the domestic front. A series of economic shocks, downturns, growing wealth inequality, a sharp recognition of natural-resource depletion and supply vulnerability, and a general rebalancing away from the US global economic domination that had characterized the decades following the Second World War combined to create a tangible public, and indeed cultural, sense that the American empire and US society itself had already begun to fall into decline during the 1970s.

The financial problems caused by the central role of the United States in global liquidity resulted in the abandonment of the Bretton Woods currency agreements, the core of the postwar global financial agreements that had thus far bound American-led global capitalist economies together. The United States had assumed such colossal economic proportions by the 1960s that its US dollar–denominated bond market had begun to act like a bank for foreign capital holders. Instead of holding on to currency or assets valued in domestic denominations, they were far more likely to hold onto US treasury bonds or other dollar assets.[49] Japan particularly became a major holder of American treasury bonds, and later US debt generally, as would China when it became economically ascendant.

The US role as the global banker was coupled with an increase in American direct and portfolio investment overseas, as well as the rise of the multinational corporation, a new type of corporate entity adapted perfectly to American world empire with sprawling financial, production, supply, and distribution networks across multiple sovereign jurisdictions. The growth of American multinational corporations was so great that by 1967 the amount of revenue generated overseas by American firms was larger than either Germany's or Japan's entire GDP.[50] With 22% of total profits derived from overseas investments, the United States held a higher portion of foreign direct investment than the entire rest of the world combined.[51] The total amount more than doubled, from $49 billion to $101 billion, in the years 1960–1968.[52]

But the sprawling global American economic order was, for reasons of overextension, exhaustion, and shifts in world power, becoming unwieldy under unilateral leadership and control, even with the institutional framework that had been designed to support it. The far greater growth in American investment abroad compared to the domestic front (471% abroad between 1958 and 1968 compared to 72% domestically)[53] meant that while businesses and investors were making more money than ever, the industrial and manufacturing lead that had formed the basis of American economic strength for decades was beginning to wither. The United States was hit by wave after wave of deindustrialization, affecting industries including textiles, steelmaking, carpentry, and low-tech consumer goods followed by high-tech consumer goods, automotives, and shipbuilding. All of this production was relocated to Asia, and particularly China, forming the industrial basis for the challenge to American world power that would rise in the decades that followed.

The massive increase in government spending on the Vietnam War and the expansion of social security and domestic government spending had begun to drive up inflation by the early 1970s. The dollars that flowed out of the United States to finance foreign investment and the ballooning costs of the Vietnam War were not being adequately recouped through trade surplus and foreign investment into the US economy.

Despite the fact that US exports had quintupled between the 1950s and the 1970s to $107 billion, 1971 marked the first year since 1894 that the United States ran a trade deficit.[54] At the same time, one of the pillars of the postwar system of embedded liberalism—low domestic unemployment—became more difficult to achieve, partially as a result of the impressive growth of foreign industrial and commercial centers in Western Europe and Japan. The drift upward of inflation and persistent currency speculation and overvaluation of the dollar led Nixon to decouple the US dollar from the gold standard established under the Bretton Woods agreements in 1971.[55]

The removal of the gold standard and the institution of floating exchange rates went some way toward decoupling industrial production from economic growth in the United States. Regulatory structures that had disincentivized making money by manipulating money were removed, and economic activity shifted away from industrial production, manufacture, and trade toward the trading stocks, bonds, currencies, and other securities.[56] This kind of finance capitalism, blamed for the rise of imperialism by Hobson and Lenin at the peak of British world power, became the major motive force of the American economy. New York, which had fallen into stagnation and decay by the 1970s, became the center of a turbocharged global financial economy and ascended to new heights of affluence and symbolic power. Historian Fernand Braudel, in his magisterial comparative study of capitalist states and empires, describes the ascendancy of finance capitalism to dominate the economic structure of an empire as the reaching of the logical maturity of the capitalist system of accumulation, and ultimately "a sign of autumn," as the productive center of the world economy would move on to greener industrial and mercantile pastures, and the old empire settled into the life of a rentier.[57]

Major inflationary shocks spread throughout the global economy when Arab oil-exporting countries proclaimed an oil embargo against nations supporting Israel in the 1973 Yom Kippur War. In 1970 the average price of a barrel of oil on the global market was $2.53; by 1980, a barrel cost around $41.[58] The price of oil imported into the United States spiked from $5 billion in 1972 to $48 billion in 1975.[59] The massive increase in liquid wealth of OPEC countries during this period saw huge amounts of US dollars paid by consumers in the United States, Europe, and Japan reinjected as investment capital from the oil-exporting states into Wall Street and the City of London. This further accelerated the financialization of the US economy and the reallocation of huge amounts of capital from the American public to investment in international economies, where financial institutions anticipated much higher rates of profit, coinciding with the stripping away of many of the New Deal restrictions on investment banking by the Securities and Exchange Commission.[60]

During the 1970s the rate of profit on capital investment in the semiperipheral countries of Asia like South Korea, Taiwan, and Indonesia was twice that of the core Western economies, which were mired in a global recession between 1973 and 1975.[61] In 1976, Citibank, one of the largest financial institutions in the United States, earned over three-quarters of its profits overseas.[62] These high-growth but comparatively small Asian economies were viewed as harbingers of the colossal profits to come should China open itself up to the global capitalist system.

Nixon's strategic legacy in Asia was continued through the Ford administration, with Kissinger remaining as secretary of state. President Carter was personally more idealistic, compromising, and open to negotiation with rivals. His influential national security advisor, Zbigniew Brzezinski, was a hawkish realist-internationalist and dedicated much of his political energy to creating a world order based around Western power and values, with the United States, Japan, and Europe at its core. This approach accepted the need for increased multipolarity but rejected Nixon and Kissinger's pragmatic pursuit of a balance between American, Soviet, and Chinese power.

Brzezinski supported closer relations with China only insofar as they could be leveraged against the Soviet Union.[63] He was instrumental in forming the Trilateral Commission with David Rockefeller in 1973, a sort of concentrated Council on Foreign Relations incorporating corporate, academic, and political leaders around the specific goal of creating a stable tripolar capitalist world order based around the United States, Japan, and Western Europe. Created largely in response to the emerging resistance of the third world to the American world order, the Trilateral Commission was an institutionalized attempt by the United States to encourage its junior partners to uphold American world empire with as much ideological zeal and material support as the United States had been willing to commit in the decades since the Second World War. The announcement under the "Carter Doctrine" of the United States' intention to respond to any threats to the supply of Middle Eastern oil to global markets was a significant example of the growing US consciousness that it would be increasingly necessary to shore up the supply of energy resources through open global markets with military power.

The most significant development in American foreign policy in Asia during the Carter administration occurred in 1978 when, after intense rounds of diplomacy, the United States and China announced their intention to fully normalize diplomatic relations. Within a week of this announcement, Deng Xiaoping, now paramount leader within the Communist Party of China, announced plans for the economic reforms that paved the way for China to emerge as the twenty-first-century colossus that it is today. Deng's model of "Socialism with Chinese Characteristics" decollectivized agriculture, opened China to foreign investment, began the drawdown of the state monopoly on business, allowing for private entrepreneurialism, and would lead to the reduction of protectionist trade barriers and price controls. While capital controls were never fully relaxed in China, significant American capital has flowed there since its economic opening. More importantly, from the view of American multinational corporations, the vast Chinese labor pool was opened to Western corporations to produce goods at a much-reduced cost, which would then be sold to Western consumers. Within weeks Coca-Cola announced that it would open a bottling plant in Shanghai. US strategic policy documents consistently cite American support for Chinese modernization, economic development, and integration into the global market as the vectors through which global capitalism would be strengthened, a more robust US-China relationship built, and a common front in confronting Soviet expansion and leadership in the third world formed.

An Unexpected Victory

Ronald Reagan, whose presidential campaign was designed to evoke a "new dawn" for the United States after the deterioration of the 1970s, made resource security a central pillar of his foreign-policy agenda. Under Reagan, minerals security was explicitly linked to superpower conflict. He campaigned on the need for preparedness for the coming "resource war" with the Soviet Union. This war was seen as being dual pronged. It involved a simultaneous Soviet drive to extend its influence in the Persian Gulf and thereby threaten global energy supplies along with a project to gain influence in southern Africa, the "Persian Gulf of nonfuel minerals," with a particular eye to forming a "supercartel." This arrangement would control global supplies of chromium, manganese, vanadium, and platinum group metals, all necessary for armaments production.[64] The renewed focus on resource security saw the elevation of the Middle East as a strategic priority over East Asia for the first time in American history.[65] Upon election, Reagan established the Strategic Minerals Task Force as an advisory body for crafting appropriate policy to conduct the "resource war." The task force included top executives from America's largest mining companies, and much of the policy advocacy emanating from the organization focused on overturning environmental protections and opening public and Native American land to miners.[66]

While strategic resource policy during this period was not focused primarily on Asia, the geopolitical dynamics that were established foreboded an increasingly important area of tension in the contemporary US-China relationship. Overreliance on China for the supply of strategic minerals upon which US defense, energy, and high-tech sectors are completely dependent has, in recent years, become a major issue in American strategic policy. Fears of Soviet domination of southern African resources, never truly realized, have now been replaced by a more imminent, market-oriented threat of Chinese industry competing for the same limited and critical resource supplies as the United States in both Africa and Latin America.

The 1980s were also a period of massive expansion of the already enormous military power of the United States. Under the Reagan administration, US defense spending doubled from $155 billion in 1980 to $320 billion in

1988. In 1980, 64% of America's military budget was spent on operating costs and 36% on new investment. By 1986, new investment had become 51% of the military budget.[67] The increasing focus on military research and investment foreshadowed the new era of a more militarized and unilaterally interventionist empire that was to come. Without detailing any concrete plans for how it would be done, outside of general and ambitious ideas of supply-side-driven growth and trickle-down wealth diffusion, Reagan had promised to both massively increase the military and outspend the Soviet Union in a reinvigorated arms race, while at the same time balancing the budget and restoring responsible stewardship of the economy, something George H. W. Bush described as "voodoo economics" during the Republican primary election campaign of 1980.

In reality, Reagan reconciled his free-market, low-taxing ideology with this massive military buildup by increasing government debt. Between 1981 and 1987 the US government racked up more debt (over $1 trillion worth) than had been accumulated in the preceding 190 years combined.[68] Deficits grew to such an extent under Reagan that by 1985, for the first time since the First World War, the United States owed more money overseas than it was owed itself, returning to the status of a debtor nation.

This meant an even greater flow of public money to private arms manufacturers like Boeing, Lockheed Martin, and Northrop Grumman, some of the largest multinational corporations on the planet. Reagan's National Security Strategy of 1982 established the reversal of Soviet control and military presence throughout the world as a guiding global objective of the US strategy.[69] Another was "to ensure the US access to foreign markets, and to ensure the US and its allies and friends access to foreign energy and mineral resources."[70] With the progressive disintegration of Soviet world power during the late 1980s and the collapse of the union itself in 1991, these objectives were achieved in a stunning closure to an epoch of world history.

The 1970s had been, in many senses, a watershed for American empire and the US role in Asia. Lessons of the limits to unilateral hegemony in Vietnam, the rapprochement with China, the strategic prioritization of forming a stable system of multipolarity, and the reemphasis of the role of strategic resources in national security all contributed to reshaping the role of the United States at the apex of world power. The 1980s did much to clarify the new structure of American empire. The decade continued and accelerated the reorientation of the American economy from one dominated by manufacturing, heavy industry, and raw materials to one dominated by finance, services, pharmaceuticals, military-industry, and a growing high-tech sector. The accounting position of the United States was inverted from its role as the world's preeminent creditor in the postwar years to a deep borrower. By 1987 the United States had become the largest debtor in the world, mostly driven by European and Japanese purchases of American treasury bonds and direct investments, which funded American purchases of their products.[71]

Eric Hobsbawm refers to the 20 years between 1973 and 1993 as the "crisis decades" of the late Cold War, when economic turmoil and global inequality skyrocketed.[72] The central fact of these decades, according to Hobsbawm, was not merely that American global capitalism had ceased functioning as well as it had during the postwar golden years but that its operations had become politically uncontrollable.[73] The institutions of "embedded liberalism" were no longer capable of constraining the market within desirable social and political limits. This relationship was now inverted, and politics and society operated within the parameters set by the global market, which progressively broke the bonds of the state institutions that had fostered it and now set the framework within which all states operated. Keynesian economics, preeminent in the West since the Second World War, began to give way to the Austrian and Chicago School neoliberal approach shaped by economists like Friedrich Hayek and Milton Friedman. Recalibration of the governing principles of the world economy were coupled with an unprecedented technological revolution, one that saw millions of jobs vanish into obsolescence, further destabilizing the system of American world power that had operated successfully along the lines of embedded liberalism in the decades after the Second World War.

The United States emerged from the Cold War in a reinforced position as the world's premier military and political power. The challenge to America's system of global capitalism that the existence of the Soviet Union embodied was destroyed at the same time as China began pivoting to a mixed market economy. The atmosphere of triumphalism and hubris at the founding of the new period of American unipolarity was so extreme that liberal political scientist Francis Fukuyama could confidently declare that history had now ended. Humanity had reached the apex of political evolution under American global leadership; the modest task that remained would be to pull along the stragglers and doubters to enjoy the full benefits of the "unabashed victory of economic and political liberalism ... and the universalization of Western liberal democracy as the final form of human government."[74]

Fukuyama pointed to China as the most important test case for liberalism at the end of history, and in 1989 he augured hopeful signs that China would follow the same path of historical development as the West.[75] Regardless of the speed of this process, Fukuyama and many others believed that with the end of the Cold War, and the economic reforms of China, there now existed no other pole toward which the world could gravitate away from American liberalism. The world had now entered a unipolar moment, led by the United States. China, recently reintegrated into the world system, was again becoming a global center of commodity production and exchange. Its place within the American global economic order would develop rapidly in the decades after the Cold War and render absurd the notion that history had ended.

PART III

FROM A UNIPOLAR GLOBAL EMPIRE TO A SHRINKING EXPLOITATIVE HEGEMONY

CHAPTER SEVEN

The Unipolar Moment
and Imperial Hubris

The United States emerged from the Cold War as the unchallenged global leader by every relevant metric of power. With the complete collapse of its ideological and geostrategic nemesis, the United States was apparently free to fulfill Isaiah's prophecy of beating swords into plowshares and use its influence to actualize the liberal dream of an international system that was truly democratic, multilateral, and institutionally capable of weathering the inevitable further shifts in the distribution of global power. In reality, however, America the empire, intoxicated by hubris, used the decades of unipolarity to expand the global Open Door and deploy its power—multilaterally when convenient, unilaterally when necessary—in an attempt to reshape the entire world in its own image. This path would, in the decades to come, lead to an epoch-defining strategic, economic, and ideological confrontation between the United States and an ascendant China.

The Pax Americana that had emerged after the Second World War, while certainly market oriented, was heavily influenced by geopolitical rivalry with the Soviet Union and concerns for stability and world order, which could come at the expense of market opportunities for the United States itself. The new American order that followed the collapse of the Soviet Union was established with no major geopolitical rival in sight. Without a serious challenger to its strategic hegemony, the United States was free to center the pursuit of market opportunities and the free flow of investment capital as the focal point of the new unipolar American world order.

The economic side of unipolar expansionism was expressed through the proliferation of hundreds of new trade agreements, most prominently the establishment of the World Trade Organization and the North American Free Trade Agreement (NAFTA); the imposition of the Washington Consensus on developing economies and former Soviet states through the Bretton Woods institutions of the IMF and the World Bank; and the massive concerted globalization of the production, exchange, and consumption of goods and services, propelled by new applications of networked digital communications technology. On the military side, a brief "peace dividend" was made redundant by the extension of military bases across areas of the world previously unoccupied by the United States, including swaths of Africa, Central Asia, and Eastern Europe; the imposition of a doctrine of "humanitarian interventionism;" the pursuit of regime-change wars in the Middle East; and the entrenchment of the pursuit of perpetual military supremacy in strategic policy planning.

Global Empire at History's End

The dominant view of the American foreign policy establishment for several decades preceding the end of the Cold War had been that the world was moving toward multipolarity. It was with some surprise then, and a great deal of triumphalism, that Washington came to appraise the emergence of a unipolar structure of world power after the fall of the Soviet Union in 1991. The United States was now the sole superpower, sometimes described as a "hyperpower," which dominated all other states in every significant domain of international affairs: economic, military, cultural, and diplomatic. After centuries of market, military, and institutional expansion, the United States had become the first ever truly global empire.

The new structure of world power made for novel twists on the dominant paradigms of international politics. The neoliberal approach, which characterized the Clinton administration's perspective on foreign affairs, saw the end of the Cold War as an opportunity to launch another round of international institution building, within which the United States would continue its position of unparalleled leadership, but which would also involve a degree of consensus building to add resilience to systemic fluctuations of the distribution of global power. This new type of liberalism was distinguished from the initial round of institution building by the United States after the Second World War by the scaling back of the government's mandate to secure domestic social and economic equity and stability within a regulated free-market framework. In the place of the stability of embedded liberalism and the Cold War balance of power came the fluctuations and growing inequality of Wall Street–led finance capitalism, progressively stripped of its earlier regulations, and the beginnings of a new stage of American "promiscuous intervention-ism" abroad.[1]

Neoconservatives viewed the end of the Cold War as a defining moment in world history which offered the United States the ability to unilaterally apply its own political and moral system upon the rest of the world. The neo-conservative approach to foreign affairs was far more formally hierarchical than the neoliberal one. This was the defining worldview of the George W. Bush administration. Notably, both approaches retained a consensus on the structure of the global economy, a continuation of the neoliberal economics that had emerged in the 1970s in which the United States played the central role in the sprawling web of global finance and corporate ownership, while production networks were increasingly shifted to low labor-cost areas of the developing world. This neoliberal economic consensus hailed an era of un-restrained global corporate capitalism, backed by the unmatched American military machine.[2]

The George H. W. Bush presidency laid the groundwork for many of the defining trends of the subsequent two administrations. The paramount Na-tional Security Strategy (NSS) paper of his presidency, which came in the same year as the formal dissolution of the Soviet Union, describes the his-torical moment as an opportunity to "grasp an extraordinary possibility that few generations have enjoyed—to build a new international system in accor-dance with our own values and ideals, as old patterns and certainties crum-ble around us."[3]

The main strategic task of the early stages of the unipolar era was man-aging Soviet decline and filling vacuums of power with American military forces. This would be undertaken by a new kind of military, reshaped in line with the "Revolution in Military Affairs" to be more technologically sophis-ticated, professionalized, mobile, and responsive, and outfitted with a new generation of "smart weapons" that would give the United States an even greater qualitative military edge.[4] Under George H. W. Bush, Chairman of the Joint Chiefs of Staff Colin Powell developed a "base force concept," through which the United States would draw down its forward presence in Europe and Asia but maintain a potent and mobile striking force to be used against "rogue states" that challenged American hegemony.[5]

In Asia, the post–Cold War focus was managing declining Russian influ-ence in its traditional satellites like Cambodia, Vietnam, and North Korea, while continuing to engage China as it "proceed[ed] inexorably towards major systemic change" of the same vein as the Soviet Union.[6] These broad strategic objectives were, as ever, inextricable from economic interests. James Baker, writing in *Foreign Affairs* as secretary of state in 1992, identified American strategic interests in Asia as continuing in the tradition of "maintaining commercial access and preventing the rise of any single hegemonic power or coalition hostile to the United States and its allies and friends," with a stronger emphasis on economic relations now than ever before.[7]

The 1991 NSS compared the current moment to the 1920s, predicting catastrophe if the United States were to again overcome critical threats to its interests only to turn inward. This time, the Bush White House argued, the United States must embrace its "pivotal and unescapable" role as the leader of a new world order.[8] The expansion of the capitalist global economy was a clear priority here. During the Cold War, the United States had doggedly supported the economic growth and stability of Western Europe and Japan, to the point of supporting competition against its own domestic industries, as part of its broader imperial grand strategy against communism and for globally integrated capitalism. With the dissipation of the communist challenge, the United States became more concerned with shoring up its own position at the apex of the global economic system, with an eye to the continuing rise of Germany and Japan as peer competitors. The 1991 NSS went as far as to state that trade negotiations with Germany and Japan "now share some of the strategic importance we have traditionally attached to arms talks with the Soviet Union."[9]

A secret defense planning paper that was produced the next year laid out US strategic objectives for the new era. It established the primary US strategic objective as the prevention of the emergence of a new hegemonic rival anywhere in the world. In a partial reversion to the model of Cold War imperial management, the planning paper explicitly called for the accommodation of the economic interests of other advanced industrial nations in Europe and Asia "to discourage them from challenging our leadership or seeking to overturn the established political and economic order."[10]

The paper, written by prominent neoconservative and future key architect of the invasion of Iraq Paul Wolfowitz, was leaked to the press, where it elicited a furious backlash over its overtly imperialistic language and strategy. It was swiftly disowned by the Defense Department, and a watered-down version was released the following January.[11] Andrew Bacevich identifies the impact of this episode on the political communications that characterized the next three presidential administrations: "its purpose was to reassure the public that the promotion of peace, democracy, and human rights and the punishment of evil-doers—not the pursuit of self-interest—defined the essence of American diplomacy."[12] The reality was that the United States was entering a new and unfettered era for its dictation of global economic structures, tied closely with geostrategic interests.

Clinton's Foreign Policy and China

The identification of foreign markets as the key to American domestic prosperity has been a constant motive force in American politics. With the election of President Bill Clinton, the centrality of the economy, and particularly the status of foreign markets, reached new levels of explicit political importance. The president was unequivocal: "Growth at home depends upon growth abroad."[13] Senior members of his administration expressed the same belief. Secretary of State Warren Christopher explained that "we've passed the point where we can sustain prosperity on sales just within the United States."[14] This attitude, combined with the receding of the Soviet military challenge and the development of a new generation of digital communications technologies, resulted in the effective melding together of American economic and strategic interests, in tandem with the further integration of the world into a unified global economy. The fall of the Soviet Union provided the opportunity to expand the global community of market economies networked under American empire.

Taken as a whole, the 1990s was a period of economic boom in the United States and one that furthered the financialization of the US economy. Unemployment dropped to 4%, its lowest level in 30 years; the rate of corporate profit reached levels not seen since the mid-1960s; and labor productivity grew steadily year on year.[15] Despite this, real wages for workers were lower in 1999 than 1968.[16] Workers' pay increased at a yearly average of 0.6% during the 1980s and 1990s, while CEO compensation increased 650% during the same period.[17] The widening gulf of socioeconomic inequality was amplified by the restructuring of the new and dynamic American economy. The traditional pillars of American industry were falling to foreign competition at the same time as American companies outsourced their production networks to developing countries with vast pools of low-cost labor. Auto manufacturing, steel production, and both heavy and light industry shed jobs on a grand scale during this period; at the same time, sectors of the high-tech economy, like computing, aerospace and defense, pharmaceuticals, and finance, grew rapidly.

The introduction of the Financial Services Modernization Act in 1999 repealed many of the regulations that had limited the casino capitalism of interinstitutional financial-product transactions that produced vast paper booms and busts, and ultimately damaged the real economy. Manufacturing in the United States continued to expand in aggregate terms, but the wealth it generated was concentrated among fewer beneficiaries. Where manufacturing had once promised a reliable path to middle-class comfort for American workers, profits were now far disproportionately being diverted to owners and upper management, as well as a ballooned sector of professional and business services, consisting of lawyers, accountants, consultants, and analysts. The broad story of the American economy under Clinton was one of massive restructuring, unequal growth, and the further integration of a single global market. The key international institutional developments during this era of globalization were the completion of the North American Free Trade Agreement (NAFTA), the establishment of the World Trade Organization (WTO), and the movement to incorporate China into the WTO framework for global trade, which was formally completed early in the administration of George W. Bush.

Clinton emphasized shifting government spending from defense to domestic priorities and initiated the 1993 "Bottom-Up Review," which aimed at such reforms in the Pentagon, early in his presidency. The overall arguments were that the United States, without a near peer competitor in the Soviet Union, could now do more with less, providing that it maintained its forward defense basing structure, through which more substantial forces could surge when required, and that American soft power—interconnected markets, international institutions, promotion of democracy, and meaningful diplomacy—would lessen the likelihood of hostility in a more interdependent world.

This document perhaps embodies the zenith of American post–Cold War hubris and "end of history" strategic thought. It envisions American leadership in a globalized world, with strategy revolving around problem-solving interventions, particularly toward recalcitrant "regional powers" like Iraq.[18] There is no recognition that any substantial foundational differences in ideology, economic systems, national interests, or hegemonic rivalry would characterize geopolitics for the foreseeable future and thus no discussion on how best to shape American strategic policy for great power conflict. Instead the United States would prevent "threats to our interests by promoting democracy, economic growth and free markets, human dignity, and the peaceful resolution of conflict."[19] This approach fit well with the sort of public-facing justification of American power that was pushed after the leak of the Wolfo-witz defense paper.

The transformed global strategic environment was further elaborated in Clinton's "engagement and enlargement" National Security Strategy paper of 1994. This drove home the message that the threat to the United States was no longer a major rival economic, political, and ideological model for world order. Rather danger lay in diverse and amorphous threats to "our open and free society," such as drug syndicates, international criminals and terrorists, demographic shifts in the developing world, refugee flows, and social unrest due to ethnic and religious tensions, which would be met with "peace oper-ations" and "strong intelligence capabilities."[20]

The emphasis on global democracy and human rights was perhaps more present in this National Security Strategy than any leading up to it, but in the same paper it was proudly touted that for "economic and strategic interests" the United States had decoupled China's most-favored-nation trading status from its record on human rights, paving the way for unfettered economic integration between American capital and Chinese labor, and American ac-cess to a Chinese economy that would grow at double-digit rates on average over the next two decades.[21] At the core of Clinton's neoliberal post–Cold War national-security strategy was "enlarging the community of market de-mocracies. . . . The more that democracy and political and economic liberal-ization take hold in the world, particularly in countries of geostrategic im-portance to us, the safer our nation is likely to be and the more our people are likely to prosper."[22]

This attitude was perhaps nowhere more prominent than in the relation-ship with China. Since Nixon, the American framework for engaging China had leaned toward strategic cooperation; China was to help balance the Asian region against the Soviet Union in a multipolar world of rival powers. By the early 1990s, the fall of the Soviet Union, China's strong reform-led economic growth, and the events of the Tiananmen Square protests and subsequent crackdown in 1989 left US policy toward China without a clear anchor. After internal disputes within the Clinton administration during 1993 and 1994, between human-rights and organized-labor factions on one side and a pro-free-trade corporate faction on the other, a heavily commercially weighted approach to China was established, which would not be seriously challenged for the next two decades. The political project to commercially engage China regardless of human-rights abuses was aggressively lobbied for by the Wall Street banks and auditing and accounting firms that oversaw the floating of

Chinese businesses on American and Asian capital markets during the period of the large-scale privatization of Chinese state-owned enterprises in the 1990s, as well as a variety of other corporate actors with interests in China and direct relationships with the Chinese government.[23]

The new consensus on China emphasized engagement and balancing. The engagement side focused on the vast economic benefits that would flow from incorporating China more closely into the global economic system. This came with the neoliberal political understanding that the habituating normative effects of closer economic ties would bring China into the American-led international political order as a stable partner. According to this theory, China would, driven by an increasingly prosperous and expanding middle class enjoying the fruits of free markets, inevitably travel the path of liberalism toward electoral democracy and a newfound respect for human rights. The "balancing" component meant reinforcing America's existing alliances in the region, maintaining American military capacities and diplomatic weight in the region to keep China conscious of the costs involved if it veered from the anticipated political and economic trajectory. Joseph Nye, a founding scholar of neoliberalism, chair of the National Intelligence Council, and assistant secretary of defense for international security affairs under Clinton, described that, in practical terms, this meant reinvigorating the Hub and Spokes regional alliances, maintaining a forward troop presence in the region, and developing regional institutions with an eye to integrating China into agreements regarding economics, military, and maritime activities.[24]

Triumphalism and the embrace of the end-of-history narrative led many politicians and China-focused political scientists in the United States to view a Chinese transition to liberal democracy as an inevitability. After visiting China, President Clinton commented that the most interesting thing he did there was visit an Internet café, remarking that "the more people know, the more opinions they're going to have; the more democracy spreads."[25] The belief in a causal link between increased economic interconnectedness, a growing middle class, and transition to democracy in China pervaded the Clinton administration's political rhetoric and policy positions. The democratizing middle-class narrative of Chinese development was paired with American economic objectives through a tenuous link between Western culture, business practices, and the promotion of human rights. Leaders of Clinton's economic team argued that "commercial considerations may seem crass when compared with human rights, but impeding commercial relations with China would impede the flow of information about Western culture, ideas, and business practices to China's emerging middle class and weaken reformers in the state and party leadership."[26]

The idea that the United States could have its cake and eat it too with China, that American profits from doing business would transmogrify into a vibrant Chinese liberal democracy, was bipartisan. It tracked closely with the approach established by President Bush in the years prior, who defended his decision to extend most-favored-nation trading status to China after the Tiananmen Square protests, saying that "no nation on Earth has discovered a way to import the world's goods and services while stopping foreign ideas at the border. Just as the democratic idea has transformed nations on every continent, so, too, change will inevitably come to China."[27]

Despite tougher rhetoric in the lead-up to his election, the next Bush administration operated under the same assumptions. Robert Zoellick, deputy secretary of state under George W. Bush, argued that "we can cooperate with the emerging China of today, even as we work for the democratic China of tomorrow," because "closed politics cannot be a permanent feature of Chinese society. It is simply not sustainable—as economic growth continues, better-off Chinese will want a greater say in their future, and pressure builds for political reform."[28]

These politicians and policymakers were accompanied by a coterie of prominent China scholars and commentators who have, for the last 30 years, repeatedly augured the imminent collapse of the Chinese one-party state for various *raisons du jour*, including corruption within the Communist Party of China, the dominance of state-run enterprises in key sectors of the economy, a precarious financial system, and environmental degradation.[29] The reality is that this collapse has never even come close to happening since the Tiananmen Square protests in 1989, and in many ways the Chinese political system seems more stable today than do many Western democracies. Professor Andrew J. Nathan, a self-confessed former diviner of China's demise, now argues that China has developed a form of "authoritarian resilience." He highlights the broadening of political participation, growing meritocracy, and institutional specialization as core reasons that the Chinese regime would not simply collapse under the weight of democratic pressure from within as the society grows wealthier.[30]

Professor John Keane has also pointed to inbuilt "virtual steam valves" in the Chinese system of government that allow for certain types of democratic civil participation, such as public opinion polling, local elections, and online public forums. These act as early warning systems of popular unrest for the

Communist Party of China, shoring up its long-term stability and building what Keane describes as a form of "phantom democracy."[31] In 2015 Nathan linked China's resurgent authoritarianism to the West's democratic decline, arguing that "the appeal of authoritarianism grows when the prestige of democracy declines" and that therefore "the most important answer to China's challenge is for the democracies to do a better job of managing themselves than they are doing today."[32] Keane has reached similar conclusions, pointing to the high degree of regime resilience and sophisticated interlinking of media, technology, phantom democracy, and state bureaucracy that characterize the new emerging type of despotic regime, posing the question of whether a Western model of liberal democracy in decline can provide an adequate challenge to this model becoming the new global norm.[33]

The president of the Council on Foreign Relations, Richard Haass, compared Clinton's record on foreign policy during the unipolar moment to an investor crowing about modest gains during the greatest bull market in history.[34] Clinton's dedication to the neoliberal reconstitution of the American economy was not paralleled with any serious commitment to the creation of a stable regional order in Asia that could outlive American unipolarity. Haass describes the Clinton administration as having left a foreign-policy void, with "no clear priorities, no consistency or thoroughness in the implementation of strategies, and no true commitment to building a domestic consensus in support of internationalism."[35] Haass was incorrect to identify no clear priorities; there was certainly a very demonstrable priority placed on forging ahead with economic globalization and forwarding American business interests on the world stage. What was lacking was any serious engagement with the task of building a world order that would be resilient once this unprecedented era of American unipolarity came to an end.

Despite the noted lack of the development of any farsighted strategic policy for the unipolar era, the military component of American empire continued its inexorable expansion. The expectation that the United States would oversee a massive reallocation of public resources from a now largely redundant military colossus was never appreciably realized. The "peace dividend" that was to follow American victory in the Cold War did see a modest reduction in American military spending, which fell progressively from 5.6% of GDP, or $624 billion (in 2018 constant dollars), in 1990 to 3.1% of GDP, or $449 billion, by 1999.[36] Considering, however, that the former Soviet Union's military budget was reduced by over 90% over the same time period, from $217 billion for the Soviet Union in 1990 to $17 billion for Russia in 1999, the result was a dramatic increase in relative American global military domi-nance.[37] By 1999 Clinton's national security advisor, Sandy Berger, was tout-ing the massive increase in American military strength gained through the years of the "peace dividend" to the Council on Foreign Relations, telling them that "our military expenditures now are larger than those of all other countries combined; our weaponry is a generation ahead of our nearest po-tential rival."[38]

The opportunity afforded to the United States by the unipolar moment was, in some ways, even greater than that enjoyed at the end of the Second World War. But with a completely different configuration of world power, American leaders faced far less pressure to invest in building imperial insti-tutions that continued to pay substantial dividends to their constituent mem-bers, or that would guarantee the security and prosperity of the United States when its waxing power began to wane. With no rival military power or eco-nomic and ideological system in sight, the United States embarked on a path of drawing down on its vast investments of political capital for the benefits of a smaller and smaller group of beneficiaries. The focus was overwhelmingly economic; farsighted strategic policy was put to the side.

The Bush Years in Asia

In his election campaign, George W. Bush touted a tough new stand on China. Rebuking Clinton's policy of engagement, Bush stated that "China is a com-petitor, not a strategic partner. We must deal with China without ill-will—but without illusions."[39] Nevertheless, the Bush years were, in many respects, a continuation of the China policy trends that predominated under Clinton, albeit with a stronger focus on strategic containment. American grand strat-egy was centered around regime-change operations and the "War on Terror" in the Middle East and South Asia, while the dynamics of the relationship with China, the only potential hegemonic challenger on the horizon, for the most part continued on the basis of the article of faith that it would be China itself that changed rather than the international balance of power and Amer-ican empire.

By the standards of relationships between a globally dominant empire and a rising competitor, the Bush administration quite successfully kept relations with China on an even keel. Engagement and balancing continued as the dominant themes. In his 2002 National Security Strategy, Bush identified the goal of his administration as building a world within which "great powers compete in peace instead of continually prepare for war."[40] War was instead to be conducted in cooperation among powerful states upon "terrorists," "rogue states," and "chaos." The world's powers were given free rein on Islamic separatists, domestic and international terrorist networks, and regional geopolitical rivals that could be designated as state sponsors of terrorism or themselves rogue states outside of the international community. With this new partnership, benefiting the United States in the Middle East and South Asia, Russia in Chechnya and Dagestan, and China in Xinjiang, also came a reduction in human-rights-centered punitive discourse directed at America's rivals. In the 2002 NSS, Bush stated that "we are also increasingly united by common values. Russia is in the midst of a hopeful transition, reaching for its democratic future and a partner in the war on terror. Chinese leaders are discovering that economic freedom is the only source of national wealth. In time, they will find that social and political freedom is the only source of national greatness."[41]

The appreciation of the Bush administration for China's cooperation in the War on Terror was exemplified by its decision not to sponsor a UN Human Rights Commission resolution condemning China for its human rights abuses, the first time the United States had declined to do so since 1989.[42]

The major feature of containment within the Bush administration's balancing strategy toward China came in the form of fortifying existing American regional alliances, notably with Japan, South Korea, and Australia, as well as in moving to incorporate India and the Indian Ocean into the Asia-Pacific strategic sphere. An emphasis was placed on directly linking the spokes of the traditional American-led regional security architecture together, moving away from the United States as the hub upon which all security arrangements solely rested. The Trilateral Security Dialogue between Australia, Japan, and the United States was established in 2002. Separate bilateral security declarations were made between Australia and Japan, and Australia and South Korea, in 2007 and 2009 respectively. Japan and India declared a "strategic partnership" in 2006.

The following year, after the United States and India concluded an agreement which conferred de facto recognition to India as a legitimate nuclear power, a quadrilateral security arrangement between the United States, India, Japan, and Australia was mooted. This arrangement was to establish an "arc of democracy" which would incorporate an alliance of democratic Asian regional powers with the United States to contain Chinese expansion. China raised serious protests about the formation of a new "small NATO" being formed against it, issuing formal diplomatic démarches to all the participants and requesting an explanation in May 2007.[43] The initiative was abandoned shortly after in the face of significant domestic political resistance within the member states, as well as the perception among foreign-policy elites that it was unnecessarily provocative of China.[44]

Alongside these moves toward strategic containment, economic engagement proceeded apace. Bush continued the policy of global free trade which was by this point near-total bipartisan orthodoxy in Washington. Between 2001 and 2008, the United States signed free trade agreements with Singapore, Australia, and South Korea. China joined the WTO under American encouragement in December 2001. Total US trade with Asia stood at $636 billion in 2001 (with a US deficit of $238 billion); by 2008 this had almost doubled to $1.184 trillion (with a US deficit of $466 billion).[45] The largest single increase in interstate trade during this period was with China, which expanded from $121 billion in 2001 ($83 billion deficit) to $407 billion in 2008 ($268 billion deficit).[46]

American direct investment in China grew at an even faster rate, more than quadrupling from $12 billion to $54 billion between 2001 and 2008.[47] The circle of strategic containment and economic engagement was squared using familiar end-of-history logic: China would soon come around to wholeheartedly embrace Western neoliberal structures and norms; in fact, the more economic engagement that occurred, the faster this transformation would be. The role of US strategy and military forces was then to coax China and other recalcitrant states along in the right direction when progress stalled or they appeared to stray from the neoliberal path. Bush explained: "A quarter century after beginning the process of shedding the worst features of the Communist legacy, China's leaders have not yet made the next series of fundamental choices about the character of their state. In pursuing advanced military capabilities that can threaten its neighbors in the Asia-Pacific region, China is following an outdated path that, in the end, will hamper its own pursuit of national greatness. In time, China will find that social and political freedom is the only source of that greatness."[48]

The War on Terror and Embracing Empire

The post–Cold War imperial hubris engendered by unipolarity and the end-of-history narrative took on a new intensity under the Bush administration. Bush's foreign-policy team consisted of a dangerous combination of hardline "national interest" conservatives, like Dick Cheney, Donald Rumsfeld, Condoleezza Rice, and Richard Armitage, and ultra-hawkish neoconservatives, like Richard Perle, Paul Wolfowitz, Douglas Feith, John Bolton, and Scooter Libby. While there was, of course, a measure of diversity of opinion within the administration, particularly between Colin Powell's State Department and Donald Rumsfeld's Pentagon, unity existed around the idea that the unipolar moment had thus far largely been squandered by Clinton and that the United States should instead use this unique historical moment to cement its power advantage permanently. This unity was most visibly manifested through the membership of the leadership of both factions of Bush's foreign-policy team in the highly influential Project for the New American Century (PNAC) think tank.

Founded in 1997, PNAC's goals were to arrest the "decline in the strength of America's defenses" (i.e., to abandon any hope for a meaningful post–Cold War "peace dividend") and, through a peerless military, to ensure that the United States could exercise global leadership in perpetuity.[49] The broad outline of the plan to cement American empire into the post–Cold War era had been contained within Paul Wolfowitz's Defense Policy Guidance in 1992. The document, which was seen as too radical by the Bush Sr. and Clinton administrations, was openly embraced by the neoconservative movement and informed many of the strategic assumptions of the Bush Jr. White House. Neoconservatism embodied a form of American exceptionalism on steroids, exhorting the United States to embrace the moral clarity and confidence to act alone in the pursuit of an American global hegemony that would supposedly benefit the world. Robert Kagan, one of the leading luminaries of the movement, described neoconservatism as representing "a potent moralism and idealism in world affairs, a belief in America's exceptional role as a promoter of the principles of liberty and democracy, a belief in the preservation of American primacy and in the exercise of power, including military power, as a tool for defending and advancing moralistic and idealistic causes, as well as a suspicion of international institutions and a tendency toward unilateralism."[50]

China was conceived of as the major emergent post–Cold War threat to American primacy by neoconservatives during the 1990s, but the terrorist attacks of September 11, 2001, provided the perfect opportunity to fully mobilize both the American government and public at large around a new war footing, one that implemented preconceived geopolitical goals in the Middle East and justified an ongoing massive expansion of both the military apparatus and the war powers of the president and the Pentagon.[51] In the wake of September 11, the shift in discourse, and indeed the general feel of American power and the state of the world, was jarring. The albeit largely delusional sense that the problems of international relations were to be managed by responsible and highly competent technocrats as the world marched along the path of progressive liberalism in relative lockstep vanished almost overnight. In its place was the articulation of a world again divided into two inherently opposed camps: America and its allies in the "free world," and Islamic terrorists and their protectors and enablers in the "axis of evil."

Bush unambiguously asserted these new fault lines of global politics in an address to the joint houses of Congress and the nation as a whole nine days after the attacks. He framed terrorism as a global enemy, intent on remaking the entire world in a fundamentalist Islamic image. Like the spread of communism before it, the new terrorist threat was not a reaction to American foreign policy or the blowback effects of the American empire but a radical ideological enemy that was driven through its Manichaean opposition to all the good things about America: "They hate what they see right here in this chamber: a democratically elected government. Their leaders are self-appointed. They hate our freedoms: our freedom of religion, our freedom of speech, our freedom to vote and assemble and disagree with each other."[52] The fight against this enemy would not consist of short and decisive campaigns that characterized the previous two administrations' military engagements but would be "a lengthy campaign unlike any other we have ever seen."[53] As in the Cold War system, all nations of the world would be compelled to take a side: "Every nation in every region now has a decision to make: Either you are with us or you are with the terrorists."[54]

The Global War on Terror reshaped American grand strategy around the Middle East and South Asia. The war, including major conflicts in Iraq and Afghanistan as well as smaller operations in over 80 countries, cost the United States' public $6.4 trillion in the years between 2001 and 2020.[55] Around 800,000 people have been killed as a result of these wars, including over 7,000 US military personal.[56] Through the process of "blowback," described by Chalmers Johnson, the war on terror had the effect of producing and reproducing terrorism as it was waged.[57] Terrorism as well as failed states, warring fiefdoms, simmering insurgencies, and well-armed autocratic regimes came to characterize the political realities of the Middle East to a higher degree than they had in any period before September 11. The spread of freedom and democracy was never achieved. The massive bloating of the US military budget, the expansion of an already immense network of bases, and the normalization of American unilateralism all did much to heighten awareness of the material realities of American empire.

The military demonstration of American imperial power was accompanied by a notable shift in the tone of political discourse. The open embrace of the word "empire" among media and political elites had probably not been seen to this degree since the advent of Wilsonian liberalism. Karl Rove, Bush's best known and closest advisor, revealed the top-down nature of the production of mediated imperial reality when he famously told a reporter for the *New York Times* that "we're an empire now, and when we act, we create our own reality. And while you're studying that reality—judiciously, as you will— we'll act again, creating other new realities, which you can study too, and that's how things will sort out. We're history's actors . . . and you, all of you, will be left to just study what we do."[58]

Among a surprisingly large section of American media and academia, empire was no longer denied. In many ways reminiscent of the discursive atmosphere at the turn of the twentieth century, the American public was encouraged to embrace the imperial realities of American power and to support their leaders in seeing the responsible management of stability, democracy, and open markets as the basis of world affairs.[59] It was during this period of imperial hubris that the United States began to renounce the treaty obligations and conventions upon which the relative international consensus over American global empire has been based since the Second World War.

In 2001 the Bush administration, notoriously entwined with the fossil-fuels sector, withdrew from the Kyoto Protocol, which sought to create a unified global approach to dealing with the effects of human-caused climate change. In 2002 the Bush administration withdrew the United States from the International Criminal Court. The same year, Bush unilaterally withdrew from the landmark Anti-Ballistic Missile Treaty that had successfully limited one component of the arms race with the Soviet Union, and later Russia, since 1971, and dropped the long-standing pledge that the United States would not use nuclear weapons against a nonnuclear state. This was done to take advantage of the clear edge in high-tech offensive and defensive capabilities that the United States enjoys over all other nations.[60] The Bush years heralded a shift from a global empire based around economic interconnectedness and a clear assortment of incentives for certain other nations to participate to one based upon total and perpetual military superiority with American interests firmly foregrounded.

It has been pointed out by historians that Bush's neoconservative foreign policy ran against long-tested imperial policies and economic interests of the United States.[61] This mode of unilateral imperialism was an aberration from the relatively stable empire that the United States had run since the Second World War. This departure was not because the United States had abandoned the long-standing principles of the international extension of the Open Door but rather because an administration was, under the influence of imperial hubris and ideological overconfidence, tempted into unilateral overextension. The goal was to reshape the Middle East in America's image: eradicating any serious challenges to American regional leadership, supporting the geopolitical ambitions of American regional allies such as Israel and Saudi Arabia, securing access for American corporations to the large oil reserves from which they had been barred in favor of French and Russian operators, and ensuring the development of regional economies along Open Door lines. This was to be done expeditiously, and the ensuing leverage that the United States held over world energy supplies could be used to apply serious pressure to China if it sought to challenge American preeminence, in Asia or elsewhere.[62]

In terms of American imperial objectives such as shaping international economic networks, ensuring global stability and domestic prosperity, and maximizing American power with regard to any potential peer competitors— these conflicts have been unmitigated disasters. The Iraq and Afghanistan Wars in particular are likely to go down in history as the critical juncture of American imperial decline, when the United States lost any hope of setting the conditions of world economic and political order far into the twenty-first century. Having unquestionably faltered at the challenge predicted by Paul Kennedy at the end of the Cold War—avoiding imperial overstretch—the United States now finds itself presented with a viable hegemonic challenger in China, which spent the last 20 years growing and mustering its resources, while the United States squandered its own in the Middle East, South Asia, and North Africa.[63]

CHAPTER EIGHT

The Sleeper Awakes

China's Rise as a World Historical Moment

In a probably apocryphal quote attributed to Napoleon Bonaparte during a meeting with Lord Amherst, British ambassador extraordinary to China, the former emperor is said to have remarked in 1817 on the British eagerness to engage China in the growing European-centered system of world trade, "China is a sleeping giant. Let her sleep. For when she wakes, she will shake the world." Whether Napoleon truly uttered these words or not, the observation that China, if ever fully accustomed to modern Western methods of organization and production, would come to supplant the West and dominate the world had become a widespread concern among Western, and particularly American, thinkers toward the end of the nineteenth century.

Adam Smith argued in *The Wealth of Nations* that by 1776 China had attained the highest level of prosperity and civilization that its institutional structure would allow. China's reticence to engage in international trade or embrace the scientific and commercial products of the enlightenment, and the industrial revolution soon to come, sealed China's fate as a secondary power in the modern world.[1] China's contemporary embrace of capitalist production and pursuit of technological advancement have turned this positionality on its head and amplified Western fears of being supplanted. Andre Gunther Frank argues that, as a result, we must "reorient" our understanding of the dynamic between East and West; we must accept that the "great divergence," when Western countries came to vastly outstrip the rest of the world in aggregate and relative economic production, prosperity, and power, was in fact a historical blip; and we must prepare for an Asia-centric world order.[2] The "Asia threat" to American power and interests that was envisaged by Charles Henry Pearson, Theodore Roosevelt, Alfred Thayer Mahan, and Brooks

Adams over a century ago is now reaching fruition as China adopts the tools of state capitalism to enrich itself and become the central pivot of the global economy—an event that holds serious questions for American military and ideological supremacy in the years to come.

As the United States hemorrhaged blood, treasure, and prestige in the Global War on Terror, China was persistently and industriously advancing toward the reassumption of its historical position as the center of the world economy. The Chinese economy had sustained a relatively high rate of growth under Maoist centralization and industrialization, while maintaining very low levels of foreign debt, albeit with massive social and human costs.[3] But by the mid-1970s, state-led autarkic industrial expansion had reached its limits. From 1979 Deng Xiaoping's program of modernization and reform spurred China's transition from the highly centralized industrial, command economy of Chairman Mao to a mixed economy that allowed for private enterprise and integration with foreign commerce. Early market reform was character-ized by the decentralization of the management of state-owned enterprises, handing over control to regional and local authorities and allowing for mar-ket mechanisms to dictate production and exchange, the decollectivization and restoration of an agrarian peasant economy, the encouragement of citi-zens to start their own businesses, and the establishment of special economic zones in various coastal regions and cities to encourage foreign investment and international trade. These reforms began the transformation of China from a largely self-contained national economy into the central hub of much of the world's system of commodity production and exchange.

Modern China's entry into the American-led global economic system has been of world historical significance in terms of its impact on the Chinese people and society, its effect on the global distribution of power, and ulti-mately the challenge it presents to American empire itself. Since 1979 Chi-na's economy has grown on average around 10% per year. This is, according to the World Bank, the fastest sustained expansion by a major economy in world history.[4] This economic expansion has seen the approximate doubling in size of the Chinese economy every eight years and lifted around 800 mil-lion people out of poverty. Over 40 years China has transitioned from a mar-ginal economic outsider to the world's largest economy (by purchasing power parity), trader, manufacturer, and holder of foreign exchange reserves.[5] China is the largest export destination for 33 countries and the largest source of imports for 65.[6] It is the biggest trading partner of the United States and the largest single holder of US treasury bonds. It is also the largest trading partner of most countries in East Asia, including all the major economies and staunchest American allies.

The relative scale and pace of China's rise is difficult to articulate in brief, but the US National Intelligence Council attempts the task by comparing it with the rise of preceding global empires. During its period of ascension to global leadership, 1830 to 1870, the British economy was increasing its share of global GDP by slightly less than 1% per decade. For the United States between 1900 and 1950, the rate was slightly above 2% per decade. For China, between 2000 and 2020, the rate per decade has been over 5%.[7] For the first time since the "great divergence" of the nineteenth century, when the newly industrialized West superseded China as the most economically productive region of the world and began the transformation of the millennia old civilization-state into a dismembered semi-colony, China is returning to its position as the pivot of the global economy.[8]

During the early decades of China's rapid economic growth and development, it did not pose a structural threat to the American-led global economic order. China's growth was highly dependent upon foreign capital investment to fund its industrial expansion, as well as Western markets to consume its manufactures. This investment capital was initially sourced from the Chinese diaspora in East Asia, with 75% of all foreign investment in China in 1990 coming from Hong Kong and Taiwan, but the long-desired growth potential of the China market soon attracted Japanese and Western investors too.[9] In 2004, at the height of China's economic boom, almost 60% of Chinese exports were manufactured in foreign-funded enterprises, a much higher figure than in the export-oriented "tiger economies" in South Korea, Taiwan, and Thailand at similar points in their boom cycle.[10] American banks, multinational corporations, and consumers all benefited in various ways from China's rise. Chinese growth only began to reshape in a way that would come to compete with, rather than simply complement, American global capitalism from the late 1990s.

In 1999 the Chinese government instituted the "Going Out Policy," which sought to increase Chinese foreign investment, largely to diversify its now massive accumulation of foreign exchange reserves into more balanced and productive investments. Foreign investment has also been used, much the same as it has been by the United States throughout its history, to secure supplies of critical energy resources and minerals and to boost the technological capacity of Chinese enterprises; this allows them to develop high-tech industries and to compete in higher value-added markets, and it provides a secure path out of the middle-income trap that has placed limits to growth on several East Asian export-oriented economies in the past. As of 2019 China had accumulated $1.34 trillion of assets through FDI, as well as credits for loans of around $1.5 trillion, while still holding slightly over $3 trillion in foreign exchange reserves.[11] China's outgoing FDI exceeded foreign investments into China for the first time in modern history in 2015, when it reached $196 billion. China is now the world's largest creditor, eclipsing the World Bank and the IMF, as well as all creditor governments of the Organisation for Economic Co-operation and Development combined.[12]

This process of Chinese economic growth, industrial restructuring, and capital accumulation has now reconfigured the economic structure of the East Asian region as a whole. Before China's economic rise, the regional economy operated under what was termed the "flying geese" model. Under this system the "lead goose," in this case Japan, having successfully passed through its own period of industrialization, technological development, and capital accumulation, would come to focus on more capital and technologically intensive areas of production. The lead goose would use the follower geese, South Korea, Taiwan, and Southeast Asia, for lower-end production, thus spurring on their own economic growth and development in turn.[13] This Japan-centric regional economic system, which the United States did so much to entrench for reasons of strategic imperial management, has now been superseded by a Sinocentric one.

Today China is by far the largest exporter of finished consumer products to Western markets, while other Asian economies provide China with components and machinery necessary for the manufacturing process. This process is undergirded through the supply of raw materials from Australia, Africa, and Latin America, and energy resources from Russia, Central Asia, and the Middle East. The Sinocentric production network was once financed by foreign investment, but today China is a net exporter of capital, much of which is destined for the development of infrastructure to support the network, which has become formalized under the framework of the Belt and Road Initiative (BRI).

The Social Impact

China's meteoric economic growth has caused myriad domestic social issues. Increasing wealth inequality, corruption and state malpractice, ill-defined property rights and a deficit in the rule of law, surging health care and education costs, and the destruction and pollution of the natural environment have all contributed in varying degrees to social unrest.[14] Taken together, these issues present a serious challenge to the enduring stability of the leadership of the Communist Party of China; this challenge is thus perceived as a highest-order priority of the Chinese state. Social stability and the people's compact with the state under Maoism was not purely ideological. It included free health care, free education, guaranteed stable employment (known colloquially in China as the "iron rice bowl"), and the provision of a basic social safety net. The dissolution of parts of these state services was offset under market reforms by rising income, professional mobility, and increased access to consumer goods. The ideology and the material compact of Maoism have now been replaced by a state-structured market, and continued economic growth, a sense of national pride and renewal, and the opportunity for improved living standards have become the foundations of a stable relationship between the Chinese state and citizenry.

Many Western politicians, scholars, and commentators have predicted that the opening of China to market forces and the growth of the middle class would lead to democratic reform.[15] It was this logic that permitted successive post–Cold War US presidential administrations to so actively work to integrate China into the global economy; the faster China got rich, the sooner it would democratize. Others have argued that the internal contradictions, economic mismanagement, and corruption of the Communist Party of China itself would inevitably result in the collapse of the Chinese state, from the ashes of which a new liberal democracy would be born.[16] Still others have foreseen China's one-party system being challenged as a result of falling into the middle-income trap and encountering serious difficulties in transitioning to a high-income economy, as its restrictive political system stifles the innovation necessary to develop an independent high-tech sector and state interference in finance leads to the failure of the banking system overburdened by bad loans.[17] Any or all of these predicted outcomes would greatly hamper the challenge that China's rise poses to American global leadership. All have proven thus far, however, to be wrong.

Sociological research in China has demonstrated that the burgeoning professional, entrepreneurial, and middle class is overwhelmingly opposed to political liberalization, out of fear that it would unleash social forces from below that would threaten their recently won privileges.[18] The one-party communist state that suppressed middle-class "capitalist roaders" under Mao has long been replaced by an authoritarian state capitalism that is run by "cadre-capitalists," families of political elites that control the gigantic state-owned enterprises of China and many of the private businesses. These elites rely upon the services and eager participation of a growing professional-managerial class of Chinese, whose interests are bound with those of the party-state. China's growing middle class, for now at least, is a stakeholder in the authoritarian system rather than an outside challenger. The anti-corruption initiatives of the Chinese government of recent years, although clearly politicized, have been widely popular and seemingly effective nonetheless.

China is now a market leader in many high-tech sectors that have been traditionally dominated by Western and Japanese companies, including computers, microprocessors, surveillance technology, and telecommunications, both in handheld devices and cellular network infrastructure.[19] The role of the government in shaping Chinese industrial development allows it to focus resources into strategic technological sectors, like microprocessor development and communications technology, in a way that the United States, particularly since the end of the Cold War, had been much less inclined to do until very recently. China has also been highly successful in leveraging access to its domestic market and labor pool to Western companies in exchange for advanced technologies and jointly conducted research and development programs.[20] China already holds almost triple the number of patents as the US does, with around half the world's total.[21] Developments in these areas do not augur systemic failure, the demise of the Chinese state, or the inevitable transition to an American-style liberal democracy.

Nevertheless, social and economic problems are serious and in some cases growing. There are around 150,000 protests, riots, and "mass incidents" in China each year.[22] Economic inequality in China is now at a level approaching the United States. The relative egalitarian communism and economic leveling of Maoist China has been replaced by the competitive, individualistic marketplace as the determiner of socioeconomic outcomes. The real income of the top 10% of Chinese grew at over three times the rate of that of the bottom 50% between 1978 and 2015.[23] Massive environmental destruction and the largest population movement in human history as China's once overwhelmingly rural peasantry moves to cities to work in industry and manufacturing are also contributing to creating conditions for social unrest.

To continue to provide economic prosperity and social stability in this environment is becoming more difficult. China's domestic market alone is incapable of driving perpetual economic growth, and an increasingly confrontational and assertive United States, conscious of the precarity of its position at the apex of global wealth and power, will no longer facilitate China's rise for the short-term commercial benefits it produces. The Chinese government has found similar solutions to those reached by American leaders during the late nineteenth century to secure ever-expanding domestic economic prosperity and social stability; it has looked abroad for secure foreign markets, resources, and investment opportunities, and is now in the early stages of reshaping the region, and quite likely ultimately the world, around these objectives.

The Belt and Road Initiative: A New Economic Order in the Making

The unprecedented speed and scale of China's economic growth has already propelled it into the position that the American economy occupied when it was assessed to have been "bursting at the seams" by Woodrow Wilson, and in need of an expanded array of export markets to ensure the livelihoods of its citizens and domestic social and political harmony.[24] Despite a concerted push by the Chinese government to vastly expand domestic consumption, the Chinese economy is facing the same economic dilemma that drove Western nations toward imperialism: underconsumption and overproduction. These domestic economic pressures arose in concert with an American push to expand and more thoroughly institutionalize its own economic and geostrategic linkages to Asia. China's response, under the notably assertive leadership of President Xi Jinping, was to announce its own formal project for the restructuring of the Eurasian economy, the Belt and Road Initiative, in October 2013.

The BRI was, in essence, the formalization of Chinese plans to secure access to foreign markets, raw materials, and China's own lines of supply, while cementing its role at the center of the Eurasian economic complex. The BRI is named after the ancient Silk Road that connected the economies of East Asia, the Middle East, North Africa, and Europe, and it symbolizes the return of China to its historic position at the center of the international economy. The initiative has been adopted as a signature policy of Xi Jinping's presidency, and its success is now closely tied to both his own personal credibility and the capacity of his government to achieve the "China Dream."[25] Under the new project, the traditional overland Silk Road through Central Asia, the Middle East, Russia, and on to Europe is complemented by a new Maritime Silk Road, a sea route with accompanying infrastructure linking China to South and Southeast Asia, East Africa, the Middle East, and Europe via the South China Sea, the Indian Ocean, and the Mediterranean. The initiative began with partnerships with 64 national economies and has since expanded to over 100 separate states involved through trade deals, infrastructure development, investment, or other agreements.[26]

The BRI represents a notable step away from the low-profile strategy initiated by Deng Xiaoping, which sought to ensure China's uninterrupted ascendance through a patient strategy of biding its time and avoiding being seen to take the lead on global initiatives, leaving American global empire unchallenged in a political sense. Under Xi Jinping's "socialism with Chinese characteristics for a new era," China is openly and actively seeking a position of economic, political, and military leadership within the international community. No longer content to wait patiently, Xi has exhorted the party and the Chinese people to "lose no time in progressing along the long march of the new era."[27] In language that would seamlessly fit with the statements of American political leaders during the boom years of the late nineteenth century, President Xi heralds a new epoch of renewed Chinese global leadership through national struggle: "The wheels of history roll on; the tides of the times are vast and mighty. History looks kindly on those with resolve, with drive and ambition, and with plenty of guts; it won't wait for the hesitant, the apathetic, or those shy of a challenge."[28]

The transcontinental infrastructure being developed under the BRI links with the interior infrastructural developments that have proceeded at an astonishing pace and massive scale within China for the past 20 years. One of the most notable features of the international infrastructure's framework is its use of overland rail connections and energy pipelines, which stands in stark contrast to the overwhelmingly maritime-oriented international resource and trade distribution network that was developed under the leadership of the United States. Between 2007 and 2014, China constructed 9,000 miles of new high-speed rail, eclipsing the combined total of the rest of the world. When this network is complete, it will connect every major Chinese city with 16,000 miles of high-speed rail track, with a total project cost of around $300 billion.[29]

This Chinese network is being integrated into a transcontinental grid of high-speed rail, energy pipelines, and logistics hubs, labeled "economic corridors," that will connect Eurasia to China's economy. The first economic corridor was launched in partnership with Germany and Russia as the New Eurasian Land Bridge in 2008. These rail connections cut the transport time of goods between Germany and China to almost half that of shipping. A direct Moscow to Beijing high-speed rail line, costing $230 billion, has also been announced, as has a China–Central Asia–West Asia route connecting China to Europe via Turkey and Iran. The east-west infrastructural links across Eurasia are interconnected with several north-south lines. In 2015 the agreement on the China-Pakistan Economic Corridor was signed, a $46 billion package that will connect the Chinese network to Pakistan with highways, high-speed rail, and pipelines. Another linkage that will connect the Chinese network to Southeast Asia, the China Indochina Peninsula Economic Corridor, is already under construction and is proposed to link with a prospective corridor connecting Bangladesh, China, India, and Myanmar via Kunming. The high-speed rail achieves the immediate instrumental goal of connecting markets through infrastructure and is also a pillar in China's ongoing project to upskill its manufacturing sector and become a market leader in key high-end industrial and engineering sectors of the future.

This vast high-speed rail network is accompanied by a complex of oil and gas pipelines that connect China with resource-rich central and west Asian states, like Kazakhstan, Turkmenistan, Uzbekistan, and Iran, as part of the China, Central Asia, West Asia Economic Corridor. The pipelines stretch thousands of miles and have the capacity to pump tens of billions of gallons and cubic meters of oil and gas to China. China has also developed the Sino-Myanmar pipeline, opened in 2013, which pumps Middle Eastern oil and Burmese natural gas for thousands of miles overland from the Bay of Bengal, bypassing the strategic bottleneck controlled by the US Navy at the Strait of Malacca. In the northeast, China is already connected to the vast network of Russian pipelines through Manchuria and Siberia for energy resources, capped with a $400 billion, 30-year deal with Gazprom, the largest gas supplier in the world, to deliver 38 billion cubic meters of natural gas annually. Historian Alfred McCoy describes the sum of all this construction as the creation of "an integrated inland energy infrastructure . . . extending across the whole of Eurasia, from the Atlantic Ocean to the South China Sea."[30]

Despite the clear geostrategic benefits that the Belt and Road Initiative holds for China itself, it is by no means a purely nationalist economic project. Like the American global economic order, it promises significant benefits for willing partners. The Chinese government states that the BRI was designed to uphold the system of global free trade and economic openness while embracing the transition to a multipolar world order.[31] The mission statement for the BRI is almost indistinguishable from the political arguments that have been made by the United States government over the past century for its own projects of liberal international economic integration:

It is aimed at promoting orderly and free flow of economic factors, highly efficient allocation of resources and deep integration of markets; encouraging the
countries along the Belt and Road to achieve economic policy coordination and
carry out broader and more in-depth regional cooperation of higher standards;
and jointly creating an open, inclusive and balanced regional economic cooperation architecture that benefits all. Jointly building the Belt and Road is in the
interests of the world community. Reflecting the common ideals and pursuit of
human societies, it is a positive endeavor to seek new models of international
cooperation and global governance, and will inject new positive energy into
world peace and development.[32]

It is in China's interest more so than that of any other nation to uphold
global free-trading principles. In 2019 China's international trade was worth
a total of $4.6 trillion, making it the world's largest trading nation, the world's
largest exporter, and the world's second largest importer of goods.[33] A major
objective of the BRI is to establish a network of free-trade areas along the
maritime and overland routes connecting Asia and Europe. These will tie in
with existing trade agreements that China is party to, including major multilateral agreements like the Regional Comprehensive Economic Partnership
(RCEP) and the Asia-Pacific Trade Agreement (APTA), as well as China's
numerous and growing bilateral free-trade agreements with countries like
South Korea, Australia, and Pakistan. The weight China holds as the world's
largest trading nation, as well as the size (both current and projected) of its
domestic consumer market, is a great inducement for other states to join the
BRI, especially as Chinese trade is becoming increasingly concentrated with
other BRI participants. The total portion of Chinese exports destined for
BRI-participating economies expanded from 19% in 2000 to 34% in 2017.[34]
Over the same period, exports destined for OECD countries fell from 61%
to 49%.[35]

The BRI will also play a major role in driving the investment in and demand for high-technology manufacturing, research, and innovation that is
crucial in further advancing the foundational Chinese goal of ensuring continued prosperity and economic stability by moving up the manufacturing
value chain. In 2015 the Chinese government announced the Made in China
2025 plan to upgrade and modernize China's manufacturing in 10 key sectors
through extensive government assistance, in order to make China internationally competitive in the highest levels of technology and manufacturing.

The target sectors include next-generation communications and information technology, robotics, aerospace, agricultural chemicals and machinery, oceanographic engineering equipment and high-technology shipping, pharmaceuticals and medical technology, renewable energy infrastructure, energy-efficient automobiles, and high-speed rail. All these areas, with the exception of high-speed rail, fueled the economic boom of the United States after the initial wave of deindustrialization during the 1970s. China's drive toward technological advancement will interface with the BRI by moving lower-tech, and often higher-polluting, economic activities to less-advanced Belt and Road countries at the same time as developing higher-tech manufacturing in China itself. This strategy will provide guaranteed market access and demand within China for the developing countries, while building the Chinese capacity to compete at the highest levels of the global economy. This will replicate the same hierarchical pattern of international economic structures that the United States and other Western countries forged through their own imperial networks. As with the postwar economic order of the United States, this Sinocentric economic order is likely to be welcomed by significant segments of the populations of the countries it engages and an overwhelming number of the political and economic elites therein.

The BRI openly embraces the market principles and private enterprise that were enshrined in the American postwar economic order, albeit with a notably different governing dynamic between the party-state and commercial actors. In the founding policy document outlining the Chinese government's vision for the BRI, explicit emphasis is given to the "decisive role of the market in resource allocation and the primary role of enterprise."[36] Adherence to free-market principles exemplifies the real impact of reforms on the political economy of China and encourages the participation of capitalist democracies in the initiative by hosting development projects themselves and providing investment capital. Most of the financing for the BRI has thus far come from Chinese state-owned banks, but direct cooperative multilateral funding from member governments also plays an important role in the operation.

To foster state-level international cooperation around regional infrastructural development, and to coordinate the allocation and distribution of state capital investment, China established the Asian Infrastructure Investment Bank (AIIB) in 2015. The AIIB has a capital reserve of $100 billion ($30 billion of which was contributed by China). It counts 57 nations as members, including close American allies like Great Britain, Australia, Germany, and South Korea, despite reported pressure emanating from Washington not to join. The total goal for investment in Asian infrastructure is estimated at $1.7 trillion per year, with the AIIB making up only a fraction of that.[37] The AIIB operates in tandem with the World Bank, the Asian Development Bank, the European Bank of Reconstruction and Development, and several other large multilateral development banks to finance BRI projects. The vast majority of investment capital driving the BRI, however, comes from China's huge state-owned banks and state-linked financial institutions. The China Development Bank, the Exim Bank, the Industrial and Commercial Bank of China, and the China Investment Corporation lead a stable of several other massive Chinese financial institutions in lending tens and sometimes hundreds of billions of dollars per year to finance Belt and Road projects.[38]

When Maoist China was evaluated as the main threat to American interests in Asia, in part due to its ideological drive for world revolution, it had very little capacity to challenge American global power. Now that China has reshaped its economy, it no longer poses an ideological threat to the survival of capitalism but is a serious challenge to America's position of leadership at the heart of it, whether this be in the form of replacing the United States as the indispensable center of the world economic system or by carving out its own international zone of privilege. By reshaping Eurasian transport, energy, trade, and investment patterns around a Chinese nexus, the BRI directly challenges the American-led postwar economic order. Paired with the project to transform China into a global leader in high-tech research and industrial sectors, and the continued development and expansion of Chinese military capabilities, the BRI makes China the most formidable rival for international power that the United States has faced since the creation of American global empire, with a far larger and more globally interconnected economy than the Soviet Union ever possessed and a materially weaker alliance structure to balance against it.

In his analysis of the foundations of America's ascendant economic supremacy at the turn of the twentieth century, Brooks Adams identified the seat of global empire as always being located at the point of exchange where the products and markets of the East have met the products and markets of the West.[39] China's Belt and Road Initiative will, if successful, move the major point of exchange from the maritime interoceanic realm that has been dominated by the United States to a Sinocentric continental system. The core regions of the initiative, Asia, Europe, and Africa, are the three constituent parts of the "World Island" in classical geopolitical thought. Mackinder's view was that who controlled the heartland controlled the World Island and thus the world, while Spykman believed that who controlled the rimland controlled the World Island and thus the world. While not yet approaching military control of either of these geopolitical pivot regions through the BRI—and perhaps not ever conceivably—China has already embarked on a project that may ultimately render it indispensable to the economic well-being of both.

Writing in the years immediately following the issuance of the Open Door Notes, J. A. Hobson predicted that China's political economy would develop in one of two ways. One possibility was that the Western powers, unified by mutual recognition of the Open Door policy and access to the Chinese labor market of such stupendous value "that it might well absorb in its development all the spare capital and business energy the advanced European countries and the United States can supply for generations," would transform into a society of dividend drawers, whose working classes were bought off with the mass importation of cheap Chinese consumer goods.[40] Under this scenario, Hobson foresaw a Western world that

> might then assume the appearance and character already exhibited by tracts of country in the South of England, in the Riviera, and in the tourist-ridden or residential parts of Italy and Switzerland, little clusters of wealthy aristocrats drawing dividends and pensions from the Far East, with a somewhat larger group of professional retainers and tradesmen and a large body of personal servants and workers in the transport trade and in the final stages of production of the more perishable goods: all the main arterial industries would have disappeared, the staple foods and manufactures flowing in as tribute from Asia and Africa.[41]

The other scenario, which Hobson believed would occur if the West were not able to assert effective political and military control over China, would see China rise through the process of Western-funded industrial development and begin to undersell Western producers in their own markets. By doing this, and refusing their Western imports in exchange, instead drawing on Western capital, China would begin "reversing the earlier process of investment until she gradually obtained financial control over her quondam patrons and civilizers."[42] Having outcompeted the West in their own markets, China would then "secure for herself what further developing work remains to be done in other undeveloped parts of the earth."[43] With China now the world's largest manufacturer, trader, holder of US dollar reserves and American debt, and architect of a new regional economic order centered around its own infrastructure, trade, and financial system, it appears that the latter of Hobson's scenarios is coming to pass. The United States has, since the Obama presidency, been searching for the most effective way to shore up its imperial leadership in the face of China's rise.

Conflicting Grand Strategies in the Pacific

The timing of the establishment of the Belt and Road Initiative and the rapidity and commitment with which it has been undertaken were in large part a response to the 2011 "Pivot to Asia," which sought to re-center the US grand strategy in the Asia-Pacific region after a decade of failure in the Middle East. Barack Obama had campaigned on a return to multilateralism and mutual respect as a key component of his foreign policy vision, in stark contrast to the unilateral neoconservatism and imperial hubris of the Bush years. While there was a strong sense that American global influence and prestige had waned considerably under Bush, this ebbing was perceived as being the result of the neoconservative agenda and policies rather than the shifting structural disposition of world power, and thus it was reversible. The structural power shift was pressing, however, and the Obama administration was committed to addressing it.

Several major American allies in Asia, particularly Japan, Taiwan, and the Philippines, had become skittish during the Bush administration over America's overwhelming focus on the Middle East as China's rapid growth threatened the strategic balance in Asia. China would surpass Japan as the region's largest economy in 2010, having been only half Japan's size five years earlier. China's military budget increased more than threefold between 2000 and 2008.[44] In November 2009, during his first trip to Asia as president, Obama sought to reassure American allies in the region by declaring his commitment "to renew American leadership and pursue a new era of engagement with the world based on mutual interests and mutual respect."[45] Obama described himself as "America's first Pacific president," and the defining foreign-policy project of his administration, the "pivot," was a grand strategic commitment to ensure the continuation of American military, economic, and diplomatic hegemony in the region in the face of China's rise.

The impression that the Bush years had seen a slide in American global power and prestige was not limited to the Obama administration or the Democratic Party. The largest and most influential organizations in American foreign-policy circles were grappling with the same questions of how to re-establish and relegitimize America's position of global leadership. The Council on Foreign Relations, the Brookings Institution, the Carnegie Endowment for International Peace, the Ford Foundation, the Center for a New American Security, and other important think tanks and philanthropic organizations were attempting to systematically articulate a new American strategic policy that could manage both the aftermath of the Global War on Terror and the much more serious structural challenges of China's rise.[46] A major report on creating a "smarter and more secure" strategic policy for the twenty-first century, produced by the Center for Strategic and International Studies and chaired by Josef Nye Jr. and Richard Armitage, whose combined experience at the highest levels of foreign- and national-security policymaking spanned all executive administrations from Reagan to Bush Jr., warned that "with Washington preoccupied in the Middle East, China has deftly stepped into the vacuum left by the United States, primarily to pursue its own economic interests, but possibly also to pursue its long-term strategic goals of becoming a global power rather than simply a regional one."[47]

In November 2011 the Pivot to Asia was unveiled by President Obama in a speech before the Australian Parliament, while on an extended tour of Asia. The Pivot would operate along six key lines of action: reinforcing bilateral security alliances; expanding American military presence in the region; working closer with emerging powers, including China; more closely fostering and engaging with regional multilateral organizations; expanding trade and investment; and advancing democracy and human rights.[48]

In the speech, Obama contrasted the preceding years of war in Afghanistan and Iraq with a new future-oriented focus on cementing America's leadership position in the Asia-Pacific. Recognizing Asia's resurgence as the center of the global economy and appreciating the strategic implications that this brought, Obama announced that he had "made a deliberate and strategic decision—as a Pacific nation, the United States will play a larger and long-term role in shaping this region and its future, by upholding core principles and in close partnership with our allies and friends."[49] Both the economic and strategic interests at play here revolved around how China's growth challenged the existing balance of power, and the economic and strategic architecture that the United States had crafted and championed since the end of the Second World War. Obama emphasized America's "profound interest in the rise of a peaceful and prosperous China."[50] But to complete its rise peacefully, China would have to work within the existent American economic and strategic architecture.

With strong parallels to Clinton and Nye's approach to China, Obama sought to use America's clear advantages in military, economic, and diplomatic power to shape China's ascendance, and to ensure that it would play by the rules of American empire and not seek to overturn the status quo. This approach, again, was mainly centered around preserving and expanding the Open Door for trade and investment in the region, operating within an American-led institutional and normative framework, while ensuring that China would not achieve the military means to overturn this system through aggression. But the approach was also couched in the language of human rights and democracy.

Obama pointedly stated that "prosperity without freedom is just another form of poverty."[51] The message was clear: despite American willingness to engage with China and further their already strong economic ties, the one-party system remained on notice. The actual program of the Pivot to Asia was a recognition that, unlike in the 1990s, the United States could no longer hold this position on its own, or with merely symbolic cooperation from traditional allies. With Chinese strength now well advanced, this would require a concerted commitment from other regional powers within a formal institutional framework of military and economic cooperation.

The month before Obama's announcement of the pivot, Secretary of State Hillary Clinton published an article in the magazine *Foreign Policy* arguing that, after 10 years of war in the Middle East, the United States now stood at a "pivot point" from whence it was necessary to ensure that its attention was firmly rooted in the Asia-Pacific, the key region of twenty-first-century global politics, economics, and strategy.[52] Clinton explicitly drew a parallel between the American economic and security architecture created after the Second World War and the plans for the Pivot to Asia. Economic recovery at home after the global financial crisis was premised on access to Asian markets for trade and investment, as they were predicted to drive a large share of the world's future economic growth.[53] The Pivot was to be a win-win because "the region is eager for our leadership and our business—perhaps more so than at any time in modern history."[54]

Asia has long been the most economically important region of the world for the United States outside of the Western Hemisphere. It surpassed Europe as the major trading partner during the 1970s, and today accounts for more than twice the annual trade quantity.[55] With China having emerged in recent decades as the new center of economic arrangements in Asia, the US government prioritized planning for the institution of a new and durable system of legal and normative arrangements that would ensure the enduring role of the United States in Asian economic life. On October 7, 2015, it was announced that the trade ministers of Australia, Brunei Darussalam, Canada, Chile, Japan, Malaysia, Mexico, New Zealand, Peru, Singapore, the United States, and Vietnam had successfully concluded the Trans-Pacific Partnership (TPP).[56] The TPP was the most significant economic agreement to be negotiated since NAFTA, with implications that stretched beyond American trade and tariff reduction to the standardization of rules and laws governing the provision of services, investment, digital commerce, competition, and environmental standards. By creating a common framework for economic interaction among these countries, which roughly amounted to 40% of global GDP combined, the United States would ensure that it remained at the nexus of global trade and investment within Asia, as the region continued its transformation into the dynamic center of the world economy.

The TPP was not designed as an ambitious plan to somehow exclude China from regional commerce. Indeed, Chinese leaders openly flirted with the idea of eventually signing on to the agreement.[57] Rather, it was an attempt by the United States to maintain its dominance over the governing rules of international commerce at a time when China and its Belt and Road Initiative were threatening this position. The emphasis on regulating and limiting the role of state-owned enterprises (SOEs) in commerce was of particular significance in this sense, as SOEs dominate almost every sector of the Chinese economy and often impede the ability of foreign private enterprise to compete for market share. Speaking on domestic opposition to the TPP, President Obama warned that "if we don't write the rules, China will write the rules out in that region."[58]

The TPP would, in accord with the other branches of the Pivot, reassert an American-led structure of regional economic integration imbued with the norms and laws of American global capitalism. The combined economic weight of the member states and the incentive to expand trade amongst them would, it was hoped, eventually shape China's economic rise along these lines. At the same time, the agreement would offer growing regional economies, like Vietnam and Malaysia, and perhaps Indonesia, Thailand, and the Philippines, an alternative to China-led growth.

In what is likely to prove a historically significant reversal of bipartisan support for the free-trading economic foundations of American empire, however, newly elected President Trump, on his first full day in office, formally withdrew the United States from the deal. Citing the damage economic globalization had caused to American workers and industry, Trump promised a new era of "America first" foreign and economic policy.[59] It was a sharp, populist, and nationalist rebuke to Obama's commitment to the multilateral and liberal model of American empire. It alienated America's closest allies in the region and left the military branch of the Pivot as by far the most prominent and stable component of the American drive for continued hegemony in Asia.

Oppositional Force Structures

The Obama administration had been eager to impress that the Pivot was not a primarily military solution to China's rise and sought constantly to highlight its diplomatic, economic, human-rights advocacy, and multilateral consensus-building facets. Kurt M. Campbell, a principal architect of the Pivot and Obama's assistant secretary of state for Pacific and East Asian affairs, dismissed the military component of the Pivot as its least important, describing perceptions of the Pivot as a primarily military venture as being the result of media hype over military affairs that are "easier-to-report-on" than complex diplomatic and economic arrangements.[60] With negotiations for the Trans-Pacific Partnership (TPP) proceeding apace during Obama's second term, there was some credence to be given to claims that the economic program eclipsed the military in terms of scale and importance. With the eventual failure of the TPP, however, and very little to show in terms of diplomatic or human-rights successes or leadership in the region, the military pivot now stands as the single major feature of America's plan for sustained regional preeminence. The United States is accelerating toward a position wherein military might acts as the primary foundation of its empire, while its economic and diplomatic pillars crumble. This is a certain sign of the intensifying risk of war.

China's rise is an open challenge to the core principle of American regional grand strategy that has stood since the Second World War: the prevention of the emergence of any potential peer-competitor or imperial rival. Calculations for balancing American cooperation with the Japanese, the Soviets, and the Chinese to limit the dominance of any one regional power were a consistent feature of American Cold War strategic planning.[61] China has now solidified as the singular strategic threat to American power in the region, and American coalition building now revolves around its containment. The renewed focus on strengthening traditional alliance, engaging other regional powers, and transitioning the Hub and Spokes model of bilateral security relationships around the American central axis toward a more deeply networked and multilateral security system was a major component of the Pivot, combining both military and diplomatic initiatives, and designed to cement a regional strategic balance that favored the United States.

The multilateralism of the Pivot was not a spontaneous eruption of regional military cooperation, although there was certainly a large reservoir of local concern over the implications of China's growth. Rather, the United States actively drove home the message that the time for sitting on the fence between the economic benefits derived from trade and investment with China and the security and stability provided by American military hegemony was at an end. Indeed, the United States government operated on the principle that the former would be impossible without the latter. Joseph Nye described the American security architecture in Asia as the oxygen that allows the region to breathe and enjoy continued economic growth and prosperity.[62] China's growth and its implicit challenge to American hegemony were increasingly seen as an imminent threat to this system. Campbell pressed this issue home in advocating for the Pivot, stating that Asian countries "must choose whether they will be stakeholders in the current system and join fully in common efforts to solve transnational problems or instead become spoilers or free riders concerned with their own narrow self-interests."[63]

The proliferation of landmark defense cooperation agreements and statements with the most important countries in the Asia-Pacific, including Japan, South Korea, India, Indonesia, Australia, Vietnam, and the Philippines, demonstrated that the United States still maintained the willing support of much of the region for its leadership.[64] Some of the military deployments that occurred under the Pivot were the setting up of a full Marine Air Ground Task Force to be permanently rotated through Darwin in Australia, in close proximity to the strategic choke point at the Malacca Strait; the construction of American facilities at five separate military bases in the Philippines; the construction of a naval facility on Jeju Island in South Korea; and the negotiation of military access to host-country bases in Australia, Singapore, and the Philippines.

With knowledge that each of these coalition partners was deeply economically entwined with China, each with its own interest in avoiding serious conflict with their much larger and more powerful neighbor, and each with the potential to fickly swing depending on domestic political concerns (with the Philippines under Duterte as a prominent case of such a swing having already occurred), a singular focus remained on the bilateral military balance between the United States and China individually. The dynamic of these oppositional military forces has revolved around the reinforcement of the American position along the island chains that have anchored its geostrategic dominance of the region since the Second World War and China's efforts to compromise it.

The aggregate military resources contained within the American regional security architecture is impressive by any standards. Well over 200 American military bases are spread across US Pacific possessions and the territories of American treaty allies, from Japan, Taiwan, the Philippines, and Australia to Guam, the Marianas, and Hawaii, with many other components in between.[65] These bases fall under the newly named US Indo-Pacific Command, which has around 400,000 military and civilian personnel; over 200 naval ships and submarines, some nuclear powered and armed with nuclear weapons; over 2,000 aircraft, missile batteries, land-, sea-, and space-based communications and surveillance arrays; Marine strike forces; and various other military assets deployed in the region and in the air and orbit above it.[66] The pearls of American Pacific forces are the five Carrier Strike Groups, each with approximately 7,500 military personnel, around 70 combat aircraft, and an accompaniment of cruisers, destroyers, frigates, and submarines for each main aircraft carrier. These military assets, often operating in conjunction with the substantial military forces of American regional allies, combine to give the United States what Barry Posen has termed "command of the commons" in the Pacific: clear dominance of the sea, air, and space in and over the ocean.[67]

Both Alfred Thayer Mahan and Sir Julian S. Corbett, the two most eminent strategic thinkers on sea power during the late nineteenth and early twentieth centuries, broadly understood "command of the sea" as the ability of a state to use the sea as it wishes while denying that use to an adversary.[68] This allowed the hegemonic sea power, at the time Great Britain, to use the world's oceans as a geopolitical amplifier of its own power and suppressant of the capabilities of its rivals. Command of the commons allows today's military hegemon, the United States, to render China incapable of conducting offensive military operations eastward across the ocean, against either the United States or its Pacific allies; it also holds the threat of blockade and trade disruption should China pursue any course of action that the United States deems an immediate and direct threat to its security. Liu Huaqing, widely viewed as the father of the modern Chinese Navy, developed the "zonal defense" model, designed to incrementally expand Chinese naval power in response to the strategic environment presented by US dominance of the Pacific.[69] The expansion of Chinese naval power and military assets capable of impacting maritime theaters of war had, by the second decade of the twenty-first century, reached such a point as to call in to question the US capacity to exert unfettered control of the Pacific.

Chinese strategists are profoundly conscious of American strategic containment and their recent history of maritime vulnerability. In *Great Wall at Sea*, professor of maritime strategy Bernard Cole quotes a PLA strategist summarizing the Chinese view of its near oceans and the threat presented by American sea command: "In the last 109 years, imperialists have repeatedly invaded China from the sea . . . 470 times, . . . 84 of these being serious invasions. The ocean has become an avenue for the aggressors to bring in their troops and haul away our wealth. . . . The ocean is not only the basic space for human survival, but also an important theatre for international political struggle. . . . The better people can control the sea, the greater they have the sea territorial rights [that have] become inseparable from a country's sovereignty."[70]

An understanding of the historical and contemporary vulnerability China faces in its maritime environment has shaped its response; an imperative to break through the first island chain by greatly expanding and modernizing its navy and air force, developing and deploying new and effective "area-denial" missile technology, militarizing the islands and reefs of the South China Sea and claiming exclusive access to their surrounding maritime environment within the nine-dash line, and ultimately pushing the American forces farther east and away from China's coastal territory and its maritime trade and energy supply corridors. It is this strategic environment that has shaped China's pursuit of anti-access/area denial (A2AD) military arsenals and the subsequent US adoption of the AirSea Battle, and later the Joint Concept for Access and Maneuver in the Global Commons (JAM-GC) doctrines, both being oppositional military postures competing under the broader strategic military Pivot to Asia.

The anti-access/area denial capabilities China has recently developed focus on deterring the United States or another rival from deploying their military assets within a defined space of strategic importance to China. In the early stages of development this space was concentrated on the Taiwan Strait but has since expanded to large areas of the East and South China Seas. China has prioritized the development of an assortment of surface-launched ballistic missiles for this task, the most notorious of which is the DF-21D anti-ship ballistic missile, or "carrier-killer," which was developed as a deterrent to the deployment of the US carrier fleet within its 1,500 kilometer range. China also fields the largest force of mid-range ballistic and cruise missiles in the world, owing to the United States having been until recently party to the Intermediate-Range Nuclear Forces Treaty with Russia, which prohibited their use. China launched its first military imaging satellites in 2000, giving its missile force the capacity to detect targets thousands of kilometers beyond ground-based radar horizon.

While China's military capabilities have expanded greatly in general, there has also been an explicit maritime focus. At the 18th Party Congress in 2012, President Hu Jintao declared that China would seek to "enhance our capacity for exploiting marine resources, develop the marine economy, protect the marine ecological environment, resolutely safeguard China's maritime rights and interests, and build China into a maritime power."[71] Within five years of this statement, the PLA Navy had overtaken the US Navy as the largest in the world, producing more modern military vessels between 2014 and 2018 than were currently serving in the entire UK Royal Navy.[72]

The US Navy still enjoys a significant lead in larger, more sophisticated vessels, but a 2015 RAND study found that China held the advantage over the United States in its capacity to destroy surface vessels and disable air bases in certain regional conflicts.[73] The 2020 deployment of the Renhai-class cruiser, with the most advanced array of A2AD capabilities in the region, further tilted the military balance in the South and East China Seas toward China.[74] The PLA Air Force is also modernizing and expanding at a rapid rate, almost doubling its fleet of modern fighters from 383 to 766 between 2010 and 2015, and now deploying a domestically produced fifth-generation fighter, the J-20, to combat the American F-35 joint strike fighter.[75] The RAND study found that, while the US continues to hold a large aggregate lead in global military capabilities, China was rapidly progressing toward the capacity to dominate its own periphery in the western Pacific, within range of its large fleet of smaller diesel-powered vessels.[76]

In 2011 the US Department of Defense compiled a special report on military and security developments in China, beginning from the assessment that China's rise was likely to stand out as a defining strategic feature of the early twenty-first century and that, in response, the United States must "continue adapting our forces, posture, and operational concepts to maintain a stable and secure East Asia environment."[77] To address this problem, the United States developed the JAM-GC doctrine, formerly known as AirSea Battle, which aims to "Disrupt, Destroy, and Defeat" enemy A2AD capabilities by integrating forces across air, sea, land, space, and cyberspace to threaten rapid air bombardment of land-based command and control centers, weapons platforms, and military formations.[78] This is essentially a plan to use overwhelming force across multiple spectrums of war fighting to destroy China's ability to deny access to its maritime approaches. The doctrine has been criticized by many observers as being inherently escalatory.[79] Even some of the biggest proponents of the AirSea Battle concept acknowledge the escalatory implications of its use of force, stating that the decision to conduct the sort of penetrating strikes outlined in the AirSea Battle concept would have to be taken at "the highest political levels" and that, for the plan to be effective, strikes against "very high-leverage targets would be essential."[80]

In describing the concept, the AirSea Battle Office stated that "at the low end of the conflict spectrum, the Concept enables decision makers to engage with partners to assure access, maintain freedom of action, conduct a show of force, or conduct limited strikes. At the high end of the conflict spectrum, the Concept preserves the ability to defeat aggression and maintain escalation advantage despite the challenges posed by advanced weapons systems."[81] When the low end of the conflict spectrum describes "assuring access," and this access can only be assured through the destruction of military assets and command and control stations in mainland China, even the low end implies dramatic conflict escalation to achieve its goals. This begs the question of how useful the concept is in fighting limited wars and necessarily evokes questions of its implications for nuclear war fighting, which cannot be dismissed when such high-value military assets within mainland China are being targeted for annihilation by US forces.

Since 2009 the United States' upgrades to its nuclear weapons arsenal across all three branches of the "nuclear triad"—land, air, and sea-launched—have increased the destructive power of American nuclear forces by up to three times.[82] During the same period, the United States has upgraded and expanded its satellite surveillance and targeting arrays and interceptor missile capabilities. With the Terminal High Altitude Area Defense (THAAD) and Aegis Ballistic Missile Defense System working in tandem with a constellation of Space Based Infrared System (SBIRS) satellites that have been progressively launched since 2011, the United States, for the moment, enjoys such an edge in nuclear-weapons deployment, detection, and interception capabilities that it could conceivably launch a nuclear attack on China and defend itself from China's second-strike capabilities.

This position undermines the logic of mutually assured destruction that has precluded the thought of a nuclear war since the 1960s, and it ensures a corresponding Chinese nuclear buildup. There are signs that this is already under way. In fact, a significant driver of China's maritime expansion is to break out of the shallow waters of the South China Sea, where the country's nuclear submarines are easily detectible, into the wide and deep waters of the Pacific to ensure that China will continue to have a stable deterrent against nuclear attack.[83] A massive increase in cyber-warfare research and capabilities, competition in the development of next-generation quantum sensing technology, and an ongoing race to militarize space, and potentially use it for kinetic and communications surveillance and targeting applications, has propelled the standoff to the forefront of twenty-first-century technological advancement.

China's advantage in pursuing anti-access/area denial weapons in the face of American command of the commons portends a possible inversion of the arms-race dynamic that saw the United States escalate Soviet spending to unsustainable levels toward the end of the Cold War. Today the United States, aggressively lobbied by the powerful arms manufacturers and pursuing full-spectrum dominance around the globe, spends trillions of dollars on ultra-expensive weapons systems that will quite possibly never be used in a war with China. Meanwhile China, free from lobbyists, builds asymmetric weapons systems, like carrier killer missiles, that cost a tiny fraction of the amount spent on the military assets that they are designed to counter.[84] America's capacity to maintain its massive levels of military spending, particularly as civil infrastructure and social services continue to crumble, is uncertain. Were dollar hegemony to end, and with it America's ability to easily service large budget deficits, the massively bloated military budget would become a huge political and economic issue.

A 2016 RAND study commissioned by the Department of Defense found that, due to China's development of A2AD military assets, the United States could no longer be confident in winning a war in the Western Pacific.[85] The researchers argued that the dynamic created by the enhanced technological capacity of both countries' militaries, now highly dependent on digitally networked sensory, guidance, and communications systems, meant that each one was incentivized to strike first before enemy forces could disable their own fragile systems.[86] The capabilities of each side to target and destroy each other's military resources would see their rapid initial depletion and result in a contest of industrial resource mobilization of the kind and scale not seen since the world wars of the twentieth century.

The study concluded that, with victory increasingly uncertain, the United

States must seriously begin to think about how to limit a war with China and its costs, rather than focus solely on how to win it.[87] The architects of the Pivot too are circumspect on the endurance of American hegemony in Asia. Campbell believes that Asia's power distribution will likely fall somewhere on the spectrum between full Chinese regional hegemony and an unstable balance of power, depending on the actions of the United States and its regional allies.[88] President Donald Trump's China policy would manifest as a refusal to accept this future and an attempt to reassert American primacy in the region while tearing up the economic and diplomatic foundations of American empire.

CHAPTER NINE

Trump, Biden, and Trouble Ahead

The election of Donald Trump to the office of president of the United States was a profound shock to the relatively stable bipartisan consensus on the management of American global empire since the end of the Second World War. Often interpreted by liberal media pundits as a historical aberration or the dying cries of a demographically diminishing white nationalism, Trump's election was, to a large extent, the consequence of misdirected resentment over the economic and political contradictions of the post–Cold War neoliberal consensus: growing inequality, the eruption of long-simmering social and racial tensions into open conflict, the cementing of a class of technocratic and managerial elites that appeared completely detached from the conditions of regular American people, and an attendant sense of alienation and cultural decay among those whose life prospects were declining amidst the wealth and splendor of late-stage American empire.

Frederick Jackson Turner identified the constant expansion of the frontier as the method by which the United States was able to achieve prosperity, democracy, and social stability during its first century. Over the course of roughly its second century of existence, the United States expanded internationally, first as a traditional imperial power in the Pacific and then as the crafter and leader of a global liberal political and economic order. The neoliberal consensus of the unipolar moment, which was to cement the achievements of centuries of continued expansion by setting the American political-economic model as the template for the world, is now compromised by both internal and external challenges. The contradictions of the highly financialized, globalized, and increasingly unequal contemporary American economy rest on the one hand, and a rising China, positioning itself as the new center of the global economy and threatening to challenge the United States at the highest levels of finance and technology, rest on the other.[1] Elected by a minority of Americans overall on a wave of anti-elitist, nationalist, and nativist sentiment, Trump promised to "Make America Great Again" through the destruction of the political status quo, or "draining the swamp," at home and through the defeat of its rival for global leadership, China, abroad.

Perhaps the most succinct distillation of the Trumpian "America first," approach to foreign policy came in a jointly penned opinion piece for the *Wall Street Journal*, written by Trump's national security adviser, H. R. McMaster, and chief economic adviser, Gary Cohn. Rejecting the foundational assumptions of liberal internationalism, they stated that "the world is not a 'global community' but an arena where nations, nongovernmental actors and businesses engage and compete for advantage. We bring to this forum unmatched military, political, economic, cultural and moral strength. Rather than deny this elemental nature of international affairs, we embrace it."[2]

This will to embrace and muster all elements of American power to pursue its direct interests in opposition to rivals was affirmed in Trump's National Security Strategy.[3] The underlying message, here and elsewhere from the Trump administration, was that the era of cooperative and coordinated American leadership of multilateral institutions and the idea that strategic rivals could be incorporated into these structures was over. In its place was a return to great power competition that characterized much of modern world history.[4]

The main fixture of this shift in the American approach to foreign affairs revolved around a direct confrontation with China. Where Obama and preceding administrations spoke of engagement and incrementally influencing the shape of China's rise through multilateral norm setting and economic cooperation, the Trump administration was far more blunt and agonistic. While this reappraisal of the balance of cooperation and competition was spearheaded by the Trump administration, it has now gained acceptance as foreign-policy orthodoxy, both between the major political parties and in the national-security and foreign-affairs establishment. Writing for the Council on Foreign Relations, former diplomat and senior national security official Robert D. Blackwill argued that the US-China relationship had now entered a new phase, much more focused on competition and less assured of the benefits of close economic ties.[5] Even Kurt Campbell, a key architect of the Pivot and President Joe Biden's serving "Asia tsar," now considers the Pivot to have been a failure. Campbell went as far as to laud Trump's first National Security

Strategy for its critical interrogation of past assumptions about the US-China relationship.[6]

Under Trump, the Pentagon openly defined China as a revisionist power, willing to accept strategic friction in pursuit of an expansive set of political, economic, and security interests, which "undermines the international system from within by exploiting its benefits while simultaneously eroding the values and principles of the rules-based order."[7] Trump's first National Security Strategy stated that China "challenge[s] American power, influence, and interests, attempting to erode American security and prosperity" while displacing it from the center of the regional security order.[8] China was accused of using its expanding power to repress its own people, influence its neighbors, and make the global economy less free and fair.[9]

John Ratcliffe, Trump's director of national intelligence, stated that "the People's Republic of China poses the greatest threat to America today, and the greatest threat to democracy and freedom world-wide since World War II."[10] Unwilling and ideologically opposed to addressing the internal problems generated by imperial political and economic structures and the grossly unequal distribution of wealth, the Trump administration focused on "unfair" Chinese economic competition as the root cause of American decline. With parallel disinterest in the myriad costs of maintaining a global military empire, the Trump administration envisioned the confrontation and containment of China, and the aggressive maintenance of the American technological and military edge, as the path toward national renewal and the continuance of the expansion of American prosperity and power.

Economic Decoupling and Strategic Resource Competition

The most immediately identifiable arena of conflict between the Trump administration and China came in the form of the trade war that began in July 2018. The United States implemented hundreds of billions of dollars of tariffs on Chinese goods, accusing it of unfair trade practices, which restricted American corporate access to the Chinese market, and infraction on intellectual property-rights agreements to which it is party, and, through this, "stealing American jobs." China responded to the tariffs in kind, while also agreeing in principle to increase purchases of American goods and to more rigorously uphold intellectual property rights. In 2018 the United States ran a $419 billion dollar trade deficit with China, which was reduced to $345 billion the following year.[11] The trade deficit was an important, but not deciding, factor in Trump's economic policy toward China. The trade war was rather the most visible and easily explicable component of a broader process of the decoupling of the US and Chinese economies, with a particular focus on the high-tech centers of future growth and innovation, which, bolstered by a massive increase in military spending, was slated by the Trump administration as the strategy through which the United States could continue enjoying its preeminent position in world affairs.

Trump's leading economic and strategic advisers warned that China would soon eclipse the United States as the world power par excellence if things continued on as they were. Measured by purchasing power parity (PPP), China already surpassed the United States as the world's largest economy in 2014.[12] The IMF projects that by 2024 the United States will have a GDP of $25.7 trillion while China's will be $40 trillion in PPP terms.[13] By 2050 the United States will account for around 12% of global GDP, down from almost 50% at the time of the creation of the US-led global economic order at end of the Second World War.[14]

Steve Bannon, Trump's former chief strategist and senior counselor, described the status-quo approach of American-China policy as "managed decline," wherein American political and economic "globalist" elites have tacitly accepted Chinese ascendance as inevitable and crafted policy around maximizing their profits under a Sinocentric economic world order to come. Giving a right-wing populist critique of neoliberal globalization and the financialization of the American economy, Bannon argued that the decoupling of the American economy from China and the reconstitution of industrial power in the United States would be the beginning of the end of managed decline.[15] Michael Pillsbury, Peter Navarro, and other prominent strategic advisers to Trump made similar arguments, placing particular emphasis on control over the high-tech research and industrial complex as the key to world power, owing to the economic and military edge it confers.[16]

Securing the American National Security Innovation Base and Defense Industrial Base has become a top priority in strategic-planning circles in the United States. In a near inversion of the liberal theory of economic integration leading to international peace, the new dominant approach to US-Chinese economic relations is that it is a threat to national security, largely because of the deleterious effects of technology transfer, open and illicit, on America's competitive edge. A Department of Defense strategic planning report describes the situation as such: "Although trade has benefited both China and its trade partners, Chinese use of espionage and theft for economic advantage, as well as diversion of acquired technology to the military, remains a significant source of economic and national security risk to all of China's trading partners."[17]

The massive prominence of digital technology in the US and Chinese economies and the much higher growth rate of the digital economy compared to the traditional economy in recent years mean that supremacy in the digital sphere will be the major determinant of relative economic power between the two countries over the coming period.[18] William Burns, director of the CIA under President Biden, has stated that technological competition will be the main arena for rivalry with China in the years ahead.[19] This raises the importance of cybersecurity to previously unknown heights. Incidences of cyberattacks and digital sabotage, including corporate and state espionage and attacks on civilian and military infrastructure, will likely increase and threaten to act as a prelude to open military conflict.

Under the Trump administration, the most comprehensive piece of policy addressing these emerging threats was the Clean Network program. This was established to exclude "untrusted" Chinese carriers from the US telecommunications network, remove Chinese applications from American mobile app stores, exclude Chinese businesses from accessing personal and proprietary information held in American cloud storage, and ensure the integrity of the physical infrastructure, like undersea cables, that underly digital networks.[20] The Clean Network program explicitly targets China alone and encourages other countries to do the same by incentivizing their own access to America's "clean" network of government and commercial digital communications. Over 30 other countries and many major telecommunications companies have already signed on to the program.[21] It is believed that locking China out of the digital economic and telecommunications networks that provide it with access to US-developed intellectual property and proprietary information will critically weaken China's capacity to compete in the high-tech economy, hamper its ability to transition to a fully modern military, and ultimately loosen the Communist Party of China's grip on power.[22]

A particularly significant action in the brewing techno-economic conflict was implemented by the Biden administration in October 2022, when it announced a set of sweeping export controls on advanced-computing and semiconductor manufacturing items to China.[23] Gregory C. Allen, director of the AI Governance Project at the Center for Strategic and International Studies, described it as the beginning of "a new U.S. policy of actively strangling large segments of the Chinese technology industry—strangling with an intent to kill."[24] The export ban followed closely on the heels of the signing of the CHIPS and Science Act, which authorized $52 billion dollars of government incentives to support the US semiconductor industry across research and development, to secure supply chains, and to ensure the "reshoring" of manufacturing.[25] Whether the ban will have the desired stifling effect on Chinese capabilities remains an open question. Some experts believe that by cutting off China's access to advanced chips today, the United States is giving up its long-term leverage over China's artificial-intelligence development programs and creating conditions for a vastly accelerated drive toward Chinese high-tech self-sufficiency.[26]

Such programs have solidified the dominant Chinese view of American strategic and political objectives toward China. While in the West, rising authoritarianism and international assertiveness under President Xi Jinping has been cast as the major driver of confrontation with China, Chinese political elites view the United States and its increasing economic hostility as being responsible for the ongoing degradation in relations. There is particularly widespread resentment toward what they perceive as the decades-long program of meddling in Chinese internal affairs with the goal of weakening the Communist Party of China and splitting China up into smaller disunited, less-threatening constituent parts, and the pilfering of the Chinese economy by Western finance and multinational corporations.[27] It is difficult to overstate the importance of the history of Western imperialism in China in cementing this skepticism of American foreign policy and the role of human-rights discourse as a branch of a larger American-led "rules-based international order." The targeted expulsion of China's leading tech companies like Huawei from Western markets is seen as an important component of this wider American policy of ramping up economic, political, and military pressure on China.

High-tech industrial sectors, particularly digital networked communications, aerospace engineering, arms manufacturing, pharmaceuticals, and green technology, will be the major areas of economic growth in the twenty-first century. It is in these fields that the competition for global market supremacy between the United States and China, and the position at the center of the global economy, will be decided. It is not an ideological challenge to the economic structures that underlie American empire that defines the dimension of the new competition between China and the United States, as it was with the Soviet Union during the Cold War, but the struggle for leadership at the new digital economic frontiers.

The United States continues to hold a significant, but narrowing, lead in research and development in these fields. Total research and development spending in the United States was $612 billion in 2019; in China it was $514 billion.[28] On the current funding trajectory, China will supersede the United States as the world's biggest investor in research and development within the next five to 10 years. The Clean Network program, trade sanctions, and continued pressure from US federal agencies on China to reform and enforce its intellectual property protections more stringently are all components of the larger effort to maintain American supremacy in these critical high-tech sectors.

In China too, strategic planning for sustaining an independent national technology base is being conducted at the highest levels. In 2018 Xi Jinping warned that "heavy dependence on imported core technology is like building our house on top of someone else's walls: No matter how big and how beautiful it is, it won't remain standing during a storm." Only by fostering its own research and industrial base in critical high-tech sectors, Xi argued, could China "truly seize the initiative in competition and development, and fundamentally safeguard our national economic security, national security, and security in other areas."[29]

Although it garnered far less attention than the trade war, the initiative of the Trump administration to renegotiate NAFTA to form what it hoped would be a credible industrial and manufacturing alternative to China was another extremely important development on the front of economic competition between the two superpowers. The new United States–Mexico–Canada Agreement (USMCA), which came into effect in July 2020, enforces, among other things, stronger protections for intellectual property rights and patents, market access for American capital, and enhanced cybersecurity protocols. Most significantly for the future world economy, it includes a clause that allows signatories to pull out of the USMCA if another country pursues a separate free-trade agreement with a "nonmarket country."[30]

Through this agreement, the United States is forcing Canada and Mexico to make a choice on their economic destiny between the United States and China. Trump White House economic adviser and National Economic Council Director Larry Kudlow said that the USMCA "sends a signal to China that we are acting as one."[31] A senior Trump administration official described the agreement as a "playbook" for the crafting of future trade deals, exemplifying a major mechanism by which the United States will seek to decouple its economic sphere from China's.[32] This is a relatively easy choice for the highly integrated economies of North America, but if the United States seeks to extend this compact beyond their continent to their allies in Asia, whose economies are now much more dependent on and integrated with China than the United States, it is likely to face stiff resistance.

The aim here is not to eliminate all economic links between China and the US but rather to create fluid connections between the economies of the United States and other states within its orbit, and barriers between this bloc and China's, which, while not affecting all trade, will certainly reduce transactions and cooperation at the level of high-tech industries and finance. There is, however, the distinct possibility that economic decoupling cannot be quarantined to just some discreet part of economic intercourse. It is unlikely that decoupling will work as a fine surgeon's tool for any great length of time. Rather, it could well be the beginning of a slope toward the development of rival autarkic economic spheres.

The threat that a system of competing economic blocs poses to international peace and stability has not gone unnoticed by world leaders outside of the United States. In a speech presenting his annual report ahead of the opening of the general assembly in 2019, UN Secretary General Antonio Guterres warned of "a new risk looming on the horizon." He described the endpoint of rising US-China tensions as entailing "the possibility of a great fracture: the world splitting in two, with the two largest economies on earth creating two separate and competing worlds, each with their own dominant currency, trade and financial rules, their own internet and artificial intelligence capacities, and their own zero sum geopolitical and military strategies."[33]

There is some room for historical analogy here. The rise of protectionism and the creation of separate trade and currency blocs during the interwar period is held to be a major factor in the lead-up to the Second World War. Indeed, American empire and the championing of the global Open Door have been justified from the beginning on the basis that they provided the conditions of international cooperation and institutional equity that would prevent a slide back toward zero-sum competition and war. It was this very stability and order that provided such fertile conditions for China's rise.

Liberal world empire is born with the seeds of hegemonic national decline, as its successes tend to strengthen other members relative to the leader.[34] The resilience of the postwar liberal global order has never been independent from American power. As the relative economic supremacy of the United States continues to erode, so too will the liberal order unravel and weaken, should no new hegemonic liberal power emerge, ultimately to be replaced by mercantilist arrangements.[35] The United States under Trump shifted toward a policy of using its deteriorating hegemony as a means of exploiting the international system for nationalist ends, rather than managing the deterioration in such a way as to incorporate a general international interest that would undergird the long-term survival of the system.[36]

President Trump's inaugural address highlighted this shift succinctly and bears quoting at length:

> For many decades, we've enriched foreign industry at the expense of American industry;
>
> Subsidized the armies of other countries while allowing for the very sad depletion of our military;
>
> ... And spent trillions of dollars overseas while America's infrastructure has fallen into disrepair and decay.
>
> We've made other countries rich while the wealth, strength, and confidence of our country has disappeared over the horizon.
>
> ... But that is the past. And now we are looking only to the future.
>
> We assembled here today are issuing a new decree to be heard in every city, in every foreign capital, and in every hall of power.
>
> From this day forward, a new vision will govern our land.
>
> From this moment on, it's going to be America First.[37]

Should this "America First" disaggregation of the global economy continue, it is likely to result in aggressive competition for markets and the strategic resources necessary to fuel a modern industry in much the same way as occurred during the 1930s. It was the singular aim of American postwar empire building that the world not be allowed to revert to the system of rival autarkic zones that characterized the interwar years and produced the crisis of the Second World War.[38] The concerted movement to "economically decouple" from China is the abandonment of the centerpiece of American imperial policy for the better part of the last century, a decision taken in response to America's inability to compete with China as the pivot of the global economy moves to the East. Even if conducted in a more diplomatic and palatable manner in the Biden era and beyond, economic decoupling, competition for resources, and the turn away from the global Open Door will further expand the points of conflict between the United States and China. The proliferation of such frictions is already well under way.

Strategic Resource Competition and Future Conflict

Competition over strategic resources is perhaps an even greater risk for great power conflict under global mercantilist arrangements than competition over trade and investment markets. The necessity of strategic minerals for industrial and military production and their scarcity and irregular geographical distribution ensure the rise of intense strategic competition for securing supply should an open international system of distribution fail. The first major scare over strategic minerals since the end of the Cold War occurred in 2010, when a border dispute between China and Japan produced fears that China would manipulate the supply of rare earth elements, in which it enjoyed a near market monopoly, to further its strategic ambitions. Although the Chinese blockade of rare earth exports never materialized, the effects of the fear are instructive as to what is likely to happen in this and other areas of critical raw material supply in the future.

Rare earths are a group of 17 elements, used most frequently for their chemical, electronic, or magnetic properties, that are critically important to the telecommunications sector, the green technology sector, and in the production of military hardware.[39] A large deposit of rare earths at Mountain Pass in California was the primary source of global supplies between the 1960s, when mining there began, and the mid-1990s, when China overtook the United States as the world's largest producer. When mining rare earths at Mountain Pass ceased in 2002, China truly came to dominate the rare earth industry. Between 2003 and 2012, Chinese production averaged over 90% of global output of rare earths, verging on 100% in some years.[40] Today, with the industry reemerging in the United States, Australia, and Russia, China accounts for around 65% of global production.[41]

The events following the September 2010 collisions between a Chinese fishing vessel and Japanese coastguard ships in disputed maritime territory surrounding the Diaoyu/Senkaku islands brought wider attention to strategic-resource vulnerability and added a sense of urgency for those already focused on it. As tensions between China and Japan flared, it was reported that Chinese customs officials were halting exports of rare earth minerals to Japan.[42] While Chinese officials denied the rumors, and some scholars suggest that the disruption to Japanese supplies was a result of an earlier decision to reduce global exports of the minerals as had been occurring progressively for several years, the threat of a minerals embargo was enough to spur anxiety in Washington and a flurry of research, reportage, and dramatic market fluctuations.[43]

A few months later, the US Department of Energy published a report on critical materials strategy, with a particular focus on the green energy sector. The report found that rare earth elements presented the highest "criticality scores" of the materials studied, with cobalt and lithium also presenting supply risks in both the short and medium term.[44] In 2011 Congress passed the Ike Skelton National Defense Authorization Act, which required the Secretary of Defense to conduct an assessment of rare earth supply chain issues and develop a plan to address any vulnerabilities. The plan, issued by the undersecretary for defense in March 2012, concluded that "the Department remains committed to pursuing a three-pronged approach to this important issue: diversification of supply, pursuit of substitutes, and a focus on reclamation of waste as part of a larger U.S. Government recycling effort."[45]

A strong focus on strategic resource policy, with a particular emphasis on China, prevailed throughout the Trump presidency. In December 2017 the Trump White House issued an executive order to develop a federal strategy to ensure secure and reliable supplies of critical minerals. In February 2018 the Department of the Interior, in coordination with the Department of Defense, issued a list of 35 critical minerals, including rare earths, upon which the United States was dependent on imports for its vital economic and national security needs. The accompanying report stated that "this dependency of the United States on foreign sources creates a strategic vulnerability for both its economy and military to adverse foreign government action."[46] For those minerals that the United States is unable to adequately source domestically, the report called for the diversification of sources of supply, with a particular focus on the strengthening of trade links and production cooperation with American allies, like Australia, that also have substantial strategic mineral endowments.[47]

On September 30, 2020, President Trump issued an executive order to address the "threat to the domestic supply chain from reliance on critical minerals from foreign adversaries."[48] In this order, China was explicitly designated as a coercive actor, using market manipulation of rare earths to gain access to intellectual property and industrial technology. President Trump declared American reliance on Chinese critical minerals a "national emergency" and instructed the Department of the Interior to lay out a plan for developing supply chains "that do not depend on resources or processing from foreign adversaries."[49] The Biden administration has continued with this initiative, conducting an extensive supply-chain review program in its first months in office. As a result of the review, the Biden White House recommended Congress provide $50 billion in funding for a federal supply-chain resilience program, the bill for which currently sits before Congress.[50]

It is the search for a reliable supply of minerals not located in the United States itself, or often anywhere nearby, that poses the greatest risk for conflict between decoupled American and Chinese economic spheres, particularly because these minerals are the ones most necessary for success in the high-tech industries of the future: green energy, aerospace, defense, and information technology and communications. These dynamics are even more perilous than those that existed during the Cold War, when the United States faced a geopolitical rival that was itself almost completely self-reliant in its supply of strategic minerals. Today the United States and China find themselves in competition for sources of supply for many of the same strategic minerals.

Researchers from the United States Geological Survey (USGS) have found that the United States and China have 11 minerals in common for which they are import reliant for at least 50% of their supplies.[51] China is also the single country upon which the United States is most reliant for 25 separate minerals that it has a greater than 50% import reliance.[52] An African or Latin American country is one of the two primary sources of supply for each of the 11 minerals identified by the USGS scholars as being shared as critically import reliant by both China and the United States.[53] Unless the continued open supply of critical materials can be guaranteed, it appears that the global south will again be a major venue for superpower conflict.

Signs of this conflict are already present. China has become the largest trading partner of both Latin America and Africa. Total trade between China and Latin America has grown from $17 billion in 2002 to almost $315 billion in 2020; Chinese investments in the region between 2005 and 2021 totaled $131 billion; and Chinese banks are the largest lenders to the region as a whole.[54] In Africa, Chinese trade was worth around $200 billion in 2018, over triple the US total.[55] Minerals and raw materials are the major exports of both regions to China and are the main destination industries of Chinese investment. This state of affairs was viewed, with some strategic reservations, as a generally valuable contribution to regional economic growth under the Bush and Obama administrations. Under Trump it was seen as an aggressive and direct threat to American power and interests.

The last National Security Strategy outline released by the Obama administration in 2015 referred to the "unprecedented scope" of American cooperation with China.[56] The first National Security Strategy of the Trump administration, released in 2017, referred to China as a challenge to American power, influence, and interests "attempting to erode American security and prosperity" and "shape a world antithetical to US values."[57] The outline went on to state that China targets its investment in the developing world to expand its influence and gain a competitive advantage over the United States, that China seeks to pull Latin America into its orbit through state-led investments and loans, and that it corrupts elites, dominates extractive industries, and locks countries into debt traps in Africa.[58]

While China expands its trade, investment, and infrastructural projects in these mineral-rich areas, the United States is strengthening its military presence. The United States established AFRICOM, the African area of strategic command, in 2007. Since then, the US political presence on the continent has steadily shifted away from an emphasis on aid and diplomacy toward military activity. Before 2005 US military assistance spending in Africa never exceeded $300 million; since the founding of AFRICOM, it has never dropped below $500 million, and at times it has surpassed $1 billion.[59] Historian Nick Turse has found that the United States now operates more than 60 military bases or outposts in at least 34 African countries, while more US Special Forces personnel are deployed in Africa than in any other region of the world besides the Middle East.[60] The potential for superpower tensions to transform into covert or open conflict of a similar pattern that occurred during the Cold War is clear.

The zone of potential conflict extends to the world's oceans. The world wars of the twentieth century demonstrated the necessity of control over the most important sea lines of communication for securing reliable material supplies. Chinese claims to territory in the South China Sea, rival interpretations of a foreign state's right to naval access to an exclusive economic zone (EEZ), the American pivot of its naval forces to Asia, the expansion of a Chinese blue-water navy, the proliferation of Chinese A2AD weaponry, and the increase in American seaborne nuclear capacity and missile defenses are just some of the many points of tension between the US and China in the sphere of maritime security. When paired with the fact that deep-sea mineral nodules are anticipated to be the next frontier of major sources for a variety of strategic minerals, the potential for resource conflict to sit at the core of maritime strategy for both states is clear too. The other new frontiers of resource exploration—the polar regions and outer space—offer similar prospects for rivalry.

Future resource conflict will be shaped by broader global economic structures. Trade wars, punitive tariffs, and the abandonment of multilateral trade agreements by the United States on the one side, and the Belt and Road Initiative, energy cooperation with Central Asia and Russia, and the continued commercial expansion that sees China as the world's largest trading nation on the other portend the continued moving away from a system of global economic integration toward one of disintegrated blocs competing for the finite resources of the periphery. With so many strategic resource vulnerabilities shared by the US and China, the rivalry between blocs in a disintegrated global economy would be fierce and hold implications for national industrial and economic survival.

Transactional International Relations, Military-Industrial Decoupling, and Strategic Recalibration

The most significant change in terms of conceptions of empire and world order under Trump was in the idea that the liberal institutional framework of trade and governance that was crafted by the United States to undergird and stabilize its power had become a vector through which the rest of the world took advantage of American economic and strategic guarantees, without shouldering an adequate share of the costs.[61] The Trump administration's response was a turn toward a transactional approach to America's international economic and strategic relationships. The imperial model through which the United States would "be willing at times to forego certain short term direct economic advantages in favor of the more substantial and enduring benefits" that has predominated in some form or another for the past 70 years was replaced under Trump with a policy of "America first."[62]

This was framed by the Trump administration as a return to traditional great power rivalry that characterized international affairs before 1945.[63] Under this new post-unipolar paradigm of world power, the administration leaned far less on liberal international institutions and far more on raw military power and alliances to provide direct material benefit for the United States in its competition with China. In this lurch away from American liberal world empire, Trump both greatly increased the likelihood of great power conflict with China in the near future and perhaps accelerated the creation of political and economic conditions needed to restructure American grand strategy in the Pacific away from the pursuit of full-spectrum strategic dominance toward a more stable position of mutual deterrence between the United States and China.

Trump's dramatic turn away from liberal institutionalism saw the withdrawal of the United States from the Trans-Pacific Partnership and the Paris climate agreement; it also saw repeated attacks from Trump and prominent members of his administration on international institutions that have formed the basis of American world order, like the United Nations, NATO, the World Health Organization, the European Union, and various international legal and human-rights bodies.[64] This approach ceded the field on global leadership in trade and sustainability to China—an opportunity which Xi Jinping embraced, proceeding apace with BRI and Regional Comprehensive Economic Partnership expansion without the obstacle of American-led alternatives, and exhorting global leaders to continue along the path of globalization and free trade, even as the United States under Trump withdrew.[65]

Under Trump, American leadership of international institutions was traded for the freedom to renegotiate economic and security ties on a bilateral and transactional basis. This placed pressure on other countries to appease American desires, particularly regarding their balance of trade and relationship with China. During his presidential campaign, Trump was particularly critical of Japan and South Korea, accusing them of freeloading off American military power and threatening to withdraw American military support unless they increased payments to cover the cost of America's extensive deployments in their countries.[66]

With the bargaining position established, however, Trump rolled back some of his demands when Asian leaders demonstrated pliability. Japanese Prime Minister Shinzo Abe reached an agreement with Trump early in his administration; the agreement offered lucrative trade and investment deals and the promise of higher commitments for military spending to maintain Japanese access to the American market in the face of new tariff regimes and to keep the American military guarantee that has underpinned their own national security since the Second World War.[67] Talks with South Korea, in which Trump reportedly demanded a 400% increase in its share of the costs of American deployments there, failed to reach a resolution.[68]

This notable change in bilateral relationship management was accompanied by a shift in America's approach to multilateral security arrangements. The approach was described as a form of "minilateralism," involving a departure from the broad regionalist approach of the past to one much more directly focused on alliances with key regional powers, who hold similarly deep-seated national security concerns over a rising China.[69] The 2017 rean-imation of the Quadrilateral Security Dialogue (the Quad) between the United States, Japan, India, and Australia is the most prominent and important ex-ample of this.

The Quad is an initiative to promote a greater degree of consultation, planning, information exchange, and military drills between the four mem-ber countries with the aim of securing "a free, open, prosperous and inclu-sive Indo-Pacific Region based on shared values and principles and respect for international law."[70] In essence, it is a statement of willingness to defend the territorial and normative status quo, and the regional balance of power, against anticipated Chinese revisionism and enlargement.

The formalization of the concept of a combined "Indo-Pacific" sphere in American strategic planning in recent years ties India, the only viable future continental rival to China, within the same strategic grouping as China's off-shore rivals. Chinese suspicions that this relatively informal grouping would gradually come to take the form of an "Asian NATO" alliance directed toward the containment of China were escalated in August 2020, when US Deputy Secretary of State Stephen Biegun spoke about Washington's aim to formal-ize the Quad into a NATO-like structure, to help to "push back against China in virtually every domain."[71]

Operating from the claim that "China seeks to displace the United States in the Indo-Pacific region, expand the reaches of its state-driven economic model, and reorder the region in its favor,"[72] the Trump administration un-ambiguously committed to maintaining its military edge over China in the near future, with a strong focus on technological-industrial superiority. The US spent $778 billion on its military in 2020, a 4.4% increase on the pre-vious year.[73] This was more than three times as much as China, which had the world's second-largest military budget of $252 billion, and greater than the combined total of the next 10 largest military budgets, most of which belonged to countries that are treaty allies of the United States.[74]

This lead in aggregate military spending is tied to a clear edge in the tech-nological and performance capabilities of the American military, an advan-tage that is amplified by the vast geostrategic network of American forces, including the communications arrays operating in land, sea, air, space, and cyberspace that coordinate it all. The US National Defense Strategy makes a clear link between the broader economic decoupling from China and Amer-ican strategic objectives, stating that "the fact that many technological devel-opments will come from the commercial sector means that state competitors and non-state actors will also have access to them, a fact that risks eroding the conventional overmatch to which our Nation has grown accustomed. Maintaining the Department's technological advantage will require changes to industry culture, investment sources, and protection across the National Security Innovation Base."[75]

The struggle for technological supremacy in world markets and military production has already begun. Continued leadership in advanced digital and communications technology has been a cornerstone in the plans for preserving American global military superiority for decades.[76] Predictably, China's emergence as a market leader in fifth-generation telecommunications technology (5G) has been met with great consternation in Washington; 5G technology will be a key driver of the internet of things, autonomous vehicle operations, drones, robotics, smart cities, and other defining technological developments of the twenty-first century. The technology will also be instrumental in improving military intelligence, surveillance, and reconnaissance, enabling new systems of command and control, and streamlining complex logistical systems.[77]

US strategists fear that the rapidly improving Chinese capabilities in this field will severely narrow America's technological-military edge and open up gateways for cyberattacks on the United States and its allies in the future. Chinese companies have already signed agreements to build 5G infrastructure in approximately 30 countries, including important American allies like Turkey. An agreement for Chinese firm Huawei to develop the United Kingdom's 5G infrastructure was reportedly canceled under duress from the Trump White House, citing geopolitical concerns over Chinese access to the communications networks of American intelligence-sharing partners.[78] A similar ban on Huawei was issued by the Australian government, another member of the Five Eyes intelligence-sharing network, in 2018.[79] Trump's secretary of state, Mike Pompeo, loudly warned the world against relying on Chinese companies for the delivery of 5G infrastructure, and Trump himself floated the possibility that Huawei would be completely banned from the US telecoms market, in accordance with the Clean Network program.[80]

The cordoning of the American Defense Innovation Base from China has been coupled with a variety of actions by the Department of Defense to increase research and development for new military technologies such as artificial intelligence, drone warfare, hypersonic weapons, directed-energy weapons, and bio and quantum technology.[81] This is being pursued through a reworked organizational structure, with the creation of a new US Space

Force and the elevation of the US Cyber Command to an independent com-batant command.[82] Building on Trump administration initiatives, President Biden has emphasized the importance of high-tech supremacy in America's bid to continue its global dominance into the twenty-first century.[83]

While in its first months the Biden administration worked assiduously to reverse course on Trumpist unilateralism, rebuilding bridges with key allies in Europe and Asia, and restating American commitments to international institutions, the Trump administration's hawkish stance on China has en-dured. Economic decoupling, strategic containment, and the diplomatic iso-lation of China are continuing apace. Indeed, with Biden's internationalist credentials, the United States is now proving markedly more successful in mustering a united Western front against China. In the first trip to Europe of his presidency, Biden managed to put a joint G7 international infrastructure financing and development program to rival China's BRI on the agenda, the Build Back Better World (B3W) partnership. Biden also left a NATO confer-ence with a joint communiqué that frames China, for the first time ever, as a systemic challenge to the international order and a threat to the security of the NATO states.[84]

On diplomatic, economic, and military-industrial fronts, the United States is preparing for an enduring conflict with China, upon which the future con-figuration of world order will hinge. At the same time, the Asia-Pacific region is host to the massive and growing highly calibrated, oppositional military forces of both sides. It is now more imperative than at any point since the Second World War that American leaders soberly assess the strategic dispo-sition of forces in the Pacific and form a farsighted strategic policy that will mitigate rather than exacerbate the likelihood of full-scale war with China.

A Post-Imperial Pacific Strategy

American security policy and military assets are now being marshaled di-rectly around rivalry with China. The Trump administration committed to withdrawing US forces from Europe, the Middle East, Latin America, and Africa to facilitate the reallocation of US military resources to the Indo-Pacific.[85] The Biden administration too has committed to centering American security policy around China and its challenge to the American world sys-tem.[86] In the first significant public strategic-policy document released under Biden, the Interim National Security Strategic Guidance, the Indo-Pacific region was explicitly elevated to the same level of importance as the Western Hemisphere to American strategic interests.[87] The management of US-China relations and the effective planning and execution of American strategic policy in the region now form the single most important factor in determining the prospects for world peace as the twenty-first century progresses.

If the decoupling of the American and Chinese economies continues apace, the United States will have effectively slammed shut the Open Door that has underpinned its foreign policy since the nineteenth century and has formed the foundations of American global empire since 1945. The major historical motive force for the pursuit of American empire in Asia will have been dismantled. A new system of competing economic spheres of influence centered around the United States and China will entail new geostrategic approaches to regional security. While strategic resource competition is likely to inflame economic and military rivalry between the United States and China in southern Africa and elsewhere, the new alignment of economic ties and security partnerships in the Asia-Pacific region could, with wise management, see the establishment of a stable balance of power and system of mutual deterrence, lessening the prospects of open superpower war as the century progresses.

There are new possibilities for American grand strategy in the Pacific in a post-unipolar world with a greater emphasis on balance of power calculations. The most dire possible future is one in which the United States continues to attempt to pursue full-spectrum military dominance over the region, with dwindling relative resources, against an opponent with greater industrial and economic capacity than it has ever faced. Under these circumstances, ever greater resources would be diverted away from productive and socially useful purposes toward an even more bloated military-industrial complex and national security state apparatus. The United States would be socially poorer, strategically more precarious, and facing an ever-increasing likelihood of war as China comes to outgrow the strategic constraints imposed by American regional military hegemony.

American empire has been, since 1945, supported by other great powers because it provided them with clear benefits. A prolonged American empire in twilight, no longer the center of the world economy and more heavily dependent upon military power for its primacy, cannot offer the same material benefits to attract great-power consent. Under this scenario, to cement cooperation from its regional allies, the United States would increasingly rely on its military assets and the implicit threat of Chinese assumption of power, rather than relying on incentives of mutual economic development or stable and equitable institutions and norms governing the use of global commons.

This is the policy of a degenerating exploitative hegemony, without the financial or industrial capabilities to reverse the global economic gravitational shift toward China but with the military capabilities to attempt a martial form of international dominance.

At the other end of the spectrum of possibilities is full strategic withdrawal to hemispheric defense. This would essentially leave India, Japan, Russia, and other Asian powers with the task of balancing against China's ascendance to regional hegemony. The concentration of material wealth and military power that China would bring to bear under conditions of hegemony over Eurasia is likely too great a threat to American national security for such a path to be taken. There is no evidence of any significant political support for such an extreme form of isolationism in the United States today, and such support is highly unlikely to develop absent a profound geopolitical crisis.

Another possibility, being advocated by a growing number of strategic scholars and planners, is built around the concepts of offshore balancing and mutual deterrence and denial, and centers "restraint" as the guiding principle for American strategic policy. Christopher Layne has been championing such an approach since the height of unipolar triumphalism during the mid-1990s.[88] This approach proceeds from the position that continued American military hegemony is impossible to achieve, undesirable to attempt, a waste of otherwise useful resources, and more than likely to result in a degraded overall national-security environment.[89] Instead, using both its own military power and, where necessary and justified, alliances with other regional powers, the United States should seek to balance against any potential Chinese expansionism or full-scale bid for regional hegemony, if and when it should occur. Responding to the symptoms of imperial overstretch and the withdrawal from global liberal economic and institutional leadership, this approach clarifies American strategic interests. America's world-spanning strategic architecture, designed to support the global Open Door, would be replaced by the simpler strategic imperative to defend US territorial integrity and balance against China's assumption of hegemony in Eurasia.[90]

Many other realist strategic scholars hold similar views to Layne and have proposed tactical and doctrinal shifts in military affairs to move the United States toward a more stable strategic disposition as Chinese power grows. Andrew Krepinevich has argued for crafting a system of "archipelagic defense" to deter possible Chinese expansionism. This builds upon the existent island-chain geostrategy but calls for reducing the focus on carrier groups and mobile naval power in the region, and enhancing allied and US land-based surface-to-air defense systems.[91] T. X. Hammes advocates a strategy centered around what he describes as "offshore control." An approach which calls for the abandonment of the objective of projecting military power over the Chinese mainland, instead focusing efforts on retaining sea denial capacity within the first island chain, and dominating air and sea theaters outside of it.[92]

Hammes proposes to use this security posture to threaten Chinese seaborne trade and energy flows in times of conflict, rather than the escalatory approach of threatening the lives and core infrastructure on mainland China. He also argues that this new posture would flip the current geographical and cost advantage enjoyed by China toward the United States; China would lose the value of the investment it has made in neutralizing US sea command, as the United States would no longer be pursuing that strategy, and the Chinese Navy would need to expand its own forces many times over to approach the ability to challenge organized US and allied sea-denial capabilities.[93]

Hammes's approach has strong parallels with Mahan's description of *guerre de course*, or commerce destroying; and while Mahan cautioned against the American faith in pursuing this as its primary naval strategy because of an absence of proximate ports to the centers of rival powers and trade routes, the modern US navy and extensive regional security architecture preclude the restraints observed by Mahan in 1890.[94] Hammes believes that focusing on economic strangulation is both less escalatory than dominance-oriented approaches and allows China to keep face in a negotiated end to the conflict, something necessary for a regime sensitive to public opinion.[95] The ongoing development of the BRI and the extensive continental infrastructure being developed for the transport of trade goods and energy supplies calls into question the long-term efficacy of this approach.

Andrew Erickson, professor of strategy at the US Naval War College, in his testimony to the House Armed Services Committee Seapower and Projection Forces Subcommittee, argued that the commercial targeting strategy advocated by Hammes is itself both escalatory and difficult to implement owing to the complexity and dynamism of modern commerce.[96] As an alternative to both full theater dominance and offshore control, Erickson proposes "deterrence by denial." This has similarities with archipelagic defense but places a greater emphasis on long-term affordability, the de-escalation of conflict with China, and the importance of regional alliances and partnerships, and their role in validating a consensus-based US military presence.[97] He also makes clear that China cannot be expected to fit neatly into preexisting Western security architecture and that the US should encourage Chinese behaviors that do not fit within these structures, but remain largely positive in terms of China's relationship with the rest of the world.[98]

In its essence, deterrence by denial would create a mutually denied maritime and air space in the Western Pacific, where neither Chinese nor US forces could achieve command of the commons and where conflict could be geographically contained, with clear boundaries for what constitutes escalation. Erickson advocates using American power and influence to work toward a balanced regional system, including a more influential Indian role, in which no one side can dominate.[99]

Perhaps the most comprehensive work done on articulating an alternative US defense strategy in Asia has been produced by a team of scholars, policy analysts, and former senior national-intelligence and military officers at the Quincy Institute for Responsible Statecraft. Their proposal for a strategy of active denial involves a restrained approach to escalation, seeking to limit the scope of conflict between nuclear superpowers, with the aim of defeating Chinese aggression, should it eventuate, in coordination with regional allies, rather than attempting to maintain full-spectrum dominance in the Western Pacific and the ability to subjugate China through war.[100] The full Quincy report constitutes an exhaustive examination of the military deployments, force structures, budgetary accounting, and broader political and strategic considerations of the United States and its regional allies in crafting a new restraint-based strategic policy in Asia, which could act as a bridge away from empire and toward a more sustainable, secure, and peaceful American foreign policy.

Whatever specific form the policy takes, planning for a system of deterrence and balance, and departing from the false hope of everlasting American dominance are necessary steps if we are to hope for a modicum of peace between a rising Chinese empire and a declining American one. Strategic forecasters tend to agree that this sort of balance of military forces is far more likely and would be in far higher accordance with the interests of the region as a whole than Chinese assumption of regional hegemony.[101] This is a vision of how a revived Quadrilateral could operate were it poised toward achieving a counter-hegemonic balance of power in the region, rather than aimed at the chimera of perpetual American leadership and military preeminence currently advocated by the Pentagon.[102]

The rise of China is an event of world historical significance. It must be planned for with the upmost sobriety and seriousness. A blind faith in the miraculous resumption of the glory days of American empire does nothing but render us ill prepared for the vast changes ahead. Those that benefited greatly in terms of security and prosperity under the last 70 years of American empire are now forced by the steady stride of history to chart a new course of peaceful and productive coexistence with those who are now rising after centuries on the outside of world imperial affairs. This is, of course, neither simple nor easy. There are myriad points of friction and legitimate criticisms of the Chinese state, its economic, political, and social policies, and how these will impact the world outside of China. Restructuring a stable, post-imperial, and counter-hegemonic strategic balance in the Asia-Pacific region as China rises will place the United States and its allies in the best possible position to navigate this difficult period while minimizing the chances of a catastrophic war.

Today's arguments for balance, deterrence, and restraint bring to mind the words of Sir Halford Mackinder, who wrote in the midst of the Second World War that, to secure an ongoing future peace, American grand strategy must recognize that "a thousand million people of ancient oriental civilization inhabit the Monsoon lands of India and China. They must grow to prosperity in the same years in which Germany and Japan are being tamed to civilization. They will then balance that other thousand million who live between the Missouri and the Yenisei. A balanced globe of human beings. And happy, because balanced and thus free."[103]

Conclusion

The United States has been in a state of near-constant expansion since its founding. Economic interests have shaped and defined the nature of this expansion; and for much of the several centuries that it has unfolded, China has been the lodestar toward which American market-driven expansionism has advanced. Strategic considerations have flowed from and worked in tandem with economic ones. The historical spread westward of American commercial interests was accompanied by the construction of a strategic military apparatus, used to both entrench and extend American commerce across the Pacific and into Asia. From the Communist victory in the Chinese Civil War in 1949 to the rapprochement of 1972, China was viewed as the major threat to American imperial interests in Asia by US strategists. After several decades of unprecedented economic growth and significant military enlargement, China has now returned to the position of preeminent challenger to American empire in Asia, no longer as a revolutionary outsider to global capitalism but as a rival center of internationally interconnected economic and military power. How the tension between the world's rising and declining superpowers is managed will be the major determinant of the prospects for world peace in the decades to come.

From the point of its first foray into formal empire in 1898 through the construction and maintenance of the American-led capitalist world order from 1945, the United States has crafted international institutions and an administrative apparatus that advance the commercial model that extends from its own particular political economy. No feature of this order has been more stable or influential than the Open Door approach to global trade and investment. While the United States sat firmly at the center of global industrial production and capital accumulation, the maintenance of an open global economic system served both to enrich America and provide a measure of stability to an international system that had passed through the most destructive period of conflict in world history prior to America's ascent to world power in 1945. Today, as the center of the global economy shifts from the United States to China, this system is facing serious and possibly terminal challenges.

French economist Francis Delaisi wrote that the golden age of any governmental regime could be identified by the harmony that reigned between its economic, administrative, and political institutions, operating under a shared set of ideological myths.[1] It is no coincidence that the United States has for the past several years been embroiled in one of its most serious periods of domestic social and political upheaval since the Civil War, concurrent with its decline in global political and economic supremacy. Since Frederick Jackson Turner first articulated his frontier thesis, a long line of historians and political scientists has recognized the codependency between social and democratic stability at home and constant market expansion abroad. The particular model of empire that this domestic political dynamic produced was historically contingent on American power in relation to the rest of the world, and through this America's capacity to shape, direct, and steward world order, international institutions, and the global economy.

The era of American preeminence that was inaugurated after the Second World War is now all but over. During the Cold War, the United States faced a near-peer military and geostrategic competitor in the Soviet Union. Today the United States faces an economic competitor in China that has already surpassed the United States by many measures and is almost certain to continue its upward trajectory. As the center of the global economy shifts toward China, the American global order will disintegrate and a new form of world order will take its place. Nothing short of the collapse of the Chinese state would seem now able to curtail this historical process. It is a sign of the times that some observers have grown anxious about the collapse of China. Despite a long list of predictions of such a collapse from American political scientists, reports of China's death are greatly exaggerated.

The shape and function of the new world order may be, in general principle, relatively similar to the American system, as the American system was relatively similar to the British-dominated one before it. The major determinants of this new order will be America's behavior as it declines, China's behavior as it rises, and to what degree the rest of the world, unified by broad common economic and balance-of-power interests, can influence these two factors. The United States will be forced to recalibrate its grand strategic policy around this emergent reality or face the very real likelihood of waging, and perhaps losing, a catastrophic war.

What was meant to be the end of history, with the United States and its model for political organization globally ascendant, was instead another belle epoque, similar to the one that preceded the First World War, when, for a large section of the world, things seemed to be improving and a new era of stable progress was taking place. We are now advancing again toward what Eric Hobsbawm once called the "strange death" of liberal world order, as it falls victim to its own successes and the social, economic, and geopolitical contradictions that they produce.[2] The long peace Europeans had by and large been conditioned to expect from their life experiences after the Napoleonic Wars was destroyed by incessant conflict and wholesale destruction during the 30 years crisis. To avoid a similar fate as this current period of global liberalism proceeds through stages of disintegration, new approaches to the management of the global economy, the international balance of power, and geostrategy must be developed, based around the shifting dynamics of global economic and military power, and the new array of crises confronting the planet.

The shape of things to come will be heavily affected by the approach taken by the United States to managing its slipping imperium. If the US seeks to exploit its continued military dominance to enforce nationalist economic advantage that dismantles the international economic order that it established and administered for the past 75 years, and if the country runs against the economic interests of its allies and rivals alike, then we are likely to be heading toward the sort of conflict-to-the-death between fully armed business concerns that Hannah Arendt viewed as the endpoint of interimperial rivalry.[3] For the United States to manage to both slam shut the Open Door of world empire as well as maintain favorable prospects for peace with China, major changes would have to occur in the political economy of America itself. A new political-economic consensus would need to be reached, one which overthrows the inherently expansionist perpetual drive for new frontiers and new wealth that has sat at the foundation of the United States since its founding, and replaces it with a sustainable and equitable national economy capable of supporting a thriving but more modest and cooperative—and less consumeristic and wasteful—society and polity.

The dramatic global economic shifts that are now taking place do afford a new possibility: the crafting of responsible, farsighted foreign and strategic policies for managing the security of the United States and promoting peace and regional stability in the Asia-Pacific that is not premised on the containment of China. These goals were perhaps impossible to expect under conditions of unchallenged American empire. Without the capacity to sustain its empire, nor the ability to reap the economic benefits that this once entailed, the United States could turn toward strategic approaches that aim for deterrence, regional balance, multilateralism, and power sharing rather than grasping for continued preeminence.

Although it runs contrary to the spirit of American hubris that has characterized the post–Cold War years, grappling with the limits of American power has a long tradition. Brooks Adams, the scribe of American imperial ascendancy, observed that the greatest catastrophes in history occur as humanity attempts to adjust itself to the movement of the international center of empire, wealth, and power.[4] At the turn of the twentieth century, well before the United States had assumed the mantle of global empire, Adams foresaw the industrial development of China as the historical catalyst which would shift this power from West to East.[5] Some farsighted American scholars and strategic planners, running against the grain of imperial hubris, have been impressing the importance of strategic planning for a transition in world power away from the United States and toward China since at least the 1960s.[6]

Seriously approaching such planning would require the development of a political bloc within the country that was truly anti-imperial, with the capacity to mobilize the majority of the population around a new political-economic consensus that did not depend upon constant international market expansion for the achievement of prosperity and social stability within the United States. Such planning would also require the breaking of the stranglehold of militarism within both major American political parties and the opening of discursive space within American society currently dominated by political and economic elites and vested interests.[7]

Despite American pride for its freedoms of speech and intellectual inquiry, there is today no single prominent politician, left or right, that speaks openly and loudly about American decline relative to China and the reality that, in many important senses, the United States will not be number one a short decade or two from today, let alone forever. A blind faith in technology, the military colossus, American ideological virtues, and national reinvention and rejuvenation has thus far prevented American political leaders from grappling with the realities of the progression of world history and geopolitical power. American empire will end, as surely as have all empires past. It is how this reality is grappled with that matters so greatly today.

The long-standing bipartisan political consensus around the Open Door has already been fractured by the Trump presidency. The Trumpian path away from the Open Door leads toward a nationalistic, exploitative American hegemony, involving more militarism and a reinforced view that the United States should dominate the world for all time. The United States would be less democratic at home, be more aggressive abroad, act unilaterally in pursuit of its economic and strategic interests, and ultimately pose a threat to world peace and the independence of nation states where these conflicted with its own narrow conception of national self-interest. The United States would come to resemble more and more the type of "new despotism" described by John Keane as coming to proliferate in the post-end-of-history world, maintaining the semblance and rhetoric of democracy but becoming increasingly reliant on covert violence, surveillance, political manipulation, the raw exertion of power, and a type of popular loyalty that masks a voluntary servitude to maintain the American social order amid declining prospects.[8] It is uncertain whether or for how long the people of the United States could stomach the raw and unvarnished militarism, the declining social conditions, and the colossal economic cost of maintaining a degenerated exploitative hegemony. Chalmers Johnson believed that, in the long run, they would not tolerate these conditions.[9] A close reading of the history of American empire leaves the issue an open question.

While the Biden administration promises a return to the liberal internationalism that characterized the Obama era and indeed almost every other presidential administration since the Second World War, this return in essence represents nothing more than a false summer of American empire. Postwar liberal institutionalism never lived up to its ideals. Promising multilateral power sharing, consensus building, and a more equal world, it delivered an imperial world order with the United States at the apex, and a coterie of allies and client states sharing in many of the benefits that came from American strategic and economic dominance. As the center of the global economy shifts toward China, the United States is becoming unable to make this system work for itself or for its other beneficiaries. Biden's America will not be able to simultaneously reinvigorate and uphold a globally integrated economic system while selectively excluding China from the major industries of twenty-first-century growth and technological development. The contradictions of American empire will persist, despite the rhetoric of international community, democracy, rule of law, and human rights. A path forward that does not reckon with the realities of a declining American empire is no path forward at all.

Under the right conditions, a third path—the embrace of a post-imperial American political system—is possible. As American power declines and the dynamic of the frontier turns from one of expansion, economic bounty, and national renewal to an exorbitantly expensive and militaristic rearguard action in defense of the geopolitical gains of the past, the political consensus on American foreign policy may change. The material realities of the American public will ultimately determine whether their ongoing consent for empire will be maintained far into the future.

One comprehensive study of the history of oligarchy, written in 2011, found that socioeconomic inequality and the distribution of political power between regular Americans and elites within the United States compared unfavorably with even the most gilded era of the Roman empire.[10] This situation has only worsened in the decade since the study's findings. Crumbling infrastructure, the failure to provide adequate health care to American citizens, even in the midst of a global pandemic, and an average net decrease in household wealth of around 20% since 2007 are realities of everyday American life.[11] These developments are occurring alongside an unprecedented explosion in the wealth of the richest Americans. A 2020 RAND study found that the bottom 90% of Americans had been stripped of around $50 trillion in wealth as a result of changes to the relative distribution of income growth since the mid-1970s.[12] Given the declining economic conditions of the average American and the supremacy of money in the American political process, the rise of populism and broad distrust of elites and elite institutions that has emerged in the United States in recent years is unsurprising.

These trends are likely to continue and quite possibly worsen as the United States ramps up military and economic competition with China. The effects of these trends may well cause the American public to become disabused of the myths of American exceptionalism and imperial destiny. As the realities of Chinese economic ascendancy become further apparent, a larger portion of the American business community will similarly begin to reevaluate the benefits of empire in decline. Whether the future of American foreign policy is to be characterized by a grasping militarized exploitative hegemony or a transition to a more sustainable great power politics will be determined by these domestic political developments and the contours of the socioeconomic consensus that underlays the American polity further into the twenty-first century.

Questions of how the United States is to manage its imperial decline must inevitably engage with the character and capabilities of the Chinese order that is being established. In striking similarity to the Americans who drew a sharp distinction between their own peculiar "empire of liberty" and European imperialism in the nineteenth century, Chinese scholars and politicians draw on tradition and culture to argue that the Chinese approach to world order is fundamentally different from the Western one and that China will not seek to impose its governing model, morals, or norms on other countries. They point to the long-lasting, peacefully maintained, and extensive international trade linkages of antiquity, China's status as a champion of the developing world, and the historical Sinocentric tributary system of regulating international relations as indicators that China will not seek to impose its will on weaker states, but bring stability and harmony;[13] in other words, that China will not be imperial in the way that we understand it.

Even in the midst of the century of humiliation, China's most influential leaders were claiming that a resurgent China would never hold expansionist ambitions. In July 1868, the same month that the Burlingame Treaty was signed between China and the United States, Zeng Guofan, the preeminent statesman and general of his era, wrote to the imperial court: "Should the day come when China gets the ascendant, and foreign nations decay and grow weak, we then should only seek to protect our own black-haired people, and have no wish to get military glory beyond the seas."[14] The sincere belief among rising imperial powers that their day will hail a new millennium of peace and justice extends at least back to the rise of Sparta, whose most distinguished general, Brasidas, during the war that would establish Spartan hegemony in Greece, declared, "We have no imperialistic ambitions; our whole effort is to put an end to imperialism."[15] Despite its assurances, China's rise will certainly present a variety of problems as the international community grapples with a new superpower that is already reshaping world order in ways favorable and familiar to itself.

The implications of a new Chinese imperium have much of the international community rightly concerned. The dramatic gulf between the geopolitical and historical conditions that favored American ascendance to world empire and those of China today provide some reassurances about the capacity of the world to achieve some semblance of equilibrium should a balancing approach be taken. The United States, having already established hegemony in the Western Hemisphere during the nineteenth century, emerged to become a twentieth-century global empire in the aftermath of the two most destructive wars in human history, which utterly decimated almost all of the United States' imperial rivals and left the country as the world's manufacturer, banker, and armory. China today is surrounded by well-armed and well-resourced neighbors, all of whom have good reason to balance Chinese influence and hedge against the threat of expansionist Chinese imperialism.

With the United States as an offshore balancer willing at times to support Japan, India, Russia, Vietnam, and others should the necessity arise, China cannot foreseeably hope to enjoy the conditions that propelled the United States to the unprecedented heights of world power in the postwar years. A wise post-imperial American foreign policy could, under these global geopolitical conditions, coexist with a larger China, with frictions, disagreements, and rivalry but without necessitating full-scale war or the development of oppositional imperial blocs, or allowing for the creation of a Sinocentric global imperialism.

To progress to this new mode of foreign policy and grand strategy, the United States would need to begin to grapple with the task of shaping its own role and identity in a post-imperial world. The national polity must first come to grips with the realities of American empire, to understand the historical process by which empire was formed and the structural reasons why it has come to decline. American scholars like Andrew Bacevich, Christopher Layne, and Alfred McCoy are today continuing in the tradition of imperial critics and historians like Charles Beard, William Appleman Williams, Gore Vidal, Norman Graebner, Paul Kennedy, Chalmers Johnson, and many others in teaching these crucial lessons to the United States itself.

J. A. Hobson saw the state of self-delusion as imperialism's gravest peril.[16] Having habituated itself to this deception and thus rendered itself incapable of self-criticism, a declining empire is likely to attempt shambolically the conversion of its slipping preeminence into an exploitative, nationalistic, militarily underwritten, shrinking hegemony.[17] This was, in essence, the vision of the Trump White House's resistance to "managed decline." Should the United States continue down this path, a near future characterized by intense and catastrophic superpower conflict is highly likely. Even with its still-considerable military edge and its continued role as the monetary pivot of the global economy, the probability of the United States achieving anything resembling a "victory" over China that improves the conditions of its own people and society, let alone the security and prosperity of the rest of the world, is negligible.[18] While the Biden White House is attempting a redefinition of American empire to one that is liberal, global, and yet firmly grounded in the containment of China, the contradictions of such an approach are already eminently visible. The path lies open for a third way, grounded in the realities of contemporary global political economy and geopolitics rather than imperial delusion, which could lead the United States off the path of empire and hubris toward a sustainable post-imperial foreign policy.

Forty years ago William Appleman Williams posed the question, "Is the idea and reality of America possible without empire?" He reasoned that in answering this question, one must either commit to imagining a new post-imperial United States or commit to the ultimately futile task of preserving the empire.[19] The decades that followed Williams's entreaty to imagine a new United States saw the resurgence of American imperial power to new heights. What was lauded as the end of history can now be definitively identified as the brief and alluring swan song of American empire. What follows will depend on the capacity to imagine a new post-imperial United States, operating to achieve its own national interests and security in accordance with the interests of its allies and the international community en masse. This new vision begins with a strong foundational understanding of the interplay between the economic and strategic forces that produced the empire itself, and a deeper accounting of the dynamics of its relationship with China.

Introduction

1. Plutarch, *Plutarch's Lives*, trans. Bernadotte Perrin (Macmillan, 1914), 363.

2. William Appleman Williams, *The Tragedy of American Diplomacy* (Norton, 1988); Frederick Jackson Turner, "The Significance of the Frontier in American History," *Annual Report of the American Historical Association* (1893).

3. John J. Mearsheimer, "China's Unpeaceful Rise," *Current History* 105, no. 690 (2006): 160–162.

4. John Darwin, *After Tamerlane: The Rise and Fall of Global Empires, 1400–2000* (Penguin UK, 2008), chapter 7, EPUB.

5. For some of the best examples, see Chalmers Johnson, *Dismantling the Empire: America's Last Best Hope* (Metropolitan Books, 2010); Andrew J. Bacevich, *American Empire* (Harvard University Press, 2009); David Harvey, *The New Imperialism* (Oxford University Press, 2005).

6. For some of the most ebullient assessments of American empire, see Niall Ferguson, *Colossus: The Rise and Fall of the American Empire* (Penguin, 2005); Max Boot, "The Case for American Empire," in *Paradoxes of Power*, ed. David Skidmore (Routledge, 2015), 88–91.

7. Joseph Alois Schumpeter, *Imperialism and Social Classes: Two Essays*, vol. 4 (Ludwig von Mises Institute, 1955), 94.

8. Schumpeter, 65.

9. Schumpeter, 5.

10. Schumpeter, 65.

11. Schumpeter, 69.

12. Schumpeter, 70.

13. Schumpeter, 73.

14. Schumpeter, 97.

15. John Atkinson Hobson, *Imperialism: A Study* (Routledge, 2018), 106.

16. Hobson, see particularly chapters 4 ("Economic Parasites of Imperialism") and 6 ("The Economic Taproot of Imperialism").

17. Hobson, 46.

18. Hobson, 47.

19. Vladimir Il'ich Lenin, *Imperialism: The Highest Stage of Capitalism* (Resistance Books, 1999).

20. Harvey, *The New Imperialism*, chapter 2 ("How America's Power Grew").

21. Harvey, 31.

22. Harvey, 126.

23. William Appleman Williams, "The Vicious Circle of American Imperialism," in *Readings in US Imperialism*, ed. Donald Clark Hodges (P. Sargent, 1971).

24. Hobson, *Imperialism*, 313–314.

25. Hobson, 314.

26. Hobson, 309.

27. Hobson, 79.

28. Hobson, 73–74.

29. Max Weber, "Politics as Vocation," in *The Vocation Lectures*, Max Weber, David S. Owen, and Tracy B. Strong (Hackett Publishing, 2004), 32.

Chapter 1 • The Long March Westward and Native Dispossession

1. Karl Polanyi, *The Great Transformation* (Farrar & Rinehart, 1944), 66.

2. See Walter LaFeber, *The American Age: United States Foreign Policy at Home and Abroad: 1750 to the Present* (Norton, 1994), chapter 1 ("The Roots of American Foreign Policy"); Peter d'Alroy Jones, *The Consumer Society: A History of American Capitalism*, vol. 780 (Penguin Books Ltd., 1965), chapter 1 ("The Economics of Dependency").

3. Patrick K. O'Brien and Stanley L. Engerman, "Exports and the Growth of the British Economy from the Glorious Revolution to the Peace of Amiens," in *Slavery and the Rise of the Atlantic System*, ed. Barbara Solow (Cambridge University Press, 1991), 177–209.

4. O'Brien and Engerman, 177–209.

5. Thomas Seward Lovering, *Minerals in World Affairs* (Prentice-Hall, 1943), 73.

6. Lovering, 74.

7. LaFeber, *The American Age*, 15.

8. LaFeber, 16–17.

9. Mary Ritter Beard and Charles Austin Beard, *History of the United States*, vol. 1 (Doubleday, Doran and Co., 2009), 59–60.

10. Beard and Beard, 29.

11. See Macabe Keliher, "Anglo-American Rivalry and the Origins of US China Policy," *Diplomatic History* 31, no. 2 (2007): 229; Norman A. Graebner, *Empire on the Pacific: A Study in American Continental Expansion* (Ronald Press, 1983), 27.

12. Thomas Jefferson, "Letter to G. K. Van Hogendorp," (October 13, 1785), Avalon Project, Documents in Law, History, and Diplomacy, Yale Law School, Lillian Goldman Law Library, accessed December 23, 2022, https://avalon.law.yale.edu/18th_century/let38.asp.

13. Russell Frank Weigley, *The American Way of War: A History of United States Military Strategy and Policy* (Indiana University Press, 1977), 40–41.

14. Weigley, 43.

15. Stacie L. Pettyjohn, *US Global Defense Posture, 1783–2011* (RAND Corporation, 2012), 16–17.

16. Colin G. Calloway, *The American Revolution in Indian Country: Crisis and Diversity in Native American Communities* (Cambridge University Press, 1995), 290.

17. Peter S. Onuf, "Imperialism and Nationalism in the Early American Republic,"

in *Empire's Twin: US Anti-Imperialism from the Founding Era to the Age of Terrorism*, ed. Ian Tyrrell and Jay Sexton (Cornell University Press, 2015), 34.

18. US Continental Congress, "The Committee, Consisting of Mr. Duane, Mr. Peters, Mr. Carrol I. E. Carroll, Mr. Hawkins and Mr. Lee, to Whom Were Referred a Report on Indian Affairs, Read in Congress on the 21st of April Last, a Letter from General Schuyler . . . With Messages to and from Certain Hostile Indians on the Subject of Peace . . . Submit the Following Detail of Facts and Resolutions," (David C. Claypoole, 1783), accessed December 23, 2022, https://www.loc.gov/item/90898080/.

19. US Continental Congress, https://www.loc.gov/item/90898080/.

20. Calloway, *The American Revolution in Indian Country*, 101–102.

21. Calloway, 106.

22. Thomas Jefferson et al., "The Declaration of Independence" (July 4, 1776), accessed December 23, 2022, https://www.archives.gov/founding-docs/declaration -transcript.

23. John Keane, *The Life and Death of Democracy* (Simon and Schuster, 2009), 363.

24. John Quincy Adams, *An Oration, Delivered at Plymouth, December 22, 1802: At the Anniversary Commemoration of the First Landing of Our Ancestors, at That Place*, vol. 2 (Russell and Cutler, 1802).

25. Robert M. Utley, *The Indian Frontier 1846–1890* (UNM Press, 2003), 36. For a summary of Jefferson's recommendations on a "civilizing" Indian policy, see Thomas Jefferson, "Jefferson to Congress January 18, 1803" (18 January, 1803), accessed December 23, 2022, https://www.loc.gov/item/mtjbib012083/.

26. See Colin G. Calloway, *The Victory with No Name: The Native American Defeat of the First American Army* (Oxford University Press, 2014).

27. "Thomas Jefferson to William H. Harrison," (The Thomas Jefferson Papers at the Library of Congress, February 27, 1803), accessed March 21, 2020, https://www.loc .gov/item/mtjbib012188/.

28. LaFeber, *The American Age*, 54.

29. Keane, *The Life and Death of Democracy*, 368.

30. Albert Katz Weinberg, *Manifest Destiny a Study of Nationalist Expansionism in American History* (Quadrangle Books, 1935), 34.

31. James Monroe, "Message Received from the President of the United States," *Journal of the Senate of the United States of America* 13 (December 2, 1823): 11.

32. Harold Adams Innis, *Empire and Communications* (Rowman & Littlefield, 2007), 13.

33. Ruth Schwartz Cowan, *A Social History of American Technology* (Oxford University Press, 1997), 83.

34. Cowan, 69.

35. Cowan, 95.

36. Cowan, 97.

37. Eric Hobsbawm, *Age of Capital: 1848–1875* (Hachette UK, 2010), 127.

38. Bhu Srinivasan, *Americana: A 400-Year History of American Capitalism* (Penguin, 2017), 85.

39. Hobsbawm, *Age of Capital*, 105.

40. Hobsbawm, 105.

41. Hobsbawm, 136.

42. Srinivasan, *Americana*, 156.

43. Beard and Beard, *History of the United States*, vol. 1, 322.

44. Peter J. Hugill, "The American Challenge to British Hegemony, 1861–1947," *Geographical Review* 99, no. 3 (2009): 405–406.

45. Lovering, *Minerals in World Affairs*, 74.

46. Richard Franklin Bensel, *The Political Economy of American Industrialization, 1877–1900* (Cambridge University Press, 2000), 4.

Chapter 2 • The China Focus in Westward Expansion

1. John H. Schroeder, *Shaping a Maritime Empire: The Commercial and Diplomatic Role of the American Navy, 1829–1861*, vol. 48 (Praeger Pub Text, 1985), 5.

2. Schroeder, 5.

3. Graebner, *Empire on the Pacific*, 218.

4. John King Fairbank, "American China Policy to 1898: A Misconception," *The Pacific Historical Review* 39, no. 4 (1970): 413.

5. "Qianlong to George III," 1793, in John Otway Percy Bland and Sir Edmund Trelawney Backhouse, *Annals and Memoirs of the Court of Peking* (Houghton Mifflin, 1914), 322–331.

6. Marshall Sahlins, "Cosmologies of Capitalism: The Trans-Pacific Sector of the World System," in *Culture/Power/History: A Reader in Contemporary Social Theory*, ed. Nicholas B. Dirks and Geoff Eley (Princeton University Press, 1994), 413.

7. Jonathan D. Spence, *Chinese Roundabout: Essays in History and Culture* (Norton, 1993), 233–235.

8. Jules Davids, *American Diplomatic and Public Papers: The United States and China. Series 1: The Treaty System and the Taiping Rebellion, 1842–1860* (Scholarly Resources, 1973), xxxvii.

9. William Appleman Williams, *The Roots of the Modern American Empire: A Study of the Growth and Shaping of Social Consciousness in a Marketplace Society* (Random House, 1969), 63.

10. See Melvyn Dubofsky, "Daniel Webster and the Whig Theory of Economic Growth: 1828–1848," *New England Quarterly* 42, no. 4 (1969): 551–572.

11. Quoted in Keliher, "Anglo-American Rivalry and the Origins of US China Policy," 227.

12. "Webster to Cushing," Cushing Correspondences, Senate Documents 138, series 457, 28th Congress, Second Session, in Davids, *American Diplomatic and Public Papers: The United States and China. Series 1: The Treaty System and the Taiping Rebellion, 1842–1860*, 150.

13. Davids, 150.

14. Schroeder, *Shaping a Maritime Empire*, vol. 48, 50.

15. Schroeder, 59.

16. Schroeder, 61.

17. John Quincy Adams, "Lecture on the War with China, Delivered before the Massachusetts Historical Society, December, 1841," *Chinese Repository* 11 (1842): 274–289.

18. Adams, 274–289.

19. Adams, 274–289.

20. Beard and Beard, *History of the United States*, vol. 1, 228.

21. Beard and Beard, 228.

22. Beard and Beard, 317.

23. Beard and Beard, 317.

24. Beard and Beard, 225.

25. De Bow, quoted in Beard and Beard, 229.

26. Williams, *The Roots of the Modern American Empire*, 76–81.

27. Quoted in Graebner, *Empire on the Pacific*, 14.

28. See Jones, *The Consumer Society*, 780; Graebner, *Empire on the Pacific,* 48; Schroeder, *Shaping a Maritime Empire*, 48.

29. Williams, *The Roots of the Modern American Empire*, 78.

30. Williams, 76.

31. Ephraim D. Adams, "English Interest in the Annexation of California," *The American Historical Review* 14, no. 4 (1909): 750–751.

32. Adams, 745.

33. Adams, 747.

34. Quoted in Graebner, *Empire on the Pacific*, 82.

35. Quoted in H. J. Raymond, "California," *The American Review: a Whig Journal of Politics, Literature, Art, And Science* 3 (January 1846): 91–92.

36. Adams, "English Interest in the Annexation of California," 762.

37. See John O'Sullivan, "Annexation," *United States Magazine and Democratic Review* 17, no. 1 (1845): 5–10.

38. James Knox Polk, *Inaugural Address, March 4, 1845* (Tennessee Presidents Trust, 1993).

39. Quoted in Alexander Gurdon, "Life of John Tyler, President of the United States up to the Close of the Second Session of the Twenty-Seventh Congress," (Harper & Bros, 1843), 129.

40. Graebner, *Empire on the Pacific*, 16.

41. Carl Schurz, "Manifest Destiny," *Harper's New Monthly Magazine* 87, no. 521 (1893), 737.

42. Weinberg, "Manifest Destiny a Study of Nationalist Expansionism in American History," 45.

43. Weinberg, 56.

44. Arnold Toynbee, *The New Europe: Some Essays in Reconstruction* (J. M. Dent and Sons Limited, 1915), 39.

45. Max Weber, *Economy and Society: An Outline of Interpretive Sociology*, vol. 1 (University of California Press, 1978), 56.

46. See "The Annexation of Hawaii" in Marion Miller, *Great Debates in American History, from the Debates in the British Parliament on the Colonial Stamp Act (1764–1765) to the Debates in Congress at the Close of the Taft Administration (1912–1913)*, vol. 3 (Current Literature Pub. Co., 1913), 169–244.

47. John Tyler, "The Tyler Doctrine," Special Message to Congress, December 30, 1842, in The Addresses and Messages of the Presidents of the United States, Inaugural, Annual, and Special, from 1789 to 1849, vol. 2 (Edward Walker, 1849), 1316–1317.

48. Tyler, 1316–1317.

49. Graebner, *Empire on the Pacific*, 84.

50. *New York Herald*, "Next Session of Congress—President's Message—Foreign

Policy of the Government," September 15, 1845, accessed December 23, 2022, https://chroniclingamerica.loc.gov/lccn/sn83030313/1845-09-15/ed-1/seq-2/.

51. Raymond, "California," 97.

52. Raymond, 94.

53. See Appendix to Mr. Benton's Speech on Oregon, "I. North American Road to India, 1819," US Congressional Globe, June 3, 1846, 920.

54. Thomas Hart Benton, US Congressional Globe, 916,

55. Thomas Hart Benton, 918.

56. Graebner, *Empire on the Pacific*, 218–228.

57. Weinberg, "Manifest Destiny a Study of Nationalist Expansionism in American History," 7.

58. US Congressional Globe, 32d Cong., 2d Sess., March 2, 1853, 1014.

59. US Congressional Globe, 31st Cong., 1st Sess., March 11, 1850, Appendix, 262.

60. US Congressional Globe, 32d Cong., 2d Sess., January 26, 1853, Appendix, 127.

61. June Mei, "Socioeconomic Origins of Emigration: Guangdong to California, 1850–1882," *Modern China* 5, no. 4 (1979): 463–501.

62. Taken from California state statistics in US Census Bureau, *Census of the United States* (1850, 1860, 1890), accessed January 29, 2018, census.gov.

63. John King Fairbank, *The United States and China* (Harvard University Press, 1983), 163.

64. Hobsbawm, *Age of Capital*, 287; Davids, *American Diplomatic and Public Papers*, xxix.

65. John R. Haddad, *America's First Adventure in China: Trade, Treaties, Opium, and Salvation* (Temple University Press, 2014), chapter 8.

66. Haddad, chapter 8.

67. Stephen R. Platt, *Autumn in the Heavenly Kingdom: China, the West, and the Epic Story of the Taiping Civil War* (Knopf, 2012), chapter 4.

68. See Davids, *American Diplomatic and Public Papers*.

69. McLane to Marcy, June 4, 1854, in Davids, document 24.

70. Davids, document 24.

71. Platt, *Autumn in the Heavenly Kingdom*, chapter 8.

72. See "Our Relations with China," *New York Times*, August 20, 1858.

73. "End of the China War," *New York Times*, August 27, 1858.

74. John S. Gregory, "British Intervention against the Taiping Rebellion," *Journal of Asian Studies* 19, no. 1 (1959): 17.

75. For a detailed account of Western intervention on the side of the Qing, see Platt, chapter 13 ("Vampires"), in *Autumn in the Heavenly Kingdom*.

76. Karl Marx, "Revolution in China and Europe," *New York Daily Tribune*, June 14, 1853, in Dona Torr, *Marx on China, 1853–1860: Articles from the* New York Daily Tribune (Lawrence and Wishart, 1951), 1.

77. Platt, *Autumn in the Heavenly Kingdom*, chap. 11 ("Crossings").

78. Jules Davids, *American Diplomatic and Public Papers, the United States and China: Series 2, the United States, China, and Imperial Rivalries, 1861–1893* (Scholarly Resources, 1979), xxv.

79. Hobsbawm, *Age of Capital*, 318.

80. Bensel, *The Political Economy of American Industrialization, 1877–1900*, 8.

81. Bensel, 4.

82. Bensel, 464.

83. Quoted in Graebner, *Empire on the Pacific*, 98.

84. Timothy Guy Phelps, "Pacific Railroad," US Congressional Globe, April 9, 1862, 1590.

85. Thomas Andrew Bailey, *A Diplomatic History of the American People* (Prentice-Hall, 1974), 392.

86. Alexander Saxton, *The Indispensable Enemy: Labor and the Anti-Chinese Movement in California* (University of California Press, 1995), 4.

87. William Whatley Pierson, "The Political Influences of an Interoceanic Canal, 1826–1926," *The Hispanic American Historical Review* 6, no. 4 (1926): 205–231.

88. US House Congressional Record, "China and Japan" March 9, 1878, 1618.

89. Williams, *The Roots of the Modern American Empire*, 21.

90. Williams, 20.

91. Williams, 22–26.

92. Williams, 29–32.

93. US Congress, "Report of the Joint Special Committee to Investigate Chinese Immigration," Government Printing Office, February 27, 1877, iv.

94. US Congress, iv.

95. US Congress, v.

96. Mr. Cleveland to Mr. Brown, San Francisco, July 27, 1868, in "Executive Documents Printed by Order of the House of Representatives, During the Third Session of the Fortieth Congress, 1868–69," ed. United States Department of State, *Foreign Relations of the United States 1868*, document no. 17, 531–543.

97. See US Senate Congressional Record, "Chinese Immigration," February 14, 1879, 1299–1316 for debate on consideration of HR Bill 2423 to restrict the immigration of Chinese to the United States; US House Congressional Record, "Chinese Immigration," March 15, 1882, 1932.

98. US House Congressional Record, "Chinese Immigration," March 15, 1882, 1939.

99. US House Congressional Record, 1939.

Chapter 3 • A Colonial Empire

1. Hobson, *Imperialism: A Study*, 308.

2. Lenin, *Imperialism: The Highest Stage of Capitalism*, 70.

3. Rosa Luxemburg, *The Accumulation of Capital* (Routledge, 2015), 426.

4. Zeng Guofan to Imperial Court, secret memorandum attached to letter Mr. Williams to Mr. Seward, Legation of the United States, Peking, July 1868, in "Executive Documents Printed by Order of the House of Representatives, During the Third Session of the Fortieth Congress, 1868–69," document no. 16, 519.

5. "Executive Documents," 519.

6. "Executive Documents," 519.

7. Polanyi, *The Great Transformation*, 167.

8. Chi-ming Hou, *Foreign Investment and Economic Development in China, 1840–1937*, Harvard East Asian Series; 21 (Harvard University Press, 1965), 7.

9. Hou, 7.

10. Charles Frederick Remer, *Foreign Investment in China* (Macmillan Company, 1933), 246.

11. Remer, 250.

12. Remer, 332.

13. Hou, *Foreign Investment and Economic Development in China, 1840–1937*, 9–10.

14. Remer, *Foreign Investment in China*, 252.

15. Brooks Adams, *America's Economic Supremacy*, ed. Marquis W. Childs (Harper, 1900), 221.

16. LaFeber, *The American Age*, 151.

17. Hannah Arendt, *The Origins of Totalitarianism* (Houghton Mifflin Harcourt, 1973), 123.

18. Arendt, 125.

19. Arendt, 138.

20. Alexis De Tocqueville, *Democracy in America*, vol. 10 (Regnery Publishing, 2003), 262.

21. De Tocqueville, 263.

22. Samuel Sullivan Cox, *Eight Years in Congress, from 1857–1865: Memoir and Speeches* (D. Appleton, 1865), 118.

23. US Census Bureau, "The Progress of the Nation," in *Census of the United States* (1890), xxxiv.

24. Turner, "The Significance of the Frontier in American History," 2.

25. Turner, 2.

26. Williams, *The Roots of the Modern American Empire*, xiv.

27. Frederick Jackson Turner, "The Problem of the West," *The Atlantic Monthly* (September 1896), 115.

28. Andrew Krepinevich and Robert O. Work, "A New Global Defense Posture for the Second Transoceanic Era," *Center for Strategic and Budgetary Assessments* (Washington DC: 2007), 39.

29. Pettyjohn, *US Global Defense Posture, 1783–2011*, 16.

30. David Vine, *Base Nation: How US Military Bases Abroad Harm America and the World* (Metropolitan Books, 2015), 36.

31. Krepinevich and Work, "A New Global Defense Posture for the Second Transoceanic Era," 42.

32. Calloway, *The Victory with No Name*, 5.

33. Calloway, 5.

34. US Census Bureau, "The Progress of the Nation," in *Census of the United States* (1890), xxxiv.

35. Thomas Jefferson, "Letter to John Jay," (Founders Online: National Archives, 23 August, 1785), accessed October 20, 2020, https://founders.archives.gov/documents/Jefferson/01-08-02-0333.

36. Jefferson, https://founders.archives.gov/documents/Jefferson/01-08-02-0333.

37. Samuel P. Huntington, "National Policy and the Transoceanic Navy," *US Naval Institute Proceedings* 80, no. 5 (1954): 615.

38. Theodore Roosevelt, "The Influence of Sea Power upon History. 1660–1783. By A. T. Mahan," *Political Science Quarterly* 9, no. 1 (1894): 171–173; "The Law of Civilisa-

tion and Decay," *The Forum* 12 (January 1987): 575; "National Life and Character," *The Sewanee Review* 2, no. 3 (1894): 353–376.

39. William Edward Burghardt Du Bois and Manning Marable, *Souls of Black Folk* (Routledge, 2015), 19.

40. Charles Henry Pearson, *National Life and Character: A Forecast* (Macmillan and Company, 1894), 89–90.

41. Pearson, 132–133.

42. Roosevelt, "National Life and Character," 353–376.

43. Roosevelt, "National Life and Character," 353–376.

44. Theodore Roosevelt to Pearson, 11 May 1894, quoted in John Tregenza, *Professor of Democracy: The Life of Charles Henry Pearson, 1830–1894, Oxford Don and Australian Radical* (Melbourne University, 1968), 231.

45. Brooks Adams, "The Spanish War and the Equilibrium of the World," paper presented at the Forum, 1898.

46. Adams, "The Spanish War."

47. Adams, "The Spanish War."

48. Brooks Adams, *The New Empire* (Macmillan, 1902), 190.

49. Alfred Thayer Mahan, "Hawaii and our Future Sea Power," (1893) in *The Interest of America in Sea Power, Present and Future* (Little, Brown, 1898), 31.

50. Mahan, 31.

51. Mahan to Theodore Roosevelt, 1 May 1897, in *The Letters and Papers of Alfred Thayer Mahan*, vol. 2, eds. Robert Seager II and Doris D. Maguire (Naval Institute Press, 1975), 506.

52. Anna K. Nelson, "Theodore Roosevelt, the Navy, and the War with Spain," in *Theodore Roosevelt, the US Navy, and the Spanish-American War* (Springer, 2001), 3.

53. Nelson, 3.

54. Hay to Roosevelt, 27 July 1898, cited in William Roscoe Thayer and John Hay, *The Life and Letters of John Hay*, vol. 2 (Houghton Mifflin, 1915), 337.

55. See "The Annexation of Hawaii," in Miller, *Great Debates in American History, from the Debates in the British Parliament on the Colonial Stamp Act (1764–1765) to the Debates in Congress at the Close of the Taft Administration (1912–1913)*, vol. 3 (Current Literature Pub. Co., 1913), 169–244.

56. Hoare quoted in "The Annexation of Hawaii," in Miller, 237.

57. Hoare, 238.

58. Quoted in Thomas J. McCormick, "Insular Imperialism and the Open Door: The China Market and the Spanish-American War," *Pacific Historical Review* 32 (1963): 161.

59. Williams, *The Tragedy of American Diplomacy*, 35–36.

60. Quoted in LaFeber, *The American Age*, 201.

61. Theodore Roosevelt, "Expansion and Peace," in *The Strenuous Life* (G. P. Putnam's, 1901), 23–36.

62. McCormick, "Insular Imperialism and the Open Door: The China Market and the Spanish-American War," 157.

63. Adam Tooze, *The Deluge: The Great War, America and the Remaking of the Global Order, 1916–1931* (Penguin Group USA, 2015), 52.

64. "What Is the 'Open Door'?," *New York Times*, January 26, 1899, 1.

65. W. M. Roger Louis and Ronald Robinson, "The Imperialism of Decolonization," *The Journal of Imperial and Commonwealth History* 22, no. 3 (1994): 462–511; McCormick, "Insular Imperialism and the Open Door: The China Market and the Spanish-American War," 169.

66. Smedley Darlington Butler, *War Is a Racket: The Antiwar Classic by America's Most Decorated Soldier* (Simon and Schuster, 2016).

67. Theodore Roosevelt, "The Roosevelt Corollary to the Monroe Doctrine," paper presented at the excerpt from president's annual message to Congress, the White House, 1904.

68. Roosevelt, "The Roosevelt Corollary."

69. Roosevelt, "The Roosevelt Corollary."

70. For an example of Jefferson's correspondence on the matter see "From Thomas Jefferson to Jean Baptiste Le Roy, 13 November 1786," Founders Online, National Archives, accessed September 29, 2019, https://founders.archives.gov/documents /Jefferson/01-10-02-0381. (Original source: Thomas Jefferson, Julian P. Boyd, and Ruth W. Lester, *The Papers of Thomas Jefferson*, vol. 10 [Princeton University Press, 1974], 524–530.) For information on the progressive initiatives of presidential administrations throughout the nineteenth century on the cutting of an isthmian canal, see Alfred Williams, *The Inter-Oceanic Canal and the Monroe Doctrine* (GP Putnam's Sons, 1880).

71. Theodore Roosevelt, "State of the Union Address, December 3, 1901," *State of the Union*, (1901), accessed December 23, 2022, https://history.state.gov/historical documents/frus1901/message-of-the-president.

72. Wilson quoted in Williams, *The Tragedy of American Diplomacy*, 66.

Chapter 4 • The 30 Years Crisis

1. William Appleman Williams, "The Legend of Isolationism in the 1920's," *Science & Society* (1954), 1–20; Bear F. Braumoeller, "The Myth of American Isolationism," *Foreign Policy Analysis* 6, no. 4 (2010): 349–371.

2. See table 6 of comparative major war materials production in Ioannis-Dionysios Salavrakos, "The Defence Industry as an Explanatory Factor of the German Defeat during World War I: Lessons for Future Conflicts," *International Journal of History and Philosophical Research* 2, no. 1 (2014): 1–34.

3. Salavrakos, 1–34.

4. Salavrakos, 1–34.

5. Sam Gindin and Leo Panitch, *The Making of Global Capitalism* (Verso Books, 2012), 10.

6. Cited in Robert Cuff, "The Dollar-a-Year Men of the Great War," *The Princeton University Library Chronicle* 30, no. 1 (1968): 10.

7. Bernard Mannes Baruch, *American Industry in the War: A Report of the War Industries Board* (Prentice-Hall, 1921), 5.

8. Darwin, *After Tamerlane.*

9. Darwin.

10. Darwin, 365.

11. Tooze, *The Deluge*, 415.

12. Giovanni Arrighi, *The Long Twentieth Century: Money, Power, and the Origins of Our Times* (Verso, 1994), 279.

13. Jones, *The Consumer Society*, vol. 780, 281.

14. Grosvenor B. Clarkson, *Industrial America in the World War: The Strategy behind the Line, 1917–1918* (Houghton Mifflin, 1923), 9.

15. Clarkson, 485.

16. Woodrow Wilson and Ollie M. James, *Speech of Governor Wilson Accepting the Democratic Nomination for President of the United States*, 62nd Congress, Second Session, Senate, doc. 903 (Government Printing Office, 1912).

17. Woodrow Wilson, "Message Regarding Tariff Duties," April 8, 1913, accessed December 23, 2022, https://millercenter.org/the-presidency/presidential-speeches /april-8-1913-message-regarding-tariff-duties.

18. Wilson and James, *Speech of Governor Wilson Accepting the Democratic Nomination*.

19. Woodrow Wilson, "Address at the Princeton Sesqui-Centennial Celebration, October 21, 1896," in August Heckscher, *The Politics of Woodrow Wilson: Selections from His Speeches and Writings* (Harper, 1956), 129.

20. Lovering, *Minerals in World Affairs*, 75.

21. Alfred E. Eckes Jr., *The United States and the Global Struggle for Minerals* (University of Texas Press, 1979), 13.

22. C. K. Leith, "Exploitation and World Progress," *Foreign Affairs* 6 (1927), 129–130.

23. Leith, 131.

24. Leith, 131.

25. Quoted in Eckes Jr., *The United States and the Global Struggle for Minerals,* 23.

26. C. K. Leith, *Minerals in the Peace Settlement*, vol. 1 (The Society, 1940), 3; Eckes Jr., *The United States and the Global Struggle for Minerals*, 28.

27. Eckes Jr., *The United States and the Global Struggle for Minerals*, 29.

28. Abraham Berglund, "The Iron and Steel Industry of Japan and Japanese Continental Policies," *Journal of Political Economy* 30, no. 5 (1922): 654.

29. Adams, *The New Empire*, 190.

30. Eckes Jr., *The United States and the Global Struggle for Minerals*, 30.

31. Theodore Roosevelt to Franklin Roosevelt, 10 May 1913, quoted in William L. Neumann, "Franklin Delano Roosevelt: A Disciple of Admiral Mahan," *United States Naval Institute Proceedings* 78 (1952): 713–14.

32. Louis Morton, "War Plan Orange: Evolution of a Strategy," *World Politics* 11, no. 2 (1959): 224.

33. Albert Gleaves, "Letter: From Commander in Chief to Secretary of the Navy. Subject: Observations on Japanese Character, with Special Reference to Japan's Ambition and Her Relation in This Connection with the United States.," September 8, 1920, ed. 12th Naval District Record Group 181 Commandant, US National Archives San Bruno, 14-5, box 2.

34. Quoted in Tooze, *The Deluge*, 30.

35. Frank Herman Schofield, "Some Effects of the Washington Conference on American Naval Strategy," lecture delivered at Army War College, Washington, DC,

Barracks, September 22, 1923, 12th Naval District, Record Group 181 Commandant, US National Archives San Bruno, 270-3, box 4.

36. Nicholas John Spykman, *America's Strategy in World Politics: The United States and the Balance of Power* (Transaction Publishers, 1942), 160.

37. Henry P. Frei, *Japan's Southward Advance and Australia: From the Sixteenth Century to World War II* (University of Hawaii Press, 1991), 125–128.

38. George H. Blackslee, "The Japanese Monroe Doctrine," *Foreign Affairs* 11 (1932): 672.

39. Remer, *Foreign Investment in China*, 77.

40. Remer, 78.

41. Remer, 76.

42. Remer, 77.

43. Eugene Staley, *War and the Private Investor: A Study in the Relations of International Politics and International Private Investment* (Doubleday, Doran & Company, 1935), 13.

44. Staley, Appendix A.

45. Fairbank, *The United States and China*, 324.

46. W. Y. Elliott, *Atlantic Monthly*, October 1933, 424, quoted in David S. Jacks and Dennis Novy, "Trade Blocs and Trade Wars during the Interwar Period," *Asian Economic Policy Review* 15, no. 1 (2020): 119.

47. Marion Clawson, *New Deal Planning: The National Resources Planning Board* (RFF Press, 2013), 121.

48. Jonathan Marshall, *To Have and Have Not: Southeast Asian Raw Materials and the Origins of the Pacific War* (University of California Press, 1995), 7–9, 33.

49. US House Congressional Record, April 25, 1939, 4771.

50. Robert Burnett Hall, "American Raw-Material Deficiencies and Regional Dependence," *Geographical Review* 30, no. 2 (1940): 183.

51. Hall, 185–186.

52. Hall, 185–186.

53. Hall, 185–186.

54. Quoted in Marshall, *To Have and Have Not*, 72.

55. Charles Faddis (D, Pennsylvania) in US House Congressional Record, "Congressional Debate on the Construction of Naval Vessels," March 12, 1940, 2744–2747.

56. Spykman, *America's Strategy in World Politics*, 468.

57. Spykman, 155.

58. Marshall, *To Have and Have Not*, 181.

59. Franklin P. Huddle, "The Evolving National Policy for Materials," *Science* 191, no. 4228 (1976): 654.

60. Elmer W. Pehrson, "The Axis and Strategic Minerals," *Engineering and Mining Journal* 143, no. 5 (1942): 42.

61. C. K. Leith, "Mineral Resources and Peace," *Foreign Affairs* 16 (1937), 522.

62. Pehrson, "The Axis and Strategic Minerals," 42.

63. Halford John Mackinder, "The Geographical Pivot of History" (The Geographical Society, 1904).

64. Halford John Mackinder, *Democratic Ideals and Reality a Study in the Politics of Reconstruction* (Diane Publishing, 1942), 106.

65. Lucian M. Ashworth, "Realism and the Spirit of 1919: Halford Mackinder, Geopolitics and the Reality of the League of Nations," *European Journal of International Relations* 17, no. 2 (2011): 284.

66. Nicholas John Spykman, *Geography of the Peace* (Harcourt, Brace and Company, 1944), 43.

67. Colin S. Gray, "Nicholas John Spykman, the Balance of Power, and International Order," *Journal of Strategic Studies* 38, no. 6 (2015): 878.

68. Spykman, *America's Strategy in World Politics*, 469.

69. Spykman, 448.

70. Spykman, 448–449.

71. Spykman, 457.

72. Franklin D. Roosevelt, "Address at University of Virginia," June 10, 1940, online by Gerhard Peters and John T. Woolley, The American Presidency Project, accessed December 23, 2022, https://www.presidency.ucsb.edu/node/209705.

73. Spykman, *America's Strategy in World Politics*, 457.

74. For an account of the reviews and misinterpretations of Spykman's work by many liberal scholars, see Gray, "Nicholas John Spykman, the Balance of Power, and International Order," 879–880.

Chapter 5 • American Hegemony

1. Paul Kennedy, *The Rise and Fall of the Great Powers* (Vintage, 2010), see chapters 5 and 6.

2. See for example De Tocqueville, *Democracy in America*, vol. 10, book 1, "Conclusion."

3. Gabriel Kolko, *The Politics of War: The World and United States Foreign Policy, 1943–1945*, vol. 631 (Random House, 1968), 245–246.

4. "An American Proposal," *Fortune Magazine*, May 1942. For a full account, see Gindin and Panitch, *The Making of Global Capitalism*, chapter 3.

5. "An American Proposal," *Fortune Magazine*. See also LaFeber, *The American Age*, 380.

6. Geir Lundestad, *The Rise and Decline of the American "Empire": Power and Its Limits in Comparative Perspective* (Oxford University Press, 2012), 12.

7. Lundestad, 12.

8. Lundestad, 12, and Geir Lundestad, "Empire by Invitation? The United States and Western Europe, 1945–1952," *Journal of Peace Research* 23, no. 3 (1986): 264.

9. Arrighi, *The Long Twentieth Century*, 284.

10. Vine, *Base Nation*, 36.

11. Quoted in Lundestad, *The Rise and Decline of the American "Empire,"* 12.

12. Darwin, *After Tamerlane*, 470–471.

13. Christopher Layne, *The Peace of Illusions: American Grand Strategy from 1940 to the Present* (Cornell University Press, 2007) 3.

14. Harold J. Laski, "America-1947," *The Nation* 13 (1947), 641.

15. Quoted in Lundestad, *The Rise and Decline of the American "Empire,"* 11.

16. George William Domhoff, *Who Rules America?*, vol. 167 (Englewood Cliffs, 1967), 74.

17. Marshall, *To Have and Have Not*, 29.

18. Kolko, *The Politics of War*, vol. 631, 247.

19. Quoted in Marshall, *To Have and Have Not*, 30.

20. Peter Grose, *Continuing the Inquiry: The Council on Foreign Relations from 1921 to 1996* (Council on Foreign Relations Press, 1996), 7.

21. Grose, 8.

22. Laurence H. Shoup and William Minter, *Imperial Brain Trust: The Council on Foreign Relations and United States Foreign Policy* (Monthly Review Press, 2004), 58.

23. Marshall, *To Have and Have Not*, 30–31; Shoup and Minter, *Imperial Brain Trust*, 128.

24. Joyce Kolko and Gabriel Kolko, *The Limits of Power: The World and United States Foreign Policy, 1945–1954* (Harper & Row, 1972), 257.

25. Kolko and Kolko, 552.

26. Woodrow Wilson Foundation and William Yandell Elliot, *The Political Economy of American Foreign Policy* (Holt, 1955), 7 and 388.

27. George Kennan, "The Sources of Soviet Conduct," *Foreign Affairs* 25, no. 4 (1947): 566–582.

28. Kennan, 575.

29. Woodrow Wilson Foundation and Elliot, *The Political Economy of American Foreign Policy*, 211.

30. Johnson, *Dismantling the Empire*, 107.

31. Christopher T. Sandars, *America's Overseas Garrisons: The Leasehold Empire* (Oxford University Press on Demand, 2000), 25.

32. Thomas J. McCormick, *America's Half-Century: United States Foreign Policy in the Cold War and After* (Johns Hopkins University Press, 1995), 57.

33. Hal M. Friedman, *Creating an American Lake: United States Imperialism and Strategic Security in the Pacific Basin, 1945–1947* (Greenwood Publishing Group, 2001), 48. Cites statements and correspondences from Secretary of the Navy James Forrestall, Fleet Admiral Chester Nimitz, and many others including the Joint Chiefs of Staff to support this sentiment.

34. Michael J. Green, *By More Than Providence: Grand Strategy and American Power in the Asia Pacific Since 1783* (Columbia University Press, 2017), 205–206.

35. Quoted in Sandars, *America's Overseas Garrisons*, 35.

36. Friedman, *Creating an American Lake*, 41.

37. Friedman, 42.

38. Green, *By More Than Providence*, 207.

39. Used in this context by Julian S. Corbett, *Principles of Maritime Strategy* (Courier Corporation, 2012), 91; and by Alfred Thayer Mahan, *The Influence of Sea Power upon History, 1660–1783* (Read Books Ltd., 2013), 539–540.

40. Quoted in Robert Frank Futrell, *Ideas, Concepts, Doctrine: Basic Thinking in the United States Air Force* (Diane Publishing, 1980), 292.

41. Sandars, *America's Overseas Garrisons*, 154.

42. Michael Schaller, *The American Occupation of Japan: The Origins of the Cold War in Asia* (Oxford University Press, 1985), 90.

43. Special Ad Hoc Committee and State-War-Navy Coordinating Committee, "(1947) Report of Committee Meeting, 21 April," *Foreign Relations of the United States* 3, 164–165.

44. George Kennan, "US State Department Policy Planning Staff Document Pps 23, Feb. 24, 1948," *Foreign Relations of the United States* 1 (1948): 509–529.

45. Kennan, 509–529.

46. Kennan, 509–529.

47. Dean Acheson, "Speech on the Far East," speech given at the National Press Club, Washington, DC (1950), accessed December 22, 2022, https://www.cia.gov /readingroom/docs/1950-01-12.pdf.

48. Lundestad, "Empire by Invitation?," 23–24.

49. Vine, *Base Nation*, 30.

50. Senate Committee on Foreign Relations, cited in Sandars, *America's Overseas Garrisons*, 9.

51. Sandars, 9.

52. Andrew Henry Thomas Berding, "Dulles on Diplomacy," (Van Nostrand, 1965), 63–64.

53. John Foster Dulles, "Security in the Pacific," *Foreign Affairs* 30, no. 2 (1952): 181–182.

54. Sandars, *America's Overseas Garrisons*.

55. Julian Go, *Patterns of Empire: The British and American Empires, 1688 to the Present* (Cambridge University Press, 2011), 142.

56. John Hargreaves, "Decolonisation: French and British Styles," in *State and Society in Francophone Africa Since Independence* (Springer, 1995), 5.

57. Louis and Robinson, "The Imperialism of Decolonization," 462–511.

58. Norman Brook to Attlee, 14 January 1948, quoted in Hargreaves, "Decolonisation: French and British Styles," 6.

59. For a full account of these, see William Blum, *Killing Hope: US Military and CIA Interventions Since World War II* (Zed Books, 2003). See also Alfred W. McCoy, *In the Shadows of the American Century: The Rise and Decline of US Global Power* (Haymarket Books, 2017), chapter 1.

60. Williams, *The Tragedy of American Diplomacy*, 53.

61. Lundestad, "Empire by Invitation?," 263–277.

62. Harry S. Truman, "Address on Foreign Economic Policy, Delivered at Baylor University," (March 6, 1947), accessed February 12, 2020, https://www.trumanlibrary .gov/library/public-papers/52/address-foreign-economic-policy-delivered-baylor -university.

63. Truman, https://www.trumanlibrary.gov/library/public-papers/52/address -foreign-economic-policy-delivered-baylor-university.

64. Quoted in Kolko, *The Politics of War*, vol. 631, 257.

65. Kolko and Kolko, *The Limits of Power*, 21.

66. Kolko and Kolko, 20–21.

67. See John Gerard Ruggie, "International Regimes, Transactions, and Change: Embedded Liberalism in the Postwar Economic Order," *International Organization* 36, no. 2 (1982): 379–415.

68. Gindin and Panitch, *The Making of Global Capitalism*, 7.

69. Harry S. Truman, "Special Message to the Congress on Greece and Turkey: The Truman Doctrine," (March 12, 1947), as delivered in person before a joint session, accessed February 12, 2020, https://quod.lib.umich.edu/p/ppotpus/4728447.1947 .001?rgn=main;view=fulltext.

70. McCormick, *America's Half-Century*, 76.
71. McCormick, 78.
72. McCormick, 78–79.
73. McCormick, 74.
74. Quoted in Schaller, *The American Occupation of Japan*, 219.
75. Schaller, 219.
76. Dulles, "Security in the Pacific," 184–185.
77. Kolko, *The Politics of War*, vol. 631, 545.
78. US Senate, *Trade Agreements Extension: Hearings before the Committee on Finance, United States Senate, Eighty-Fourth Congress, First Session, on H.R. 1*, 1256 (1955).

Chapter 6 • War with Asia, Recession, and Resurgence

1. Acheson, "Speech on the Far East."
2. US National Security Council, "United States Objectives and Programs for National Security," (April 14, 1950), 6.
3. US National Security Council, 4.
4. McCormick, *America's Half-Century*, 98.
5. US National Security Council, "United States Objectives and Programs for National Security," 30.
6. Green, *By More Than Providence*, 271; Walton S. Moody, Walter S. Poole, and David A. Armstrong, "History of the Joint Chiefs of Staff: The Joint Chiefs of Staff and the First Indochina War, 1947–1954," (Joint Chiefs of Staff Joint History Office, 2004), 36.
7. Green, *By More Than Providence*, 275.
8. McCormick, *America's Half-Century*, 105.
9. McCormick, 105.
10. Kolko and Kolko, *The Limits of Power*, 642.
11. Kolko and Kolko, 642–643.
12. Kolko and Kolko, 644.
13. Arrighi, *The Long Twentieth Century*, 307.
14. Green, *By More Than Providence*, 287.
15. Moody, Poole, and Armstrong, "History of the Joint Chiefs of Staff," 35.
16. Dwight D. Eisenhower, "Remarks at the Governors' Conference, Seattle, Washington," The American Presidency Project, August 4, 1953, accessed December 22, 2022, https://www.presidency.ucsb.edu/documents/remarks-the-governors-conference-seattle-washington.
17. Eisenhower, "Remarks at the Governors' Conference."
18. Dwight D. Eisenhower, "The President's News Conference," The American Presidency Project, April 7, 1954, accessed December 22, 2022, https://www.presidency.ucsb.edu/documents/the-presidents-news-conference-361.
19. Richard M. Nixon, "Asia after Viet Nam," *Foreign Affairs* 46, no. 1 (1967): 111.
20. Kolko and Kolko, *The Limits of Power*, 683–684.
21. For more on the CIA's role in this and many other military coups during this era, see McCoy, *In the Shadows of the American Century*, chapter 2.
22. Robert McNamara, "Draft Memorandum from Secretary of Defense McNamara to President Johnson," Washington National Records Center, RG 330, McNamara Files,

FRC 71 A 3470, South Vietnam, Statements and Supporting Papers, Top Secret, November 3, 1965.

23. McNamara, RG 330.

24. McNamara, RG 330.

25. See McCormick, *America's Half-Century*, 115.

26. Arthur M. Schlesinger, *The Bitter Heritage: Vietnam and American Democracy, 1941–1968* (Fawcett Publications, 1968), 7.

27. Stephen Pelz, "John F. Kennedy's 1961 Vietnam War Decisions," *Journal of Strategic Studies* 4, no. 4 (1981): 356.

28. Quoted in Michael H. Hunt, *Lyndon Johnson's War: America's Cold War Crusade in Vietnam, 1945–1968* (Macmillan, 1997), 77.

29. For a detailed analysis of the signals-intelligence mishandling that concludes no attack occurred, published in the classified internal journal of NSA *Cryptologic Quarterly,* see Robert J. Hanyok, *Skunks, Bogies, Silent Hounds, and the Flying Fish: The Gulf of Tonkin Mystery, 2–4 August 1964* (Center for Cryptologic History, National Security Agency, 1998). For the digital archive of declassified National Security Agency documents on the incident see https://www.nsa.gov/news-features/declassified-documents /gulf-of-tonkin/ (accessed February 10, 2020).

30. Quoted in Hanyok, 46.

31. Carl Berger, *The United States Air Force in Southeast Asia, 1961–1973* (Office of Air Force History, 1977), 366.

32. Ziad Obermeyer, Christopher J. L. Murray, and Emmanuela Gakidou, "Fifty Years of Violent War Deaths from Vietnam to Bosnia: Analysis of Data from the World Health Survey Programme," *British Medical Journal* 336, no. 7659 (2008): 1482–1486.

33. US National Security Council, "U.S. Plan of Action to Curb the Threat of Chinese Communist Infiltration in Southeast Asia," (US Declassified Documents Online, 25 September, 1959), accessed July 23, 2018, http://tinyurl.galegroup.com/tinyurl/ 6nFpZ3.

34. Hans J. Morgenthau, *United States Policy toward Asia, Hearings before the Subcommittee on the Far East and the Pacific of the Committee on Foreign Affairs*, 89th Congress House of Respresentatives, Second Session, 128 (January 25, 26, 27, and February 1, 2, 3, 1966).

35. Jacob Javits in US Senate Congressional Record, "Legislative Proposals Relating to the War in Southeast Asia," 92nd Congress, First Session, 104 (April 21, 1971).

36. Richard M. Nixon, "Informal Remarks in Guam with Newsmen," The American Presidency Project, July 25, 1969, accessed June 12, 2020, https://www.presidency.ucsb .edu/documents/informal-remarks-guam-with-newsmen.

37. Nixon, https://www.presidency.ucsb.edu/documents/informal-remarks-guam -with-newsmen.

38. Richard M. Nixon, "First Annual Report to the Congress on United States Foreign Policy for the 1970's," The American Presidency Project, February 18, 1970, accessed December 23, 2022, https://www.presidency.ucsb.edu/documents/first -annual-report-the-congress-united-states-foreign-policy-for-the-1970s.

39. Green, *By More Than Providence*, 339.

40. Earl C. Ravenal, "The Nixon Doctrine and Our Asian Commitments," *Foreign Affairs* 49, no. 2 (1971): 202.

41. Nixon, "Asia after Viet Nam," 113.

42. Nixon, "Asia after Viet Nam," 119.

43. Green, *By More Than Providence*, 319–320.

44. Henry A. Kissinger, "Central Issues of American Foreign Policy," *Agenda for the Nation* (Brookings Institution, 1968), 585–614.

45. Kissinger, 585–614.

46. "Summary of Kissinger Speech to U.S. Ambassadors," *New York Times*, April 7, 1976.

47. "Summary of Kissinger Speech," *New York Times*.

48. White House, "David Aaron and Michel Oksenberg Provide Vice President Walter Mondale with a List of U.S. Objectives for Mondale's Trip to China," US Declassified Documents Online, August 18, 1979, Memo, accessed December 23, 2022, https://tinyurl.com/4ca8t3zd.

49. Gindin and Panitch, *The Making of Global Capitalism*, 126.

50. McCormick, *America's Half-Century*, 157.

51. McCormick, 157.

52. LaFeber, *The American Age*, 581.

53. LaFeber, 611.

54. LaFeber, 610.

55. Peter M. Garber, "The Collapse of the Bretton Woods Fixed Exchange Rate System," in *A Retrospective on the Bretton Woods System: Lessons for International Monetary Reform* (University of Chicago Press, 1993), 469–470.

56. Joseph Vogl, *The Ascendancy of Finance* (John Wiley & Sons, 2017), 401–402.

57. Fernand Braudel, *Civilization and Capitalism, 15th–18th Century, Vol. III: The Perspective of the World* (University of California Press, 1992), 246.

58. Eric J. Hobsbawm and Marion Cumming, *Age of Extremes: The Short Twentieth Century, 1914–1991* (Abacus London, 1995), 474.

59. McCormick, *America's Half-Century*, 164.

60. Gindin and Panitch, *The Making of Global Capitalism*, 122.

61. McCormick, *America's Half-Century*, 166.

62. McCormick, 166.

63. Green, *By More Than Providence*, 368.

64. Jock A. Finlayson and David G. Haglund, "Whatever Happened to the Resource War?," *Survival* 29, no. 5 (1987): 403; Susan Gilpin, "Minerals and Foreign Policy," *Africa Report* 27, no. 3 (1982): 16.

65. US National Security Council, "Two Versions of a Draft on US National Strategy Suggest: US Needs to Counter Soviet Influence over the Oil Producing States in the Persian Gulf Region; and Communist Persuasion Could Undermine the Viability of NATO and Cause Economic Disruptions in Europe, Japan and the US," US Declassified Documents Online, December 20, 1980, Memo, accessed December 23, 2022, https://tinyurl.com/2p8v2knx.

66. Al Gedicks, *The New Resource Wars: Native and Environmental Struggles against Multinational Corporations*, vol. 210 (Black Rose Books Ltd., 1994), 41.

67. McCormick, *America's Half-Century*, 217.

68. LaFeber, *The American Age*, 667.

69. Ronald Reagan, "National Security Decision Directive Number 32," Washington,

DC, May 20, 1982, accessed December 23, 2022, https://irp.fas.org/offdocs/nsdd/23
-1618t.gif.

70. Reagan, "National Security."

71. McCormick, *America's Half-Century*, 194.

72. Hobsbawm and Cumming, *Age of Extremes*, 403.

73. Hobsbawm and Cumming, 408.

74. Francis Fukuyama, "The End of History?," *The National Interest*, no. 16 (1989):
3–4.

75. Fukuyama, 11.

Chapter 7 • *The Unipolar Moment and Imperial Hubris*

1. Andrew J. Bacevich, "Ending Endless War: A Pragmatic Military Strategy," *Foreign Affairs* 95, no. 5 (2016): 36.

2. Andrew J. Bacevich, *The Age of Illusions: How America Squandered Its Cold War Victory* (Metropolitan Books, 2020), 12.

3. George H. W. Bush, *National Security Strategy of the United States* (White House, 1991), v, accessed December 23, 2022, https://history.defense.gov/Portals/70 /Documents/nss/nss1991.pdf?ver=3sIpLiQwmknO-RplyPeAHw%3d%3d.

4. Bacevich, *The Age of Illusions*, 122.

5. Colin L. Powell, "US Forces: Challenges Ahead," *Foreign Affairs* 71, no. 5 (1992): 32–45.

6. Bush, *National Security Strategy of the United States*, 9.

7. James A. Baker III, "America in Asia: Emerging Architecture for a Pacific Community," *Foreign Affairs* 70, no. 1 (1990): 3–4.

8. Bush, *National Security Strategy of the United States*, 2.

9. Bush, 6.

10. Paul Wolfowitz, "Defense Planning Guidance, FY 1994–1999 (Declassified 2008)," (National Security Council).

11. Bacevich, *American Empire*, 45.

12. Bacevich, 46.

13. Clinton quoted in Bacevich, 86.

14. Christopher quoted in Bacevich, 85.

15. Gindin and Panitch, *The Making of Global Capitalism*, 184.

16. Gindin and Panitch, 184.

17. Gindin and Panitch, 184.

18. Les Aspin, *Report on the Bottom-up Review* (US Department of Defense, October 1993), 1, accessed December 23, 2022, https://history.defense.gov/Portals/70 /Documents/dod_reforms/Bottom-upReview.pdf.

19. Aspin, 3.

20. William J. Clinton, *A National Security Strategy of Engagement and Enlargement* (White House, July 1994), 1, 13–14, accessed December 23, 2022, https://history .defense.gov/Portals/70/Documents/nss/nss1994.pdf.

21. Clinton, 24.

22. Clinton, 2.

23. See Ho-fung Hung, "The Periphery in the Making of Globalization: The China

Lobby and the Reversal of Clinton's China Trade Policy, 1993–1994," *Review of International Political Economy* 28, no. 4, (2020): 1–24; and "The US-China Rivalry Is About Capitalist Competition," *Jacobin*, November 7, 2020, accessed July 13, 2020, https://www.jacobinmag.com/2020/07/us-china-competition-capitalism-rivalry.

24. Joseph S. Nye Jr., "The Case for Deep Engagement," *Foreign Affairs* 74, no. 4 (1995): 94–95, 100.

25. William J. Clinton, "Remarks to the World Economic Forum and a Question-and-Answer Session in Davos, Switzerland," Online by Gerhard Peters and John T. Woolley, The American Presidency Project, accessed December 23, 2022, https://www.presidency.ucsb.edu/node/227554.

26. W. Bowman Cutter, Joan Spero, and Laura D'Andrea Tyson, "New World, New Deal: A Democratic Approach to Globalization," *Foreign Affairs* 79, no. 2 (2000): 88.

27. George H. W. Bush, "Remarks at the Yale University Commencement Ceremony in New Haven, Connecticut, May 27, 1991," *Public Papers of the Presidents* (1991), 567.

28. Robert B. Zoellick, "Whither China: From Membership to Responsibility?," Remarks to National Committee on U.S.-China Relations, New York City, September 21, 2005, accessed December 23, 2022, https://2001-2009.state.gov/s/d/former/zoellick/rem/53682.htm.

29. For some of the most prominent examples, see Gordon G. Chang, *The Coming Collapse of China* (Random House, 2010); Minxin Pei, *China's Trapped Transition* (Harvard University Press, 2006); and David Shambaugh, "The Coming Chinese Crackup," *Wall Street Journal*, March 6, 2015.

30. Andrew J. Nathan, "China's Changing of the Guard: Authoritarian Resilience," in *Critical Readings on the Communist Party of China*, 4 vols. set (Brill, 2017), 86.

31. John Keane, *When Trees Fall, Monkeys Scatter: Rethinking Democracy in China* (World Scientific, 2017), 152.

32. Andrew J. Nathan, "China's Challenge," *Journal of Democracy* 26, no. 1 (2015): 168.

33. John Keane, *The New Despotism* (Harvard University Press, 2020), 234.

34. Richard N. Haass, "The Squandered Presidency: Demanding More from the Commander-in-Chief," *Foreign Affairs* 79, no. 1 (2000): 136.

35. Haass, 139.

36. "Military expenditure by country as percentage of gross domestic product, 1988–2019," DB SIPRI, Sipri Military Expenditure Database, (Stockholm International Peace Research Institute Solna, 2019), accessed May 26, 2020, https://www.sipri.org/databases/milex.

37. "Military expenditure by country, in constant (2018) US$ m., 1988–2019," DB SIPRI, https://www.sipri.org/databases/milex.

38. Samuel R. Berger, "American Power: Hegemony, Isolationism or Engagement," Address to the Council on Foreign Relations, October 21, 1999, accessed December 23, 2022, https://clintonwhitehouse4.archives.gov/textonly/WH/EOP/NSC/html/speeches/19991021.html.

39. George W. Bush, "A Distinctly American Internationalism," November 19, 1999, speech delivered at Ronald Reagan Presidential Library, Simi Valley, California, in *The George W. Bush Foreign Policy Reader: Presidential Speeches with Commentary*, John W. Dietrich (Taylor & Francis Group, 2005), 26.

40. Bush, "The National Security Strategy of the United States of America," (Executive Office of the President, 2002), ii, accessed December 23, 2022, https://georgewbush-whitehouse.archives.gov/nsc/nss/2002/.

41. Bush, ii.

42. Warren I. Cohen, *America's Response to China: A History of Sino-American Relations* (Columbia University Press, 2019), 270.

43. David Brewster, "The Australia–India Security Declaration," *Security Challenges* 6, no. 1 (2010): 3.

44. Brewster, 3.

45. US Census Bureau, "US International Trade Data: Trade in Goods with Asia," accessed June 25, 2020, https://www.census.gov/foreign-trade/balance/c0016.html.

46. US Census Bureau, "US International Trade Data: Trade in Goods with China," accessed June 25, 2020, https://www.census.gov/foreign-trade/balance/c5700.html.

47. US Department of Commerce, "Balance of Payments and Direct Investment Position Data: US-China," ed. Bureau of Economic Analysis (2020), accessed June 26, 2020, https://apps.bea.gov/iTable/iTable.cfm?ReqID=2&step=1#reqid=2&step=10&isuri=1&202=1&203=30&204=10&205=1,2&200=1&201=1&207=56,55,52,49,48,43,42,41,40,39,38,37,36,35,34,33,32,31&208=2&209=1.

48. Bush, "The National Security Strategy of the United States of America," 27.

49. Donald Kagan and Thomas Donnelly, *Rebuilding America's Defences: Strategy, Forces and Resources For a New Century, A Report of The Project for the New American Century* (Washington, DC: 2000), i.

50. Robert Kagan, "Neocon Nation: Neoconservatism, C. 1776," *World Affairs* 170, no. 4 (2008): 13–35.

51. See Kagan and Donnelly, *Rebuilding America's Defences.*

52. *Washington Post*, "Transcript: President Bush Addresses the Nation," September 20, 2001, accessed December 23, 2022, https://www.washingtonpost.com/wp-srv/nation/specials/attacked/transcripts/bushaddress_092001.html.

53. *Washington Post*, https://www.washingtonpost.com/wp-srv/nation/specials/attacked/transcripts/bushaddress_092001.html.

54. *Washington Post*, https://www.washingtonpost.com/wp-srv/nation/specials/attacked/transcripts/bushaddress_092001.html.

55. Neta C. Crawford, "United States Budgetary Costs of the Post-9/11 Wars through FY2020: $6.4 Trillion Spent and Obligated," Watson Institute for International & Public Affairs, Brown University, 2019, accessed December 23, 2022, https://watson.brown.edu/costsofwar/figures/2019/budgetary-costs-post-911-wars-through-fy2020-64-trillion.

56. Neta C. Crawford and Catherine Lutz, "Human Cost of Post-9/11 Wars: Direct War Deaths in Major War Zones," Watson Institute for International & Public Affairs, Brown University, 2019, accessed December 23, 2022, https://watson.brown.edu/costsofwar/figures/2021/WarDeathToll.

57. See Chalmers Johnson, *Blowback: The Costs and Consequences of American Empire* (Macmillan, 2000).

58. Ron Suskind, "Faith, Certainty and the Presidency of George W. Bush," *New York Times*, October 17, 2004.

59. Some notable examples of this approach include Michael Ignatieff, "The Ameri-

can Empire (Get Used to It)," *New York Times Magazine*, January 6, 2003; Ferguson, *Colossus: The Rise and Fall of the American Empire*.

60. Eric Hobsbawm, *On Empire: America, War, and Global Supremacy* (Pantheon, 2008), 51–52.

61. Hobsbawm, 55; and Eric Hobsbawm, "America's Imperial Delusion," *Guardian*, June 13, 2003.

62. For more on this theme, see Harvey, *The New Imperialism*, 24–25.

63. Kennedy, *The Rise and Fall of the Great Powers*, 515.

Chapter 8 • The Sleeper Awakes

1. Adam Smith, *The Wealth of Nations: An Inquiry into the Nature and Causes of the Wealth of Nations* (Harriman House Limited, 2010), 78, 529.

2. See Andre Gunder Frank, *Reorient: Global Economy in the Asian Age* (University of California Press, 1998).

3. Ho-fung Hung, *The China Boom: Why China Will Not Rule the World* (Columbia University Press, 2015), 50.

4. "China at a Glance," World Bank, accessed July 6, 2020, https://www.worldbank .org/en/country/china/testpagecheck#:~:text=China%20At%2DA%2DGlance&text =GDP%20growth%20has%20averaged%20nearly,MDGs)%20by%20201... (page discontinued).

5. Wayne M. Morrison, *China's Economic Rise: History, Trends, Challenges, and Implications for the United States* (Congressional Research Service, 2019).

6. Jonathan Woetzel, "China and the World: Inside the Dynamics of a Changing Relationship," McKinsey Global Institute, July 1, 2019, 2, accessed December 23, 2022, https://www.mckinsey.com/featured-insights/china/china-and-the-world-inside-the -dynamics-of-a-changing-relationship.

7. National Intelligence Council, *Global Trends 2030: Alternative Worlds* (Central Intelligence Agency, 2013), 2.

8. For more on the "great divergence," see Kenneth Pomeranz, *The Great Divergence: China, Europe, and the Making of the Modern World Economy* (Princeton University Press, 2000).

9. Giovanni Arrighi, *Adam Smith in Beijing: Lineages of the Twenty-First Century* (Verso Trade, 2007), 352.

10. Hung, *The China Boom*, 56.

11. Section 11-13, "Utilization of Foreign Capital," and Section 18-7, "Gold and Foreign Currency Reserves," China Statistical Yearbook 2019, National Bureau of Statistics of China, accessed July 7, 2020, http://www.stats.gov.cn/tjsj/ndsj/2019 /indexeh.htm.

12. Sebastian Horn, Carmen M. Reinhart, and Christoph Trebesch, "How Much Money Does the World Owe China," *Harvard Business Review*, February 26, 2020, accessed December 23, 2022, https://hbr.org/2020/02/how-much-money-does-the -world-owe-china.

13. For a full account of this system see, Kiyoshi Kojima, "The 'Flying Geese' Model of Asian Economic Development: Origin, Theoretical Extensions, and Regional Policy Implications," *Journal of Asian Economics* 11, no. 4 (2000): 375–401.

14. Chih-Jou Jay Chen, "Growing Social Unrest and Emergent Protest Groups in

China," in *Rise of China: Beijing's Strategies and Implications for the Asia-Pacific*, ed. Hsin-Huang Michael Hsiao and Cheng-Yi Lin (Routledge, 2009), 87.

15. For examples of this approach, see Ronald Inglehart and Christian Welzel, "How Development Leads to Democracy: What We Know About Modernization," *Foreign Affairs* 88, no. 2 (2009): 33–48; Bruce Gilley, *China's Democratic Future: How It Will Happen and Where It Will Lead* (Columbia University Press, 2004).

16. For examples of this approach, see Chang, *The Coming Collapse of China*; Minxin Pei, *China's Crony Capitalism* (Harvard University Press, 2016).

17. For context on the debates surrounding this issue, see Arie Y. Lewin, Martin Kenney, and Johann Peter Murmann, *China's Innovation Challenge: Overcoming the Middle-Income Trap* (Cambridge University Press, 2016); Xielin Liu et al., "Beyond Catch-up—Can a New Innovation Policy Help China Overcome the Middle Income Trap?," *Science and Public Policy* 44, no. 5 (2017): 656–659; Wing Thye Woo, "China Meets the Middle-Income Trap: The Large Potholes in the Road to Catching-Up," *Journal of Chinese Economic and Business Studies* 10, no. 4 (2012): 313–336.

18. Hung, *The China Boom*, 60.

19. "China Makes Gains against US in High-Tech Markets," *Nikkei Asian Review*, July 9, 2019, accessed December 23, 2022, https://asia.nikkei.com/Business/Business-trends/China-makes-gains-against-US-in-high-tech-markets2.

20. Naubahar Sharif, "China as the World's Technology Leader in the 21st Century: Dream or Reality?," 2016, HKUST Institute for Emerging Market Studies, Thought Leadership Brief Series, accessed December 23, 2022, https://ideas.repec.org/p/hku/briefs/201611.html.

21. McCoy, *In the Shadows of the American Century*, chapter 8.

22. Keane, *When Trees Fall, Monkeys Scatter*, 2.

23. Facundo Alvaredo et al., "Global Inequality Dynamics: New Findings from WID.World," *American Economic Review* 107, no. 5 (2017): 406.

24. Wilson and James, *Speech of Governor Wilson Accepting the Democratic Nomination for President of the United States*.

25. Yong Deng, "How China Builds the Credibility of the Belt and Road Initiative," *Journal of Contemporary China* 30, no. 131 (2021): 739.

26. OECD, "The Belt and Road Initiative in the Global Trade, Investment and Finance Landscape," in *OECD Business and Finance Outlook* (OECD, 2018), 9.

27. Xi Jinping, "Secure a Decisive Victory in Building a Moderately Prosperous Society in All Respects and Strive for the Great Success of Socialism with Chinese Characteristics for a New Era," paper presented at the 19th National Congress of the Communist Party of China, October 18, 2017, *China Daily*, accessed December 23, 2022, https://www.chinadaily.com.cn/china/19thcpcnationalcongress/2017-11/04/content_34115212.htm.

28. Jinping, "Secure a Decisive Victory."

29. McCoy, *In the Shadows of the American Century*, 141.

30. McCoy, 142.

31. National Development Reform Commission, "Vision and Actions on Jointly Building Silk Road Economic Belt and 21st-Century Maritime Silk Road," Ministry of Commerce of the People's Republic of China Ministry of Foreign Affairs, with State Council authorization (2015), accessed December 23, 2022, https://www.fmprc.gov.cn

/eng/topics_665678/2015zt/xjpcxbayzlt2015nnh/201503/t20150328_705553.html#
:~:text=The%20initiative%20to%20jointly%20build,spirit%20of%20open%20
regional%20cooperation.

32. National Development Reform Commission, https://www.fmprc.gov.cn/eng
/topics_665678/2015zt/xjpcxbayzlt2015nnh/201503/t20150328_705553.html#:~:text
=The%20initiative%20to%20jointly%20build,spirit%20of%20open%20regional%20
cooperation.

33. "China Trade Statistics: Exports, Imports, Products, Tariffs, GDP and Related
Development Indicator," (2020), World Bank, accessed July 29, 2020, https://wits
.worldbank.org/CountryProfile/en/CHN.

34. OECD, "The Belt and Road Initiative in the Global Trade, Investment and
Finance Landscape," 30.

35. OECD, 30.

36. National Development Reform Commission, "Vision and Actions," https://www
.fmprc.gov.cn/eng/topics_665678/2015zt/xjpcxbayzlt2015nnh/201503/t20150328
_705553.html#:~:text=The%20initiative%20to%20jointly%20build,spirit%20of%20
open%20regional%20cooperation.

37. "Asia Infrastructure Needs Exceed $1.7 Trillion Per Year, Double Previous
Estimates," Asia Development Bank, February 28, 2017, https://www.adb.org/news
/asia-infrastructure-needs-exceed-17-trillion-year-double-previous-estimates.

38. OECD, "The Belt and Road Initiative in the Global Trade, Investment and
Finance Landscape," 18–19.

39. Adams, *America's Economic Supremacy*, 12.

40. Hobson, *Imperialism*, 311–315.

41. Hobson, 311–315.

42. Hobson, 309.

43. Hobson, 309.

44. DB SIPRI, Sipri Military Expenditure Database, accessed December 23, 2022,
https://www.sipri.org/databases/milex.

45. Barack Obama, "Remarks by President Barack Obama at Suntory Hall," *The
White House Office of the Press Secretary* 14 (2009).

46. For details, see Bastiaan Van Apeldoorn and Naná De Graaff, *American Grand
Strategy and Corporate Elite Networks: The Open Door since the End of the Cold War*
(Routledge, 2015), chapter 6.

47. Richard Lee Armitage and Joseph S. Nye, *CSIS Commission on Smart Power:
A Smarter, More Secure America* (CSIS, 2007), 25.

48. Hillary Clinton, "America's Pacific Century," *Foreign Policy* 189, no. 1 (2011):
56–63.

49. Barack Obama, "Remarks by President Obama to the Australian Parliament"
(2011), https://obamawhitehouse.archives.gov/the-press-office/2011/11/17/remarks
-president-obama-australian-parliament.

50. Obama, "Remarks."

51. Obama, "Remarks."

52. Clinton, "America's Pacific Century."

53. Clinton, "America's Pacific Century."

54. Clinton, "America's Pacific Century."

55. David Shambaugh, "Assessing the US 'Pivot' to Asia," *Strategic Studies Quarterly* 7, no. 2 (2013): 11.

56. "'TPP Ministers' statement, October 2015," Australian Department of Foreign Affairs and Trade, accessed July 6, 2020, https://www.dfat.gov.au/trade/agreements /not-yet-in-force/tpp/Pages/ministers-statement.

57. Michael J. Green and Matthew P. Goodman, "After TPP: The Geopolitics of Asia and the Pacific," *The Washington Quarterly* 38, no. 4 (2015): 23.

58. Gerald F. Seib, "Obama Presses Case for Asia Trade Deal, Warns Failure Would Benefit China," *Wall Street Journal,* April 27, 2015.

59. Peter Baker, "Trump Abandons Trans-Pacific Partnership, Obama's Signature Trade Deal," *New York Times,* January 23, 2017.

60. Kurt Campbell and Brian Andrews, "Explaining the US 'Pivot' to Asia," Chatham House, August 2013, 8.

61. While the US accord with China aimed at containing Soviet expansion in 1972 is well known, there were also calls in US foreign-policy circles in the other direction. In "Asia After Vietnam," Richard Nixon references the movement to seek an "anti-Chinese alliance with European powers, even the Soviet Union." Nixon, "Asia after Viet Nam," 122.

62. Nye Jr., "The Case for Deep Engagement," 91.

63. Kurt Campbell, *The Pivot: The Future of American Statecraft in Asia* (Hachette UK, 2016), 154.

64. For details on these agreements, see Campbell, 27.

65. For a full account of American military installations in the region, see US Department of Defense, "Base Structure Report—Fiscal Year 2018 Baseline Summary," accessed September 5, 2020, https://www.acq.osd.mil/eie/Downloads/BSI/Base%20 Structure%20Report%20FY18.pdf.

66. US Department of Defense, "Indo-Pacific Strategy Report: Preparedness, Partnership, and Promoting a Networked Region," (US Department of Defense, 2019), 19.

67. Barry R. Posen, "Command of the Commons: The Military Foundation of US Hegemony," *International Security* 28, no. 1 (2003): 5–46.

68. Used in this context by Corbett, *Principles of Maritime Strategy*, 91; and by Mahan, *The Influence of Sea Power upon History, 1660–1783*, 539–540; among many other examples.

69. Leszek Buszynski, "The South China Sea: Oil, Maritime Claims, and US-China Strategic Rivalry," *The Washington Quarterly* 35, no. 2 (2012): 146.

70. "Chen Wanjun, 'Interview with Sr. Capt. Yu Guoquan (Director of Division of Ships, Dept. of Armaments and Technology, PLAN)' *Jianchuan Zhishi* (Beijing), 07 July 1995, 2-3, in FBIS-CST-96-014," in Bernard D. Cole, *Great Wall at Sea* (Naval Institute Press, 2012), xxiv.

71. "Full Text of Hu Jintao's Report at 18th Party Congress," November 27, 2012, Embassy of the People's Republic of China in the United States, accessed August 12, 2020, http://www.china-embassy.org/eng/zt/18th_CPC_National_Congress_Eng /t992917.htm.

72. "How Is China Modernising Its Navy?," *China Power*, Center for Strategic and International Studies, accessed August 12, 2020, https://chinapower.csis.org/china -naval-modernization/.

73. Eric Heginbotham et al., *The US-China Military Scorecard: Forces, Geography, and the Evolving Balance of Power, 1996–2017* (RAND Corporation, 2015), xxix.

74. Zachary Williams, "The Plan's Renhai-Class Cruiser and the Future of Anti-Access and Area Denial," *The Diplomat,* April 29, 2020, accessed December 23, 2022, https://thediplomat.com/2020/04/the-plans-renhai-class-cruiser-and-the-future -of-anti-access-and-area-denial/.

75. Heginbotham et al., *The US-China Military Scorecard,* 75.

76. Heginbotham et al., xxx.

77. US Department of Defense, "Military and Security Developments Involving the People's Republic of China 2011," (US Department of Defense, 2011), 1.

78. US Department of Defense, *Air-Sea Battle: Service Collaboration to Address Anti-Access & Area Denial Challenges* (Air-Sea Battle Office, 2013), 7.

79. See for example Amitai Etzioni, "The Air-Sea Battle 'Concept': A Critique," *International Politics* 51, no. 5 (2014): 577–596; Green, *By More Than Providence,* 530.

80. Jan van Tol et al., "Airsea Battle: A Point-of-Departure Operational Concept," (Center for Strategic and Budgetary Assessments Washington DC, 2010), 66.

81. US Department of Defense, *Air-Sea Battle,* 7.

82. Hans M. Kristensen, Matthew McKinzie, and Theodore A. Postol, "How US Nuclear Force Modernization Is Undermining Strategic Stability: The Burst-Height Compensating Super-Fuze," *Bulletin of the Atomic Scientists,* March 1, 2017, accessed December 23, 2022, https://thebulletin.org/2017/03/how-us-nuclear-force-moderni zation-is-undermining-strategic-stability-the-burst-height-compensating-super-fuze/.

83. Rory Medcalf, "Undersea Deterrence and Strategic Competition in the Indo-Pacific," in *The Future of the Undersea Deterrent: A Global Survey,* ed. Rory Medcalf (ANU National Security College, 2020), 2; James Goldrick, "Maritime and Naval Power in the Indo-Pacific," in *The Future of the Undersea Deterrent,* ed. Medcalf, 5.

84. Kishore Mahbubani, *Has China Won? The Chinese Challenge to American Primacy* (Hachette UK, 2020), 62–63.

85. David C. Gompert, Astrid Stuth Cevallos, and Cristina L. Garafola, *War with China: Thinking through the Unthinkable* (RAND Corporation, 2016), iv–v.

86. Gompert, x.

87. Gompert, iv–v.

88. Campbell, *The Pivot,* 156.

Chapter 9 • Trump, Biden, and Trouble Ahead

1. For further reading on growing inequality in the United States under neoliberalism, especially since the global financial crisis, see Juliana Menasce Horowitz, Ruth Igielnik, and Rakesh Kochhar, "Most Americans Say There Is Too Much Economic Inequality in the US, but Fewer Than Half Call It a Top Priority," Pew Research Center, January 8, 2020, accessed December 23, 2022, https://www.pewresearch.org/social -trends/2020/01/09/most-americans-say-there-is-too-much-economic-inequality -in-the-u-s-but-fewer-than-half-call-it-a-top-priority/; and Alvaredo et al., "Global Inequality Dynamics: New Findings from WID.World."

2. Herbert R. McMaster and Gary D. Cohn, "America First Doesn't Mean America Alone," *Wall Street Journal,* May 30, 2017.

3. Donald J. Trump, "National Security Strategy of the United States of America," (Executive Office of the President, 2017), 26.

4. For more on this, see Elbridge A. Colby and A. Wess Mitchell, "The Age of Great-Power Competition: How the Trump Administration Refashioned American Strategy," *Foreign Affairs* 99, no. 1 (2020): 118.

5. Robert D. Blackwill, *Implementing Grand Strategy toward China: Twenty-Two US Policy Prescriptions* (Council on Foreign Relations, 2020), iv–v.

6. Kurt M. Campbell and Ely Ratner, "The China Reckoning: How Beijing Defied American Expectations," *Foreign Affairs* 97, no. 2 (2018): 70.

7. US Department of Defense, "Indo-Pacific Strategy Report: Preparedness, Partnership, and Promoting a Networked Region," 7.

8. Trump, "National Security Strategy of the United States of America," 2, 25.

9. Trump, 2, 25.

10. John Ratcliffe, "China Is National Security Threat No. 1," *Wall Street Journal*, December 3, 2020, accessed December 23, 2022, https://www.wsj.com/articles/china -is-national-security-threat-no-1-11607019599.

11. US Census Bureau, "US International Trade Data: Trade in Goods with China," accessed December 23, 2022, https://www.census.gov/foreign-trade/balance/c5700.html.

12. International Monetary Fund, "World Economic Outlook: Legacies, Clouds, Uncertainties," October 2014, accessed December 23, 2022, https://www.imf.org/en /Publications/WEO/Issues/2016/12/31/Legacies-Clouds-Uncertainties.

13. International Monetary Fund, "World Economic Outlook Database," 2020, accessed July 7, 2020, https://www.imf.org/external/pubs/ft/weo/2019/01/weodata /weorept.aspx?pr.x=66&pr.y=10&sy=2017&ey=2024&scsm=1&ssd=1&sort=country&ds= .&br=1&c=193%2C273%2C223%2C138%2C156%2C924%2C922%2C456%2C132%2C184 %2C134%2C146%2C534%2C536%2C186%2C136%2C158%2C112%2C111%2C542&s =NGDPD%2CPPPGDP%2CNGDPDPC%2CPPPSH&grp=0&a=#cs79.

14. John Hawksworth, Hannah Audino, and Rob Clarry, "The Long View: How Will the Global Economic Order Change by 2050," February 2017, accessed December 23, 2022, https://www.pwc.com/gx/en/world-2050/assets/pwc-the-world-in-2050-full -report-feb-2017.pdf.

15. "Full Interview with Steve Bannon and Kyle Bass on 'Phase One' Trade Deal," CNBC, January 15, 2020, accessed December 23, 2022, https://www.cnbc.com/video /2020/01/15/watch-cnbcs-full-interview-with-steve-bannon-and-kyle-bass-on-phase -one-trade-deal.html.

16. See Peter Navarro, "Donald Trump Is Standing Up for American Interests," *Financial Times*, April 9, 2018; and Michael Pillsbury, *The Hundred-Year Marathon: China's Secret Strategy to Replace America as the Global Superpower* (Henry Holt and Company, 2015).

17. US Department of Defense, "Indo-Pacific Strategy Report," 9.

18. Yan Xuetong, "Bipolar Rivalry in the Early Digital Age," *The Chinese Journal of International Politics* 13, no. 3 (2020): 323–324.

19. William Burns, interview by NPR, July 22, 2021, accessed December 23, 2022, https://www.npr.org/2021/07/22/1017900583/transcript-nprs-full-conversation-with -cia-director-william-burns.

20. Michael R. Pompeo, "Announcing the Expansion of the Clean Network to Safeguard America's Assets," US Department of State news release, August 5, 2020, accessed December 23, 2022, https://2017-2021.state.gov/announcing-the-expansion -of-the-clean-network-to-safeguard-americas-assets/index.html.

21. Pompeo, "Announcing the Expansion."

22. Trump, "National Security Strategy of the United States of America," 21, 29–32.

23. US Bureau of Industry and Security, "Commerce Implements New Export Controls on Advanced Computing and Semiconductor Manufacturing Items to the People's Republic of China (PRC)," October 7, 2022, accessed December 23, 2022, https://www.bis.doc.gov/index.php/documents/about-bis/newsroom/press-releases /3158-2022-10-07-bis-press-release-advanced-computing-and-semiconductor-manu facturing-controls-final/file.

24. Gregory C. Allen, "Choking Off China's Access to the Future of AI," Center for Strategic and International Studies, October 11, 2022, accessed December 23, 2022, https://www.csis.org/analysis/choking-chinas-access-future-ai.

25. White House, "Fact Sheet: CHIPS and Science Act Will Lower Costs, Create Jobs, Strengthen Supply Chains, and Counter China," August 9, 2022, accessed January 15, 2023, https://www.whitehouse.gov/briefing-room/statements-releases/2022/08 /09/fact-sheet-chips-and-science-act-will-lower-costs-create-jobs-strengthen-supply -chains-and-counter-china/.

26. Paul Scharre, "Decoupling Wastes U.S. Leverage on China," *Foreign Policy*, January 13, 2023, accessed January 15, 2023, https://foreignpolicy.com/2023/01/13 /china-decoupling-chips-america/?tpcc=onboarding_trending.

27. Wang Jisi, "The Plot against China?: How Beijing Sees the New Washington Consensus," *Foreign Affairs* 100, no. 4 (2021): 48.

28. OECD, "Gross Domestic Spending on R&D (Indicator)," OECD Data 2021, accessed May 18, 2021, https://data.oecd.org/rd/gross-domestic-spending-on-r-d.htm.

29. "Core Technology Depends on One's Own Efforts: President Xi," *CRI Online*, April 19, 2019, accessed December 23, 2022, http://en.people.cn/n3/2018/0419/c90000 -9451186.html.

30. Gerry Shih, "Trump's New North American Trade Deal Also Aimed at Bigger Target: China," *Washington Post*, October 3, 2018.

31. Quoted in Naomi Powell, "Tethering Canada, Containing China: Will USMCA Boost Trump's Efforts to Isolate Beijing?," *Financial Post*, October 4, 2018, accessed December 23, 2022, https://financialpost.com/news/economy/tethering-canada -containing-china-will-usmca-boost-trumps-efforts-to-isolate-beijing.

32. Quoted in Shih, "Trump's New North American Trade Deal."

33. "In 'World of Disquiet,' UN Must Deliver for the People, Guterres Tells General Assembly," *UN News*, September 24, 2019.

34. David P. Calleo, *Beyond American Hegemony: The Future of the Western Alliance*, vol. 1 (Wheatsheaf Books, 1987), 143.

35. Ruggie, "International Regimes, Transactions, and Change," 381.

36. A process described as a common behavior of declining hegemons in Calleo, *Beyond American Hegemony*, vol. 1, 142.

37. Donald J. Trump, "Inaugural Address: Remarks of President Donald J. Trump—

as Prepared for Delivery," January 20, 2017, accessed December 23, 2022, https://trump whitehouse.archives.gov/briefings-statements/the-inaugural-address/.

38. Kolko and Kolko, *The Limits of Power*, 3.

39. Volker Zepf, "An Overview of the Usefulness and Strategic Value of Rare Earth Metals," in *Rare Earths Industry* (Elsevier, 2016), 3–17.

40. See US Geological Survey, "Mineral Commodities Summary: Rare Earths," years 2003 through 2012.

41. US Geological Survey, "Mineral Commodities Summary: Rare Earths " 2020, 132, accessed December 23, 2022, https://pubs.er.usgs.gov/publication/mcs2020.

42. Keith Bradsher, "Amid Tension, China Blocks Vital Exports to Japan," *New York Times*, September 22, 2010.

43. Amy King and Shiro Armstrong, "Did China Really Ban Rare Earth Metals Exports to Japan?," *East Asia Forum,* August 18, 2013, accessed December 23, 2022, https://www.eastasiaforum.org/2013/08/18/did-china-really-ban-rare-earth-metals -exports-to-japan/.

44. US Department of Energy, "Critical Materials Strategy," 2010, Appendix A, 111, accessed December 7, 2020, http://energy.gov/sites/prod/files/piprod/documents/cms _dec_17_full_web.pdf.

45. US Department of Defense, "Report to Congress: Rare Earth Materials in Defense Applications," March 2012, accessed December 7, 2020, https://www.hsdl.org /?abstract&did=704803.

46. US Department of the Interior, "Final List of Critical Minerals," (Federal Register, May 18, 2018).

47. Donald J. Trump, Executive Order 13817: A Federal Strategy to Ensure Secure and Reliable Supplies of Critical Minerals, the White House, December 20, 2017, accessed December 23, 2022, https://www.federalregister.gov/documents/2017/12 /26/2017-27899/a-federal-strategy-to-ensure-secure-and-reliable-supplies-of-critical -minerals.

48. Donald J. Trump, Executive Order 13953: Addressing the Threat to the Domestic Supply Chain from Reliance on Critical Minerals from Foreign Adversaries, the White House September 30, 2020, accessed December 23, 2022, https://trumpwhite house.archives.gov/presidential-actions/executive-order-addressing-threat-domestic -supply-chain-reliance-critical-minerals-foreign-adversaries/.

49. Trump, Executive Order 13953.

50. White House, Building Resilient Supply Chains, Revitalizing American Manufacturing, and Fostering Broad-Based Growth: 100-Day Reviews under Executive Order 14017, June 2021 and 117th Congress, First Session, Supply Chain Security and Resilience Act, H. R. 5505 (2021).

51. Andrew L. Gulley, Nedal T. Nassar, and Sean Xun, "China, the United States, and Competition for Resources That Enable Emerging Technologies," *Proceedings of the National Academy of Sciences* 115, no. 16 (2018): 4111.

52. US Geological Survey, "Mineral Commodity Summaries," (2019), 6, accessed December 12, 2020, https://doi.org/10.3133/70202434.

53. Gulley, Nassar, and Xun, "China, the United States, and Competition for Resources," 4113.

54. Mark P. Sullivan and Thomas Lum, "China's Engagement with Latin America and the Caribbean," (Congressional Research Service, 2021).

55. "China-Africa Bilateral Trade Data," China Africa Research Initiative, Johns Hopkins University, 2019, accessed December 23, 2022, http://www.sais-cari.org/data -china-africa-trade.

56. Barack Obama, "National Security Strategy" (Executive Office of the President, 2015).

57. Trump, "National Security Strategy of the United States of America."

58. Trump, "National Security Strategy of the United States of America."

59. Nathaniel D. F. Allen, "Assessing a Decade of US Military Strategy in Africa," *Orbis* 62, no. 4 (2018): 655–699.

60. Nick Turse, "The U.S. Military's Best Kept Secret," *The Nation*, November 17, 2015, accessed December 23, 2022, https://www.thenation.com/article/the-us -militarys-best-kept-secret/; and Nick Turse, Sam Mednick, and Amanda Sperber, "Exclusive: Inside the Secret World of US Commandos in Africa," *Globe and Mail*, August 11, 2020.

61. This is a consistent theme of Trump's speeches and comments at world forums. See for example Donald J. Trump, "Remarks by President Trump at the 2020 Salute to America," White House news release, July 4, 2020, accessed December 23, 2022, https://ge.usembassy.gov/remarks-by-president-trump-at-the-2020-salute-to-america -july-4/; and "Trump Says Other Countries 'Taking Advantage' of US—Video," *Guardian*, July 20, 2018, accessed December 23, 2022, https://www.theguardian.com/us-news /video/2018/jul/20/trump-says-other-countries-advantage-of-us-china-surplus -video.

62. Woodrow Wilson Foundation and Elliot, *The Political Economy of American Foreign Policy*, 7.

63. Trump, "National Security Strategy of the United States of America," 27; US Department of Defense, "Indo-Pacific Strategy Report," 53.

64. Anne Applebaum, "Trump Hates the International Organizations That Are the Basis of U.S. Wealth, Prosperity and Military Power," *Washington Post*, July 3, 2018, accessed December 23, 2022, https://www.aclu.org/blog/human-rights/five-ways -trump-administration-has-attacked-un-and-international-human-rights; Financial Times Editorial Board, "Trump Administration Extends Its Assault on Multilateralism," *Financial Times*, September 15, 2018, accessed December 23, 2022, https://www.ft.com /content/729e1bf6-b826-11e8-bbc3-ccd7de085ffe.

65. Xi Jinping, "Keynote Speech at World Economic Forum Annual Meeting, Davos. Jointly Shoulder Responsibility of Our Times, Promote Global Growth," news release, 17 January, 2017, accessed December 10, 2020, https://america.cgtn.com/2017/01/17 /fulltext-of-xi-jinping-keynote-at-the-world-economic-forum (page discontinued).

66. David E. Sanger and Maggie Haberman, "Highlights from Our Interview with Donald Trump on Foreign Policy," *New York Times*, March 26, 2016, accessed December 23, 2022, https://www.nytimes.com/2016/03/27/us/politics/donald-trump-interview -highlights.html.

67. White House, "Joint Statement from President Donald J. Trump and Prime Minister Shinzo Abe," (February 10, 2017).

68. Ryan Browne, "US and South Korea Fail to Reach Cost Sharing Agreement for

US Troops," CNN, December 18, 2019, accessed December 23, 2022, https://edition.cnn
.com/2019/12/18/politics/us-south-korea-troop-cost-sharing-fail/index.html.

69. For more on minilateralism, see Joel Wuthnow, "US 'Minilateralism'in Asia and
China's Responses: A New Security Dilemma?," *Journal of Contemporary China* 28, no.
115 (2019): 133–150.

70. " 'Quad' Reviews Situation in Indo-Pacific Region," *Economic Times*, November
4, 2019.

71. Quoted in Jesse Johnson, "With Eye on China, U.S. Aims to 'Formalize' Four-
Nation 'Quad' Security Grouping," *Japan Times*, September 1, 2020, accessed December
23, 2022, https://www.japantimes.co.jp/news/2020/09/01/asia-pacific/china-us-quad/.

72. Trump, "National Security Strategy of the United States of America," 25.

73. DB SIPRI, Sipri Military Expenditure Database, accessed December 23, 2022,
https://www.sipri.org/databases/milex.

74. DB SIPRI, Sipri Military Expenditure Database.

75. Jim Mattis, "Summary of the 2018 National Defense Strategy of the United
States of America," (Department of Defense, 2018), 3.

76. See for example US Joint Chiefs of Staff, "Joint Vision 2010," US Government
Printing Office, June 1996), 25–27.

77. J. R. Hoehn and K. M. Sayler, "National Security Implications of Fifth Generation (5G) Mobile Technologies," *Congressional Research Service* (2019), 1.

78. Toby Helm, "Pressure from Trump Led to 5G Ban, Britain Tells Huawei,"
Guardian, July 18, 2020, accessed December 23, 2022, https://www.theguardian.com
/technology/2020/jul/18/pressure-from-trump-led-to-5g-ban-britain-tells-huawei.

79. Michael Slezak, "Huawei Banned from 5G Mobile Infrastructure Rollout in
Australia," *ABC News*, August 23, 2018.

80. Matthew Lee, "Pompeo, in Slovenia, Pushes 5G Security, Warns about China,"
Associated Press, August 14, 2020, accessed December 23, 2022, https://apnews.com
/article/international-news-europe-eastern-europe-politics-slovenia-7764f3b6cb
3820191068d798401fad92; and Yun Li, "Trump Says US Government Won't Do Business with Huawei, Not Ready to Make a Trade Deal with China," *CNBC*, August 9, 2019,
accessed December 23, 2022, https://www.cnbc.com/2019/08/09/trump-says-us-is
-not-going-to-do-business-with-huawei-not-ready-to-make-a-trade-deal-with-china
.html.

81. Ronald O'Rourke, "Renewed Great Power Competition: Implications for
Defense—Issues for Congress," (Congressional Research Service, 2020), 10.

82. O'Rourke, 4.

83. Joseph R. Biden Jr., "Remarks as Prepared for Delivery by President Biden—
Address to a Joint Session of Congress," April 28, 2021, accessed June 15, 2021, https://
www.whitehouse.gov/briefing-room/speeches-remarks/2021/04/28/remarks-as
-prepared-for-delivery-by-president-biden-address-to-a-joint-session-of-congress/;
and "Interim National Security Strategic Guidance," (Executive Office of the President,
2021).

84. White House, "President Biden and G7 Leaders Launch Build Back Better
World (B3W) Partnership," June 12, 2021, accessed June 20, 2021, https://www.white
house.gov/briefing-room/statements-releases/2021/06/12/fact-sheet-president-biden
-and-g7-leaders-launch-build-back-better-world-b3w-partnership/; and NATO, "Brus-

sels Summit Communiqué: Issued by the Heads of State and Government Participating in the Meeting of the North Atlantic Council in Brussels," June 14, 2021, accessed June 20, 2021, https://www.nato.int/cps/en/natohq/news_185000.htm.

85. O'Rourke, "Renewed Great Power Competition," 4.

86. Biden Jr., "Interim National Security Strategic Guidance," 8.

87. Biden Jr., 10.

88. Christopher Layne, "From Preponderance to Offshore Balancing: America's Future Grand Strategy," *International Security* 22, no. 1 (1997): 86–124.

89. For an excellent example of these arguments, see Layne, *The Peace of Illusions*, in particular 134–205.

90. Layne, "From Preponderance to Offshore Balancing," 112.

91. Andrew F. Krepinevich Jr., "How to Deter China: The Case for Archipelagic Defense," *Foreign Affairs* 94, no. 2, (2015): 78.

92. Thomas X. Hammes, "Offshore Control: A Proposed Strategy for an Unlikely Conflict," Institute for National Strategic Studies, June 2012, 4, accessed December 23, 2022, https://ndupress.ndu.edu/Portals/68/Documents/stratforum/SF-278.pdf.

93. Hammes, "Offshore Control." https://ndupress.ndu.edu/Portals/68/Documents/stratforum/SF-278.pdf.

94. Mahan, *The Influence of Sea Power Upon History, 1660–1783*, 32.

95. Hammes, "Offshore Control," 6, https://ndupress.ndu.edu/Portals/68/Documents/stratforum/SF-278.pdf.

96. Andrew S. Erickson, "China's Naval Modernization: Implications and Recommendations," *testimony in hearing on US Asia-Pacific Strategic Considerations Related to PLA Naval Forces, Before the House Armed Services Committee Seapower and Projection Forces Subcommittee,*11 (2013), 10.

97. Erickson, 12.

98. Erickson, 15.

99. Erickson, 15.

100. Rachel Esplin Odell et al., "Active Denial: A Roadmap to a More Effective, Stabilizing, and Sustainable U.S. Defense Strategy in Asia," *Quincy Report* (June 2022), 3–4.

101. Stephen Biddle and Ivan Oelrich, "Future Warfare in the Western Pacific: Chinese Antiaccess/Area Denial, US Airsea Battle, and Command of the Commons in East Asia," *International Security* 41, no. 1 (2016): 12.

102. US Department of Defense, "Indo-Pacific Strategy Report," 16.

103. Halford John Mackinder, "The Round World and the Winning of the Peace," *Foreign Affairs* 21, no. 4 (1942): 605.

Conclusion

1. Francis Delaisi, *Political Myths and Economic Realities* (Kennikat Press, 1927), 57.

2. Eric Hobsbawm, *Age of Empire: 1875–1914* (Hachette UK, 2010), 10.

3. Arendt, *The Origins of Totalitarianism*, 126.

4. Adams, *America's Economic Supremacy*, vi.

5. Adams, vi.

6. See for example Morgenthau, *United States Policy toward Asia. Hearings before the Subcommittee on the Far East and the Pacific of the Committee on Foreign Affairs*, 129.

7. Bacevich, *American Empire*, 221; and *The Age of Illusions*, chapter 8.

8. Keane, *The New Despotism*.

9. Johnson, *Blowback*, 221.

10. Jeffrey A. Winters, *Oligarchy* (Cambridge University Press, 2011), 92, 217.

11. "Survey of Consumer Finances," Board of Governors of the Federal Reserve System, accessed May 25, 2021, https://www.federalreserve.gov/econres/scf/dataviz /scf/chart/#series:Net_Worth;demographic:all;population:1;units:median2020.

12. Carter C. Price and Kathryn A. Edwards, "Trends in Income from 1975 to 2018," RAND Corporation, 2020, https://www.rand.org/pubs/working_papers/WRA516-1 .html.

13. For a particularly important example of this, see Xi Jinping, "Work Together to Build the Silk Road Economic Belt and the 21st Century Maritime Silk Road," a keynote speech at the opening ceremony of the Belt and Road Forum (BRF) for International Cooperation in Beijing, China, May 20, 2017, http://cy.china-embassy.gov.cn/eng/xwdt /201705/t20170520_3123364.htm.

14. Zeng Guofan to Imperial Court, secret memorandum attached to Mr. Williams to Mr. Seward, Legation of the United States, Peking, July 1868, in "Executive Documents Printed by Order of the House of Representatives, during the Third Session of the Fortieth Congress, 1868–69," 519.

15. Charles Forster Smith, *Thucydides: History of the Peloponnesian War*, vol. 108 (W. Heinemann, 1962), 280.

16. Hobson, *Imperialism*, 212.

17. Calleo, *Beyond American Hegemony*, vol. 1, 142.

18. Eric Hobsbawm reaches a similar conclusion in Hobsbawm, *On Empire*, 53.

19. William Appleman Williams, *Empire as a Way of Life: An Essay on the Causes and Character of America's Present Predicament, Along with a Few Thoughts About an Alternative* (Oxford University Press, 1980), 119.

Acheson, Dean. "Speech on the Far East." Speech given at the National Press Club. Washington, DC, 1950. https://www.cia.gov/readingroom/docs/1950-01-12.pdf.

Adams, Brooks. *America's Economic Supremacy*. Edited by Marquis W. Childs. Harper, 1900.

———. *The New Empire*. Macmillan, 1902.

———. "The Spanish War and the Equilibrium of the World." Paper presented at the Forum, 1898.

Adams, Ephraim D. "English Interest in the Annexation of California." *American Historical Review* 14, no. 4 (1909): 744–763.

Adams, John Quincy. "Lecture on the War with China, Delivered before the Massachusetts Historical Society, December, 1841." *Chinese Repository* 11 (1842): 274–289.

———. *An Oration, Delivered at Plymouth, December 22, 1802: At the Anniversary Commemoration of the First Landing of Our Ancestors, at That Place*. Vol. 2. Russell and Cutler, 1802.

Allen, Gregory C. "Choking Off China's Access to the Future of AI." Center for Strategic and International Studies. October 11, 2022. https://www.csis.org/analysis/choking -chinas-access-future-ai.

Allen, Nathaniel D. F. "Assessing a Decade of US Military Strategy in Africa." *Orbis* 62, no. 4 (2018): 655–669.

Alvaredo, Facundo, Lucas Chancel, Thomas Piketty, Emmanuel Saez, and Gabriel Zucman. "Global Inequality Dynamics: New Findings from WID.World." *American Economic Review* 107, no. 5 (2017): 404–409.

Applebaum, Anne. "Trump Hates the International Organizations That Are the Basis of U.S. Wealth, Prosperity and Military Power." *Washington Post*, July 3, 2018. https:// www.aclu.org/blog/human-rights/five-ways-trump-administration-has-attacked -un-and-international-human-rights.

Arendt, Hannah. *The Origins of Totalitarianism*. Houghton Mifflin Harcourt, 1973.

Armitage, Richard Lee, and Joseph S. Nye. *CSIS Commission on Smart Power: A Smarter, More Secure America*. CSIS, 2007.

Arrighi, Giovanni. *Adam Smith in Beijing: Lineages of the Twenty-First Century*. Verso Trade, 2007.

———. *The Long Twentieth Century: Money, Power, and the Origins of Our Times*. Verso, 1994.

Ashworth, Lucian M. "Realism and the Spirit of 1919: Halford Mackinder, Geopolitics and the Reality of the League of Nations." *European Journal of International Relations* 17, no. 2 (2011): 279–301.

Asia Development Bank. "Asia Infrastructure Needs Exceed $1.7 Trillion Per Year, Double Previous Estimates." February 28, 2017. https://www.adb.org/news/asia-infrastructure-needs-exceed-17-trillion-year-double-previous-estimates.

· Aspin, Les. *Report on the Bottom-up Review.* US Department of Defense, October 1993. https://history.defense.gov/Portals/70/Documents/dod_reforms/Bottom-upReview.pdf.

Australian Department of Foreign Affairs and Trade. "TPP Ministers' statement, October 2015." https://www.dfat.gov.au/trade/agreements/not-yet-in-force/tpp/Pages/ministers-statement.

Bacevich, Andrew J. *The Age of Illusions: How America Squandered Its Cold War Victory.* Metropolitan Books, 2020.

———. *American Empire.* Harvard University Press, 2009.

———. "Ending Endless War: A Pragmatic Military Strategy." *Foreign Affairs* 95, no. 5 (2016): 36–44.

Bailey, Thomas Andrew. *A Diplomatic History of the American People.* Prentice-Hall, 1974.

Baker III, James A. "America in Asia: Emerging Architecture for a Pacific Community." *Foreign Affairs* 70, no.1 (1990): 1.

Baker, Peter. "Trump Abandons Trans-Pacific Partnership, Obama's Signature Trade Deal." *New York Times*, January 23, 2017.

Baruch, Bernard Mannes. *American Industry in the War: A Report of the War Industries Board.* Prentice-Hall, 1921.

Beard, Mary Ritter, and Charles Austin Beard. *History of the United States.* Vol. 1. New York: Doubleday, Doran, and Co., 2009.

Bensel, Richard Franklin. *The Political Economy of American Industrialization, 1877–1900.* Cambridge University Press, 2000.

Berding, Andrew Henry Thomas. "Dulles on Diplomacy." Van Nostrand, 1965.

Berger, Carl. *The United States Air Force in Southeast Asia, 1961–1973.* Office of Air Force History, 1977.

Berger, Samuel R. "American Power: Hegemony, Isolationism or Engagement." Address to the Council on Foreign Relations, October 21, 1999. https://clintonwhitehouse4.archives.gov/textonly/WH/EOP/NSC/html/speeches/19991021.html.

Berglund, Abraham. "The Iron and Steel Industry of Japan and Japanese Continental Policies." *Journal of Political Economy* 30, no. 5 (1922): 623–654.

Biddle, Stephen, and Ivan Oelrich. "Future Warfare in the Western Pacific: Chinese Antiaccess / Area Denial, US Airsea Battle, and Command of the Commons in East Asia." *International Security* 41, no. 1 (2016): 7–48.

Biden Jr., Joseph R. "Interim National Security Strategic Guidance." Washington, DC: Executive Office of the President, 2021.

———. "Remarks as Prepared for Delivery by President Biden—Address to a Joint Session of Congress." April 28, 2021. https://www.whitehouse.gov/briefing-room/speeches-remarks/2021/04/28/remarks-as-prepared-for-delivery-by-president-biden-address-to-a-joint-session-of-congress.

Blackslee, George H. "The Japanese Monroe Doctrine." *Foreign Affairs* 11 (1932): 671–681.

Blackwill, Robert D. *Implementing Grand Strategy toward China: Twenty-Two US Policy Prescriptions*. Council on Foreign Relations, 2020.

Bland, John Otway Percy, and Sir Edmund Trelawney Backhouse. *Annals and Memoirs of the Court of Peking*. Boston and New York: Houghton Mifflin, 1914.

Blum, William. *Killing Hope: US Military and CIA Interventions since World War II*. Zed Books, 2003.

Board of Governors of the Federal Reserve System. "Survey of Consumer Finances." https://www.federalreserve.gov/econres/scf/dataviz/scf/chart/#series:Net_Worth ;demographic:all;population:1;units:median.

Boot, Max. "The Case for American Empire." In *Paradoxes of Power*, edited by David Skidmore, 88–91. Routledge, 2015.

Bradsher, Keith. "Amid Tension, China Blocks Vital Exports to Japan." *New York Times*, September 22, 2010.

Braudel, Fernand. *Civilization and Capitalism, 15th–18th Century, Vol. III: The Perspective of the World*. University of California Press, 1992.

Braumoeller, Bear F. "The Myth of American Isolationism." *Foreign Policy Analysis* 6, no. 4 (2010): 349–371.

Brewster, David. "The Australia-India Security Declaration." *Security Challenges* 6, no. 1 (2010): 1–9.

Browne, Ryan. "US and South Korea Fail to Reach Cost Sharing Agreement for US Troops." CNN, December 18, 2019. https://edition.cnn.com/2019/12/18/politics /us-south-korea-troop-cost-sharing-fail/index.html.

Burns, William. "Transcript: NPR's Full Conversation with CIA Director William Burns." NPR, July 22, 2021. https://www.npr.org/2021/07/22/1017900583/tran script-nprs-full-conversation-with-cia-director-william-burns.

Bush, George H. W. *National Security Strategy of the United States*. Washington, DC: White House, 1991. https://history.defense.gov/Portals/70/Documents/nss/nss1991 .pdf?ver=3sIpLiQwmknO-RplyPeAHw%3d%3d.

———. "Remarks at the Yale University Commencement Ceremony in New Haven, Connecticut, May 27, 1991." *Public Papers of the Presidents* (1991).

Bush, George W. "A Distinctly American Internationalism." Speech delivered at Ronald Reagan Presidential Library, Simi Valley, California, November 19, 1999. In *The George W. Bush Foreign Policy Reader: Presidential Speeches with Commentary*, John W. Dietrich, 26. Taylor & Francis Group, 2005.

———. "The National Security Strategy of the United States of America." Washington, DC: Executive Office of the President, 2002. https://georgewbush-whitehouse .archives.gov/nsc/nss/2002/.

Buszynski, Leszek. "The South China Sea: Oil, Maritime Claims, and US–China Strategic Rivalry." *Washington Quarterly* 35, no. 2 (2012): 139–156.

Butler, Smedley Darlington. *War Is a Racket: The Antiwar Classic by America's Most Decorated Soldier*. Simon and Schuster, 2016.

Calleo, David P. *Beyond American Hegemony: The Future of the Western Alliance*. Vol. 1. Wheatsheaf Books, 1987.

Calloway, Colin G. *The American Revolution in Indian Country: Crisis and Diversity in Native American Communities*. Cambridge University Press, 1995.

———. *The Victory with No Name: The Native American Defeat of the First American Army*. Oxford University Press, 2014.

Campbell, Kurt. *The Pivot: The Future of American Statecraft in Asia*. Hachette UK, 2016.

Campbell, Kurt, and Brian Andrews. "Explaining the US 'Pivot' to Asia." Chatham House, August 2013.

Campbell, Kurt M., and Ely Ratner. "The China Reckoning: How Beijing Defied American Expectations." *Foreign Affairs* 97, no. 2 (2018): 60.

Center for Strategic and International Studies. "How Is China Modernising Its Navy?" *China Power*. https://chinapower.csis.org/china-naval-modernization/.

Chang, Gordon G. *The Coming Collapse of China*. Random House, 2010.

Chen, Chih-Jou Jay. "Growing Social Unrest and Emergent Protest Groups in China." In *Rise of China: Beijing's Strategies and Implications for the Asia-Pacific*, edited by Hsin-Huang Michael Hsiao and Cheng-Yi Lin, 87–106. Routledge, 2009.

China Africa Research Initiative. "China-Africa Bilateral Trade Data." Johns Hopkins University, 2019. http://www.sais-cari.org/data-china-africa-trade.

Clarkson, Grosvenor B. *Industrial America in the World War: The Strategy Behind the Line, 1917–1918*. Houghton Mifflin, 1923.

Clawson, Marion. *New Deal Planning: The National Resources Planning Board*. RFF Press, 2013.

Clinton, Hillary. "America's Pacific Century." *Foreign Policy* 189, no. 1 (2011): 56–63.

Clinton, William J. *A National Security Strategy of Engagement and Enlargement*. Washington, DC: White House, July 1994. https://history.defense.gov/Portals/70/Documents/nss/nss1994.pdf.

———. "Remarks to the World Economic Forum and a Question-and-Answer Session in Davos, Switzerland." Online by Gerhard Peters and John T. Woolley, The American Presidency Project. https://www.presidency.ucsb.edu/node/227554.

CNBC. "Full Interview with Steve Bannon and Kyle Bass on 'Phase One' Trade Deal." January 15, 2020. https://www.cnbc.com/video/2020/01/15/watch-cnbcs-full-interview-with-steve-bannon-and-kyle-bass-on-phase-one-trade-deal.html.

Cohen, Warren I. *America's Response to China: A History of Sino-American Relations*. Columbia University Press, 2019.

Colby, Elbridge A., and A. Wess Mitchell. "The Age of Great-Power Competition: How the Trump Administration Refashioned American Strategy." *Foreign Affairs* 99, no. 1 (2020): 118.

Cole, Bernard D. *Great Wall at Sea*. Naval Institute Press, 2012.

Corbett, Julian S. *Principles of Maritime Strategy*. Courier Corporation, 2012.

Cowan, Ruth Schwartz. *A Social History of American Technology*. New York: Oxford University Press, 1997.

Cox, Samuel Sullivan. *Eight Years in Congress, from 1857–1865: Memoir and Speeches*. D. Appleton, 1865.

Crawford, Neta C. "United States Budgetary Costs of the Post-9/11 Wars through FY2020: $6.4 Trillion Spent and Obligated." Watson Institute for International & Public Affairs, Brown University, 2019. https://watson.brown.edu/costsofwar/figures/2019/budgetary-costs-post-911-wars-through-fy2020-64-trillion.

Crawford, Neta C., and Catherine Lutz. "Human Cost of Post-9/11 Wars: Direct War

Deaths in Major War Zones." Watson Institute for International & Public Affairs, Brown University, 2019. https://watson.brown.edu/costsofwar/figures/2021/War DeathToll.

CRI Online. "Core Technology Depends on One's Own Efforts: President Xi." April 19, 2019. http://en.people.cn/n3/2018/0419/c90000-9451186.html.

Cuff, Robert. "The Dollar-a-Year Men of the Great War." *Princeton University Library Chronicle* 30, no. 1 (1968): 10–24.

Cutter, W. Bowman, Joan Spero, and Laura D'Andrea Tyson. "New World, New Deal: A Democratic Approach to Globalization." *Foreign Affairs* 79, no. 2 (2000): 80–98.

Darwin, John. *After Tamerlane: The Rise and Fall of Global Empires, 1400–2000*. Penguin UK, 2008. EPUB.

Davids, Jules. *American Diplomatic and Public Papers, the United States and China: Series 2, the United States, China, and Imperial Rivalries, 1861–1893*. Wilmington, DE: Scholarly Resources, 1979.

———. *American Diplomatic and Public Papers: The United States and China. Series 1: The Treaty System and the Taiping Rebellion, 1842–1860*. Wilmington, DE: Scholarly Resources, 1973.

DB SIPRI. Sipri Military Expenditure Database. Stockholm International Peace Research Institute Solna, 2019. https://www.sipri.org/databases/milex.

De Tocqueville, Alexis. *Democracy in America*. Vol. 10. Regnery Publishing, 2003.

Delaisi, Francis. *Political Myths and Economic Realities*. Kennikat Press, 1927.

Deng, Yong. "How China Builds the Credibility of the Belt and Road Initiative." *Journal of Contemporary China* 30, no. 131 (2021): 734–750.

Domhoff, George William. *Who Rules America?* Vol. 167. Englewood Cliffs, 1967.

Du Bois, William Edward Burghardt, and Manning Marable. *Souls of Black Folk*. Routledge, 2015.

Dubofsky, Melvyn. "Daniel Webster and the Whig Theory of Economic Growth: 1828–1848." *New England Quarterly* 42, no.4 (1969): 551–572.

Dulles, John Foster. "Security in the Pacific." *Foreign Affairs* 30, no. 2 (1952): 175–187.

Eckes Jr., Alfred E. *The United States and the Global Struggle for Minerals*. University of Texas Press, 1979.

Economic Times. "'Quad' Reviews Situation in Indo-Pacific Region." November 4, 2019.

Eisenhower, Dwight D. "The President's News Conference." The American Presidency Project, April 7, 1954. https://www.presidency.ucsb.edu/documents/the-presidents -news-conference-361.

———. "Remarks at the Governors' Conference, Seattle, Washington." The American Presidency Project, August 4, 1953. https://www.presidency.ucsb.edu/documents /remarks-the-governors-conference-seattle-washington.

Embassy of the People's Republic of China in the United States. "Full Text of Hu Jintao's Report at 18th Party Congress." November 27, 2012. http://www.china -embassy.org/eng/zt/18th_CPC_National_Congress_Eng/t992917.htm.

Erickson, Andrew S. "China's Naval Modernization: Implications and Recommendations." *Testimony in Hearing on US Asia-Pacific Strategic Considerations Related to PLA Naval Forces, before the House Armed Services Committee Seapower and Projection Forces Subcommittee*, Washington, DC, 11 (2013).

Etzioni, Amitai. "The Air-Sea Battle 'Concept': A Critique." *International Politics* 51, no. 5 (2014): 577–596.

Fairbank, John King. "American China Policy to 1898: A Misconception." *Pacific Historical Review* 39, no. 4 (1970): 409–420.

———. *The United States and China.* Harvard University Press, 1983.

Ferguson, Niall. *Colossus: The Rise and Fall of the American Empire.* Penguin, 2005.

Financial Times Editorial Board. "Trump Administration Extends Its Assault on Multilateralism." *Financial Times,* September 15, 2018. https://www.ft.com/content/729e1bf6-b826-11e8-bbc3-ccd7de085ffe.

Finlayson, Jock A., and David G. Haglund. "Whatever Happened to the Resource War?" *Survival* 29, no. 5 (1987): 403–415.

Fortune Magazine. "An American Proposal." May 1942.

Frank, Andre Gunder. *Reorient: Global Economy in the Asian Age.* University of California Press, 1998.

Frei, Henry P. *Japan's Southward Advance and Australia: From the Sixteenth Century to World War II.* University of Hawaii Press, 1991.

Friedman, Hal M. *Creating an American Lake: United States Imperialism and Strategic Security in the Pacific Basin, 1945–1947.* Greenwood Publishing Group, 2001.

Fukuyama, Francis. "The End of History?" *The National Interest,* no. 16 (1989): 3–18.

Futrell, Robert Frank. *Ideas Concepts Doctrine: Basic Thinking in the United States Air Force.* Diane Publishing, 1980.

Garber, Peter M. "The Collapse of the Bretton Woods Fixed Exchange Rate System." In *A Retrospective on the Bretton Woods System: Lessons for International Monetary Reform,* 461–494. University of Chicago Press, 1993.

Gedicks, Al. *The New Resource Wars: Native and Environmental Struggles against Multinational Corporations.* Vol. 210. Black Rose Books Ltd., 1994.

Gilley, Bruce. *China's Democratic Future: How It Will Happen and Where It Will Lead.* Columbia University Press, 2004.

Gilpin, Susan. "Minerals and Foreign Policy." *Africa Report* 27, no. 3 (1982): 16.

Gindin, Sam, and Leo Panitch. *The Making of Global Capitalism.* Verso Books, 2012.

Gleaves, Albert. "Letter: From Commander in Chief to Secretary of the Navy. Subject: Observations on Japanese Character, with Special Reference to Japan's Ambition and Her Relation in This Connection with the United States." September 8, 1920. Edited by 12th Naval District, Record Group 181 Commandant, US National Archives San Bruno, 14-5, box 2.

Go, Julian. *Patterns of Empire: The British and American Empires, 1688 to the Present.* Cambridge University Press, 2011.

Gompert, David C., Astrid Stuth Cevallos, and Cristina L. Garafola. *War with China: Thinking through the Unthinkable.* RAND Corporation, 2016.

Graebner, Norman A. *Empire on the Pacific: A Study in American Continental Expansion.* New York: Ronald Press, 1983.

Gray, Colin S. "Nicholas John Spykman, the Balance of Power, and International Order." *Journal of Strategic Studies* 38, no. 6 (2015): 873–897.

Green, Michael J., and Matthew P. Goodman. "After TPP: The Geopolitics of Asia and the Pacific." *Washington Quarterly* 38, no. 4 (2015): 19–34.

Green, Michael J. *By More Than Providence: Grand Strategy and American Power in the Asia Pacific Since 1783.* Columbia University Press, 2017.

Gregory, John S. "British Intervention against the Taiping Rebellion." *Journal of Asian Studies* 19, no. 1 (1959): 11–24.

Grose, Peter. *Continuing the Inquiry: The Council on Foreign Relations from 1921 to 1996.* Council on Foreign Relations Press, 1996.

Guardian. "Trump Says Other Countries 'Taking Advantage' of US—Video." July 20, 2018. https://www.theguardian.com/us-news/video/2018/jul/20/trump-says-other -countries-advantage-of-us-china-surplus-video.

Gulley, Andrew L., Nedal T. Nassar, and Sean Xun. "China, the United States, and Competition for Resources That Enable Emerging Technologies." *Proceedings of the National Academy of Sciences* 115, no. 16 (2018): 4111–4115.

Gurdon, Alexander. "Life of John Tyler, President of the United States up to the Close of the Second Session of the Twenty-Seventh Congress." New York: Harper & Bros., 1843.

Haass, Richard N. "The Squandered Presidency: Demanding More from the Commander-in-Chief." *Foreign Affairs* 79, no. 1 (2000): 136–140.

Haddad, John R. *America's First Adventure in China: Trade, Treaties, Opium, and Salvation.* Temple University Press, 2014.

Hall, Robert Burnett. "American Raw-Material Deficiencies and Regional Dependence." *Geographical Review* 30, no. 2 (1940): 177–186.

Hammes, Thomas X. "Offshore Control: A Proposed Strategy for an Unlikely Conflict." Institute for National Strategic Studies. June 2012. https://ndupress.ndu.edu /Portals/68/Documents/stratforum/SF-278.pdf.

Hanyok, Robert J. *Skunks, Bogies, Silent Hounds, and the Flying Fish: The Gulf of Tonkin Mystery, 2–4 August 1964.* Center for Cryptologic History, National Security Agency, 1998.

Hargreaves, John. "Decolonisation: French and British Styles." In *State and Society in Francophone Africa since Independence*, 3–15. Springer, 1995.

Harvey, David. *The New Imperialism.* Oxford University Press, 2005.

Hawksworth, John, Hannah Audino, and Rob Clarry. "The Long View: How Will the Global Economic Order Change by 2050." 2017. https://www.pwc.com/gx/en /world-2050/assets/pwc-the-world-in-2050-full-report-feb-2017.pdf.

Heckscher, August. *The Politics of Woodrow Wilson: Selections from His Speeches and Writings.* New York: Harper, 1956.

Heginbotham, Eric, Michael Nixon, Forrest E. Morgan, Jacob L. Heim, Jeff Hagen, Sheng Li, Jeffrey Engstrom, et al. *The US-China Military Scorecard: Forces, Geography, and the Evolving Balance of Power, 1996–2017.* RAND Corporation, 2015.

Helm, Toby. "Pressure from Trump Led to 5G Ban, Britain Tells Huawei." *Guardian*, July 18, 2020. https://www.theguardian.com/technology/2020/jul/18/pressure -from-trump-led-to-5g-ban-britain-tells-huawei.

Hobsbawm, Eric. *Age of Capital: 1848–1875.* Hachette UK, 2010.

——. *Age of Empire: 1875–1914.* Hachette UK, 2010.

——. "America's Imperial Delusion." *Guardian,* June 13, 2003, 21.

——. *On Empire: America, War, and Global Supremacy.* Pantheon, 2008.

Hobsbawm, Eric J., and Marion Cumming. *Age of Extremes: The Short Twentieth Century, 1914–1991*. Abacus London, 1995.

Hobson, John Atkinson. *Imperialism: A Study*. Routledge, 2018.

Hodges, Donald Clark. *Readings in US Imperialism*. P. Sargent, 1971.

Hoehn, J. R., and K. M. Sayler. "National Security Implications of Fifth Generation (5G) Mobile Technologies." *Congressional Research Service*. 2019.

Horn, Sebastian, Carmen M. Reinhart, and Christoph Trebesch. "How Much Money Does the World Owe China." *Harvard Business Review*, February 26, 2020. https://hbr.org/2020/02/how-much-money-does-the-world-owe-china.

Horowitz, Juliana Menasce, Ruth Igielnik, and Rakesh Kochhar. "Most Americans Say There Is Too Much Economic Inequality in the US, but Fewer Than Half Call It a Top Priority." Pew Research Center, January 8, 2020. https://www.pewresearch.org/social-trends/2020/01/09/most-americans-say-there-is-too-much-economic-inequality-in-the-u-s-but-fewer-than-half-call-it-a-top-priority/.

Hou, Chi-ming. *Foreign Investment and Economic Development in China, 1840–1937*. Harvard East Asian Series 21. Cambridge: Harvard University Press, 1965.

Huddle, Franklin P. "The Evolving National Policy for Materials." *Science* 191, no. 4228 (1976): 654–659.

Hugill, Peter J. "The American Challenge to British Hegemony, 1861–1947." *Geographical Review* 99, no. 3 (2009): 403–425.

Hung, Ho-fung. *The China Boom: Why China Will Not Rule the World*. Columbia University Press, 2015.

——. "The Periphery in the Making of Globalization: The China Lobby and the Reversal of Clinton's China Trade Policy, 1993–1994." *Review of International Political Economy* 28, no. 4 (2020): 1–24.

——. "The US-China Rivalry Is about Capitalist Competition." *Jacobin*, November 7, 2020. https://www.jacobinmag.com/2020/07/us-china-competition-capitalism-rivalry.

Hunt, Michael H. *Lyndon Johnson's War: America's Cold War Crusade in Vietnam, 1945–1968*. Macmillan, 1997.

Huntington, Samuel P. "National Policy and the Transoceanic Navy." *US Naval Institute Proceedings* 80, no. 5 (1954): 615.

Ignatieff, Michael. "The American Empire (Get Used to It)." *New York Times Magazine*, January 6, 2003, 22–27.

Inglehart, Ronald, and Christian Welzel. "How Development Leads to Democracy: What We Know about Modernization." *Foreign Affairs* 88, no. 2, (2009): 33–48.

Innis, Harold Adams. *Empire and Communications*. Rowman & Littlefield, 2007.

International Monetary Fund. "World Economic Outlook Database." 2020. https://www.imf.org/external/pubs/ft/weo/2019/01/weodata/weorept.aspx?pr.x=66&pr.y=10&sy=2017&ey=2024&scsm=1&ssd=1&sort=country&ds=.&br=1&c=193%2C273%2C223%2C138%2C156%2C924%2C922%2C456%2C132%2C184%2C134%2C146%2C534%2C536%2C186%2C136%2C158%2C112%2C111%2C542&s=NGDPD%2CPPPGDP%2CNGDPDPC%2CPPPPSH&grp=0&a=#cs79.

——. "World Economic Outlook: Legacies, Clouds, Uncertainties." October 2014. https://www.imf.org/en/Publications/WEO/Issues/2016/12/31/Legacies-Clouds-Uncertainties.

Jacks, David S., and Dennis Novy. "Trade Blocs and Trade Wars During the Interwar Period." *Asian Economic Policy Review* 15, no. 1 (2020): 119–136.

Jefferson, Thomas. "Jefferson to Congress January 18, 1803." January 18, 1803. https://www.loc.gov/item/mtjbib012083/.

———. "Letter to G. K. Van Hogendorp." October 13, 1785. Avalon Project, Documents in Law, History, and Diplomacy, Yale Law School, Lillian Goldman Law Library. https://avalon.law.yale.edu/18th_century/let38.asp.

———. "Letter to John Jay." August 23, 1785. Founders Online, National Archives. https://founders.archives.gov/documents/Jefferson/01-08-02-0333.

———. "Thomas Jefferson to William H. Harrison." February 27, 1803. The Thomas Jefferson Papers at the Library of Congress.

Jefferson, Thomas, Julian P. Boyd, and Ruth W. Lester. *The Papers of Thomas Jefferson.* Vol. 10. Princeton, NJ: Princeton University Press, 1974.

Jefferson, Thomas et al. "The Declaration of Independence." July 4, 1776. https://www.archives.gov/founding-docs/declaration-transcript.

Jinping, Xi. "Keynote Speech at World Economic Forum Annual Meeting, Davos. Jointly Shoulder Responsibility of Our Times, Promote Global Growth." News release, January 17, 2017. https://america.cgtn.com/2017/01/17/fulltext-of-xi-jinping-keynote-at-the-world-economic-forum (page discontinued).

———. "Secure a Decisive Victory in Building a Moderately Prosperous Society in All Respects and Strive for the Great Success of Socialism with Chinese Characteristics for a New Era." Paper presented at the 19th National Congress of the Communist Party of China, October 18, 2017. *China Daily.* https://www.chinadaily.com.cn/china/19thcpcnationalcongress/2017-11/04/content_34115212.htm.

———. "Work Together to Build the Silk Road Economic Belt and the 21st Century Maritime Silk Road." A keynote speech at the opening ceremony of the Belt and Road Forum (BRF) for International Cooperation in Beijing, China, May 20, 2017. http://cy.china-embassy.gov.cn/eng/xwdt/201705/t20170520_3123364.htm.

Jisi, Wang. "The Plot against China?: How Beijing Sees the New Washington Consensus." *Foreign Affairs* 100, no. 4 (2021): 48.

Johnson, Chalmers. *Blowback: The Costs and Consequences of American Empire.* Macmillan, 2000.

———. *Dismantling the Empire: America's Last Best Hope.* Metropolitan Books, 2010.

Johnson, Jesse. "With Eye on China, U.S. Aims to 'Formalize' Four-Nation 'Quad' Security Grouping." *Japan Times,* September 1, 2020. https://www.japantimes.co.jp/news/2020/09/01/asia-pacific/china-us-quad/.

Jones, Peter d'Alroy. *The Consumer Society: A History of American Capitalism.* Vol. 780. Penguin Books Ltd., 1965.

Kagan, Donald, and Thomas Donnelly. *Rebuilding America's Defences: Strategy, Forces and Resources For a New Century, A Report of The Project for the New American Century.* Washington, DC: 2000.

Kagan, Robert. "Neocon Nation: Neoconservatism, C. 1776." *World Affairs* 170, no. 4 (2008): 13–35.

Keane, John. *The Life and Death of Democracy.* Simon and Schuster, 2009.

———. *The New Despotism.* Harvard University Press, 2020.

——. *When Trees Fall, Monkeys Scatter: Rethinking Democracy in China*. World Scientific, 2017.

Keliher, Macabe. "Anglo-American Rivalry and the Origins of US China Policy." *Diplomatic History* 31, no. 2 (2007): 227–257.

Kennan, George. "The Sources of Soviet Conduct." *Foreign Affairs* 25, no. 4 (1947): 566–582.

——. "US State Department Policy Planning Staff Document Pps 23, Feb. 24, 1948." *Foreign Relations of the United States* 1 (1948): 509–529.

Kennedy, Paul. *The Rise and Fall of the Great Powers*. Vintage, 2010.

King, Amy and Shiro Armstrong. "Did China Really Ban Rare Earth Metals Exports to Japan?" *East Asia Forum*, August 18, 2013. https://www.eastasiaforum.org/2013/08/18/did-china-really-ban-rare-earth-metals-exports-to-japan/.

Kissinger, Henry A. "Central Issues of American Foreign Policy." *Agenda for the Nation*. 585–614. Washington: Brookings Institution, 1968.

Kojima, Kiyoshi. "The 'Flying Geese' Model of Asian Economic Development: Origin, Theoretical Extensions, and Regional Policy Implications." *Journal of Asian Economics* 11, no. 4 (2000): 375–401.

Kolko, Gabriel. *The Politics of War: The World and United States Foreign Policy, 1943–1945*. Vol. 631. New York: Random House, 1968.

Kolko, Joyce, and Gabriel Kolko. *The Limits of Power: The World and United States Foreign Policy, 1945–1954*. New York: Harper & Row, 1972.

Krepinevich, Andrew, and Robert O. Work. "A New Global Defense Posture for the Second Transoceanic Era." *Center for Strategic and Budgetary Assessments*. Washington, DC, 2007.

Krepinevich Jr., Andrew F. "How to Deter China: The Case for Archipelagic Defense." *Foreign Affairs* 94, no. 2, (2015): 78.

Kristensen, Hans M., Matthew McKinzie, and Theodore A. Postol. "How US Nuclear Force Modernization Is Undermining Strategic Stability: The Burst-Height Compensating Super-Fuze." *Bulletin of the Atomic Scientists*, March 1, 2017. https://thebulletin.org/2017/03/how-us-nuclear-force-modernization-is-undermining-strategic-stability-the-burst-height-compensating-super-fuze/.

LaFeber, Walter. *The American Age: United States Foreign Policy at Home and Abroad: 1750 to the Present*. New York: Norton, 1994.

Laski, Harold J. "America-1947." *The Nation* 13 (1947): 641–644.

Layne, Christopher. "From Preponderance to Offshore Balancing: America's Future Grand Strategy." *International Security* 22, no. 1 (1997): 86–124.

——. *The Peace of Illusions: American Grand Strategy from 1940 to the Present*. Cornell University Press, 2007.

Lee, Matthew. "Pompeo, in Slovenia, Pushes 5G Security, Warns About China." *Associated Press*, 14 August, 2020. https://apnews.com/article/international-news-europe-eastern-europe-politics-slovenia-7764f3b6cb3820191068d798401fad92.

Leith, C. K. "Exploitation and World Progress." *Foreign Affairs* 6 (1927): 128.

——. "Mineral Resources and Peace." *Foreign Affairs* 16 (1937): 515–524.

——. *Minerals in the Peace Settlement*. Vol. 1. The Society, 1940.

Lenin, Vladimir Il'ich. *Imperialism: The Highest Stage of Capitalism*. Resistance Books, 1999.

Lewin, Arie Y., Martin Kenney, and Johann Peter Murmann. *China's Innovation Challenge: Overcoming the Middle-Income Trap.* Cambridge University Press, 2016.

Li, Yun. "Trump Says US Government Won't Do Business with Huawei, Not Ready to Make a Trade Deal with China." *CNBC,* August 9, 2019. https://www.cnbc.com /2019/08/09/trump-says-us-is-not-going-to-do-business-with-huawei-not-ready -to-make-a-trade-deal-with-china.html.

Liu, Xielin, Sylvia Schwaag Serger, Ulrike Tagscherer, and Amber Y. Chang. "Beyond Catch-up—Can a New Innovation Policy Help China Overcome the Middle Income Trap?" *Science and Public Policy* 44, no. 5 (2017): 656–669.

Louis, W. M. Roger, and Ronald Robinson. "The Imperialism of Decolonization." *The Journal of Imperial and Commonwealth History* 22, no. 3 (1994): 462–511.

Lovering, Thomas Seward. *Minerals in World Affairs.* Prentice-Hall, 1943.

Lundestad, Geir. "Empire by Invitation? The United States and Western Europe, 1945– 1952." *Journal of Peace Research* 23, no. 3 (1986): 263–277.

——. *The Rise and Decline of the American"Empire": Power and Its Limits in Comparative Perspective.* Oxford University Press, 2012.

Luxemburg, Rosa. *The Accumulation of Capital.* Routledge, 2015.

Mackinder, Halford John. *Democratic Ideals and Reality a Study in the Politics of Reconstruction.* Diane Publishing, 1942.

——. "The Geographical Pivot of History." The Geographical Society, 1904.

——. "The Round World and the Winning of the Peace." *Foreign Affairs* 21, no. 4 (1942): 595–605.

Seager II, Robert, and Doris D. Maguire, eds. *The Letters and Papers of Alfred Thayer Mahan* Vol. 2. Annapolis, MD: Naval Institute Press, 1975.

Mahan, Alfred Thayer. *The Influence of Sea Power upon History, 1660–1783.* Read Books Ltd., 2013.

——. *The Interest of America in Sea Power, Present and Future.* Little, Brown, 1898.

Mahbubani, Kishore. *Has China Won?: The Chinese Challenge to American Primacy.* Hachette UK, 2020.

Marshall, Jonathan. *To Have and Have Not: Southeast Asian Raw Materials and the Origins of the Pacific War.* University of California Press, 1995.

Mattis, Jim. "Summary of the 2018 National Defense Strategy of the United States of America." Washington, DC: Department of Defense, 2018.

McCormick, Thomas J. *America's Half-Century: United States Foreign Policy in the Cold War and After.* Johns Hopkins University Press, 1995.

——. "Insular Imperialism and the Open Door: The China Market and the Spanish-American War." *Pacific Historical Review* 32 (1963): 155.

McCoy, Alfred W. *In the Shadows of the American Century: The Rise and Decline of US Global Power.* Haymarket Books, 2017.

McMaster, Herbert R., and Gary D. Cohn. "America First Doesn't Mean America Alone." *Wall Street Journal,* May 30, 2017.

McNamara, Robert. "Draft Memorandum from Secretary of Defense McNamara to President Johnson." Washington National Records Center, RG 330, McNamara Files: FRC 71 A 3470, South Vietnam, Statements and Supporting Papers. Top Secret. November 3, 1965.

Mearsheimer, John J. "China's Unpeaceful Rise." *Current History* 105, no. 690 (2006): 160–162.

Medcalf, Rory, ed. *The Future of the Undersea Deterrent: A Global Survey*. ANU National Security College, 2020.

Mei, June. "Socioeconomic Origins of Emigration: Guangdong to California, 1850–1882." *Modern China* 5, no. 4 (1979): 463–501.

Miller, Marion. *Great Debates in American History, from the Debates in the British Parliament on the Colonial Stamp Act (1764–1765) to the Debates in Congress at the Close of the Taft Administration (1912–1913)*. Vol. 3. New York: Current Literature Pub. Co., 1913.

Monroe, James. "Message Received from the President of the United States." *Journal of the Senate of the United States of America* 13 (December 2, 1823).

Moody, Walton S., Walter S. Poole, and David A. Armstrong. "History of the Joint Chiefs of Staff: The Joint Chiefs of Staff and the First Indochina War, 1947–1954." Washington, DC: Joint Chiefs of Staff Joint History Office, 2004.

Morgenthau, Hans J. *United States Policy toward Asia. Hearings before the Subcommittee on the Far East and the Pacific of the Committee on Foreign Affairs*. 89th Congress House of Respresentatives, Second Session, January 25, 26, 27, and February 1, 2, 3, 1966.

Morrison, Wayne M. *China's Economic Rise: History, Trends, Challenges, and Implications for the United States*. Washington, DC: Congressional Research Service 2019.

Morton, Louis. "War Plan Orange: Evolution of a Strategy." *World Politics* 11, no. 2 (1959): 221–250.

Nathan, Andrew J. "China's Challenge." *Journal of Democracy* 26, no. 1 (2015): 156–170.

——. "China's Changing of the Guard: Authoritarian Resilience." In *Critical Readings on the Communist Party of China*. 4 Vols. Set, 86–99. Brill, 2017.

National Bureau of Statistics of China. China Statistical Yearbook, 2019. http://www.stats.gov.cn/tjsj/ndsj/2019/indexeh.htm.

National Development Reform Commission. "Vision and Actions on Jointly Building Silk Road Economic Belt and 21st-Century Maritime Silk Road." Ministry of Commerce of the People's Republic of China Ministry of Foreign Affairs, with State Council authorization, 2015. https://www.fmprc.gov.cn/eng/topics_665678/2015zt/xjpcxbayzlt2015nnh/201503/t20150328_705553.html#:~:text=The%20initiative%20to%20jointly%20build,spirit%20of%20open%20regional%20cooperation.

National Intelligence Council. *Global Trends 2030: Alternative Worlds*. Central Intelligence Agency, 2013.

NATO. "Brussels Summit Communiqué: Issued by the Heads of State and Government Participating in the Meeting of the North Atlantic Council in Brussels." June 14, 2021. https://www.nato.int/cps/en/natohq/news_185000.htm.

Navarro, Peter. "Donald Trump Is Standing Up for American Interests." *Financial Times*, April 9, 2018.

Nelson, Anna K. "Theodore Roosevelt, the Navy, and the War with Spain." In *Theodore Roosevelt, the US Navy, and the Spanish-American War*, 1–5. Springer, 2001.

Neumann, William L. "Franklin Delano Roosevelt: A Disciple of Admiral Mahan." *United States Naval Institute Proceedings* 78 (1952): 713–14.

New York Herald. "Next Session of Congress—President's Message—Foreign Policy of

the Government." September 15, 1845. https://chroniclingamerica.loc.gov/lccn
/sn83030313/1845-09-15/ed-1/seq-2/.

New York Times. "End of the China War." August 27, 1858.

New York Times. "Our Relations with China." August 20, 1858.

New York Times. "Summary of Kissinger Speech to U.S. Ambassadors." April 7, 1976, 16.

New York Times. "What Is the 'Open Door'?" January 26, 1899.

Nikkei Asian Review. "China Makes Gains against US in High-Tech Markets." July 9,
2019. https://asia.nikkei.com/Business/Business-trends/China-makes-gains-against
-US-in-high-tech-markets2.

Nixon, Richard M. "Asia after Viet Nam." *Foreign Affairs* 46, no. 1 (1967): 111–125.

———. "First Annual Report to the Congress on United States Foreign Policy for
the 1970's." The American Presidency Project, February 18, 1970. https://www
.presidency.ucsb.edu/documents/first-annual-report-the-congress-united-states
-foreign-policy-for-the-1970s.

———. "Informal Remarks in Guam with Newsmen." The American Presidency Project,
July 25, 1969. https://www.presidency.ucsb.edu/documents/informal-remarks
-guam-with-newsmen.

Nye Jr., Joseph S. "The Case for Deep Engagement." *Foreign Affairs* 74, no. 4 (1995):
90–102.

O'Brien, Patrick K., and Stanley L. Engerman. "Exports and the Growth of the British
Economy from the Glorious Revolution to the Peace of Amiens." In *Slavery and the
Rise of the Atlantic System*, edited by Barbara Solow, 177–209. Cambridge University
Press, 1991.

O'Rourke, Ronald. "Renewed Great Power Competition: Implications for Defense—
Issues for Congress." Washington, DC: Congressional Research Service, 2020.

O'Sullivan, John. "Annexation." *United States Magazine and Democratic Review* 17, no. 1
(1845): 5–10.

Obama, Barack. "National Security Strategy." Executive Office of the President, 2015.

———. "Remarks by President Barack Obama at Suntory Hall." *The White House Office
of the Press Secretary* 14 (2009).

———. "Remarks by President Obama to the Australian Parliament." *Parliament House,
Canberra, Australia* 17 (2011).

Obermeyer, Ziad, Christopher J. L. Murray, and Emmanuela Gakidou. "Fifty Years
of Violent War Deaths from Vietnam to Bosnia: Analysis of Data from the World
Health Survey Programme." *British Medical Journal* 336, no. 7659 (2008): 1482–
1486.

Odell, Rachel Esplin, et al. "Active Denial: A Roadmap to a More Effective, Stabilizing,
and Sustainable U.S. Defense Strategy in Asia." *Quincy Report* (June 2022).

OECD. "The Belt and Road Initiative in the Global Trade, Investment and Finance
Landscape." In *OECD Business and Finance Outlook*. Paris: OECD, 2018.

———. "Gross Domestic Spending on R&D (Indicator)." OECD Data 2021. https://data
.oecd.org/rd/gross-domestic-spending-on-r-d.htm.

Pearson, Charles Henry. *National Life and Character: A Forecast*. Macmillan and Company, 1894.

Pehrson, Elmer W. "The Axis and Strategic Minerals." *Engineering and Mining Journal*
143, no. 5 (1942): 42.

Pei, Minxin. *China's Crony Capitalism*. Harvard University Press, 2016.

———. *China's Trapped Transition*. Harvard University Press, 2006.

Pelz, Stephen. "John F. Kennedy's 1961 Vietnam War Decisions." *Journal of Strategic Studies* 4, no. 4 (1981): 356–385.

Pettyjohn, Stacie L. *US Global Defense Posture, 1783–2011*. RAND Corporation, 2012.

Pierson, William Whatley. "The Political Influences of an Interoceanic Canal, 1826–1926." *The Hispanic American Historical Review* 6, no. 4 (1926): 205–231.

Pillsbury, Michael. *The Hundred-Year Marathon: China's Secret Strategy to Replace America as the Global Superpower*. Henry Holt and Company, 2015.

Platt, Stephen R. *Autumn in the Heavenly Kingdom: China, the West, and the Epic Story of the Taiping Civil War*. Knopf, 2012.

Plutarch. *Plutarch's Lives*. Translated by Bernadotte Perrin. New York: Macmillan Company, 1914.

Polanyi, Karl. *The Great Transformation*. New York: Farrar & Rinehart, 1944.

Polk, James Knox. *Inaugural Address, March 4, 1845*. Tennessee Presidents Trust, 1993.

Pomeranz, Kenneth. *The Great Divergence: China, Europe, and the Making of the Modern World Economy*. Princeton University Press, 2000.

Pompeo, Michael R. "Announcing the Expansion of the Clean Network to Safeguard America's Assets." News release, August 5, 2020. https://2017-2021.state.gov /announcing-the-expansion-of-the-clean-network-to-safeguard-americas-assets /index.html.

Posen, Barry R. "Command of the Commons: The Military Foundation of US Hegemony." *International Security* 28, no. 1 (2003): 5–46.

Powell, Colin L. "US Forces: Challenges Ahead." *Foreign Affairs* 71, no. 5 (1992): 32–45.

Powell, Naomi. "Tethering Canada, Containing China: Will USMCA Boost Trump's Efforts to Isolate Beijing?" *Financial Post*, October 4, 2018. https://financialpost .com/news/economy/tethering-canada-containing-china-will-usmca-boost-trumps -efforts-to-isolate-beijing.

Price, Carter C., and Kathryn A. Edwards. "Trends in Income from 1975 to 2018." RAND Corporation, 2020. https://www.rand.org/pubs/working_papers/WRA516 -1.html.

Odell, Rachel Esplin et al. "Active Denial: A Roadmap to a More Effective, Stabilizing, and Sustainable U.S. Defense Strategy in Asia." *Quincy Report* (June 2022).

Ratcliffe, John. "China Is National Security Threat No. 1." *Wall Street Journal*, December 3, 2020. https://www.wsj.com/articles/china-is-national-security-threat-no-1 -11607019599.

Ravenal, Earl C. "The Nixon Doctrine and Our Asian Commitments." *Foreign Affairs* 49, no. 2 (1971): 201–217.

Raymond, H. J. "California." *The American Review: a Whig Journal of Politics, Literature, Art, And Science* 3 (January 1846).

Reagan, Ronald. "National Security Decision Directive Number 32." Washington, DC, May 20, 1982. https://irp.fas.org/offdocs/nsdd/23-1618t.gif.

Remer, Charles Frederick. *Foreign Investment in China*. New York: Macmillan Company, 1933.

Roosevelt, Franklin D. "Address at University of Virginia." June 10, 1940. Online by

Gerhard Peters and John T. Woolley, The American Presidency Project. https://www.presidency.ucsb.edu/node/209705.

Roosevelt, Theodore. "The Influence of Sea Power upon History. 1660–1783. By A. T. Mahan." *Political Science Quarterly* 9, no. 1 (1894): 171–173.

——. "The Law of Civilisation and Decay." *The Forum* 12 (January 1987): 575.

——. "National Life and Character." *The Sewanee Review* 2, no. 3 (1894): 353–376.

——. "The Roosevelt Corollary to the Monroe Doctrine." Paper presented at the excerpt from president's annual message to Congress. The White House, 1904.

——. "State of the Union Address, December 3, 1901." *State of the Union.* 1901. https://history.state.gov/historicaldocuments/frus1901/message-of-the-president.

——. *The Strenuous Life.* New York: G. P. Putnam's, 1901.

Ruggie, John Gerard. "International Regimes, Transactions, and Change: Embedded Liberalism in the Postwar Economic Order." *International Organization* 36, no. 2 (1982): 379–415.

Sahlins, Marshall. "Cosmologies of Capitalism: The Trans-Pacific Sector of 'the World System.'" In *Culture/Power/History: A Reader in Contemporary Social Theory*, edited by Nicholas B. Dirks and Geoff Eley, 412–455. Princeton University Press, 1994.

Salavrakos, Ioannis-Dionysios. "The Defence Industry as an Explanatory Factor of the German Defeat during World War I: Lessons for Future Conflicts." *International Journal of History and Philosophical Research* 2, no. 1 (2014): 1–34.

Sandars, Christopher T. *America's Overseas Garrisons: The Leasehold Empire.* Oxford University Press on Demand, 2000.

Sanger, David E., and Maggie Haberman. "Highlights from Our Interview with Donald Trump on Foreign Policy." *New York Times*, March 26 2016. https://www.nytimes.com/2016/03/27/us/politics/donald-trump-interview-highlights.html.

Saxton, Alexander. *The Indispensable Enemy: Labor and the Anti-Chinese Movement in California.* University of California Press, 1995.

Schaller, Michael. *The American Occupation of Japan: The Origins of the Cold War in Asia.* Oxford University Press, 1985.

Scharre, Paul. "Decoupling Wastes U.S. Leverage on China." *Foreign Policy*, January 13, 2023. https://foreignpolicy.com/2023/01/13/china-decoupling-chips-america/?tpcc=onboarding_trending.

Schlesinger, Arthur M. *The Bitter Heritage: Vietnam and American Democracy, 1941–1968.* Fawcett Publications, 1968.

Schofield, Frank Herman. "Some Effects of the Washington Conference on American Naval Strategy." Lecture delivered at Army War College, Washington, DC, Barracks. September 22, 1923. 12th Naval District, Record Group 181 Commandant, US National Archives San Bruno, 270-3, box 4.

Schroeder, John H. *Shaping a Maritime Empire: The Commercial and Diplomatic Role of the American Navy, 1829–1861.* Vol. 48. Praeger Pub Text, 1985.

Schumpeter, Joseph Alois. *Imperialism and Social Classes: Two Essays.* Vol. 4. Ludwig von Mises Institute, 1955.

Schurz, Carl. "Manifest Destiny." *Harper's New Monthly Magazine* 87, no. 521 (1893): 737–746.

Seib, Gerald F. "Obama Presses Case for Asia Trade Deal, Warns Failure Would Benefit China." *Wall Street Journal*, April 27, 2015.

Shambaugh, David. "Assessing the US 'Pivot' to Asia." *Strategic Studies Quarterly* 7, no. 2 (2013): 10–19.

——. "The Coming Chinese Crackup." *Wall Street Journal*, March 6, 2015, 382.

Sharif, Naubahar. "China as the World's Technology Leader in the 21st Century: Dream or Reality?" HKUST Institute for Emerging Market Studies, Thought Leadership Brief Series. 2016. https://ideas.repec.org/p/hku/briefs/201611.html.

Shih, Gerry. "Trump's New North American Trade Deal Also Aimed at Bigger Target: China." *Washington Post*, October 3, 2018.

Shoup, Laurence H., and William Minter. *Imperial Brain Trust: The Council on Foreign Relations and United States Foreign Policy*. New York: Monthly Review Press, 2004.

Slezak, Michael. "Huawei Banned from 5G Mobile Infrastructure Rollout in Australia." *ABC News*, 23 August, 2018.

Smith, Adam. *The Wealth of Nations: An Inquiry into the Nature and Causes of the Wealth of Nations*. Harriman House Limited, 2010.

Smith, Charles Forster. *Thucydides: History of the Peloponnesian War*. Vol. 108. W. Heinemann, 1962.

Special ad hoc Committee and State-War-Navy Coordinating Committee. "(1947) Report of Committee Meeting, 21 April." *Foreign Relations of the United States* 3: 164–165.

Spence, Jonathan D. *Chinese Roundabout: Essays in History and Culture*. Norton, 1993.

Spykman, Nicholas John. *America's Strategy in World Politics: The United States and the Balance of Power*. Transaction Publishers, 1942.

——. *Geography of the Peace*. New York: Harcourt, Brace and Company, 1944.

Srinivasan, Bhu. *Americana: A 400-Year History of American Capitalism*. Penguin, 2017.

Staley, Eugene. *War and the Private Investor: A Study in the Relations of International Politics and International Private Investment*. Doubleday, Doran & Company, 1935.

Sullivan, Mark P., and Thomas Lum. "China's Engagement with Latin America and the Caribbean." Congressional Research Service, 2021.

Suskind, Ron. "Faith, Certainty and the Presidency of George W. Bush." *New York Times*, October 17, 2004, 17.

Thayer, William Roscoe, and John Hay. *The Life and Letters of John Hay*. Vol. 2. Houghton Mifflin, 1915.

Tooze, Adam. *The Deluge: The Great War, America and the Remaking of the Global Order, 1916–1931*. Penguin Group USA, 2015.

Torr, Dona. *Marx on China, 1853–1860: Articles from the New York Daily Tribune*. London: Lawrence and Wishart, 1951.

Toynbee, Arnold. *The New Europe: Some Essays in Reconstruction*. London and Toronto: J. M. Dent and Sons Limited, 1915.

Tregenza, John. *Professor of Democracy: The Life of Charles Henry Pearson, 1830–1894, Oxford Don and Australian Radical*. Melbourne University, 1968.

Truman, Harry S. "Address on Foreign Economic Policy, Delivered at Baylor University." March 6, 1947. https://www.trumanlibrary.gov/library/public-papers/52 /address-foreign-economic-policy-delivered-baylor-university.

——. "Special Message to the Congress on Greece and Turkey: The Truman Doctrine."

March 12, 1947. https://quod.lib.umich.edu/p/ppotpus/4728447.1947.001?rgn
=main;view=fulltext.

Trump, Donald J. Executive Order 13817: A Federal Strategy to Ensure Secure and
Reliable Supplies of Critical Minerals. The White House. December 20, 2017.
https://www.federalregister.gov/documents/2017/12/26/2017-27899/a-federal
-strategy-to-ensure-secure-and-reliable-supplies-of-critical-minerals.

———. Executive Order 13953: Addressing the Threat to the Domestic Supply Chain
from Reliance on Critical Minerals from Foreign Adversaries. The White House.
September 30, 2020. https://trumpwhitehouse.archives.gov/presidential-actions
/executive-order-addressing-threat-domestic-supply-chain-reliance-critical
-minerals-foreign-adversaries/.

———. "Inaugural Address: Remarks of President Donald J. Trump—as Prepared for
Delivery." Washington, DC, January 20, 2017. https://trumpwhitehouse.archives
.gov/briefings-statements/the-inaugural-address/.

———. "National Security Strategy of the United States of America." Executive Office of
the President. Washington, DC, 2017.

———. "Remarks by President Trump at the 2020 Salute to America." News release,
July 4, 2020. https://ge.usembassy.gov/remarks-by-president-trump-at-the-2020
-salute-to-america-july-4/.

Turner, Frederick Jackson. "The Problem of the West." *The Atlantic Monthly*, September 1896.

———. "The Significance of the Frontier in American History." *Annual Report of the
American Historical Association*. 1893.

Turse, Nick. "The U.S. Military's Best Kept Secret." *The Nation*, November 17, 2015.
https://www.thenation.com/article/the-us-militarys-best-kept-secret/.

Turse, Nick, Sam Mednick, and Amanda Sperber. "Exclusive: Inside the Secret World
of US Commandos in Africa." *Globe and Mail*, August 11, 2020.

Tyler, John. "The Tyler Doctrine." Special Message to Congress. December 30, 1842. In
*The Addresses and Messages of the Presidents of the United States, Inaugural, Annual,
and Special, from 1789 to 1849*. Vol. 2, 1316–1317. New York: Edward Walker, 1849.

Tyrrell, Ian, and Jay Sexton. *Empire's Twin: US Anti-Imperialism from the Founding Era
to the Age of Terrorism*. Cornell University Press, 2015.

UN News. "In 'World of Disquiet,' UN Must Deliver for the People, Guterres Tells
General Assembly." September 24, 2019.

US Bureau of Industry and Security. "Commerce Implements New Export Controls
on Advanced Computing and Semiconductor Manufacturing Items to the People's
Republic of China (PRC)." October 7, 2022. https://www.bis.doc.gov/index.php
/documents/about-bis/newsroom/press-releases/3158-2022-10-07-bis-press
-release-advanced-computing-and-semiconductor-manufacturing-controls-final
/file.

US Census Bureau. *Census of the United States*. 1850, 1860, 1890.

———. "The Progress of the Nation." In *Census of the United States*. 1890.

———. "US International Trade Data: Trade in Goods with Asia." https://www.census
.gov/foreign-trade/balance/c0016.html.

———. "US International Trade Data: Trade in Goods with China." https://www.census
.gov/foreign-trade/balance/c5700.html.

US Congress. "Report of the Joint Special Committee to Investigate Chinese Immigra-
tion." Washington, DC: Government Printing Office, February 27, 1877.
US Congressional Globe. June 3, 1846.
——. "31st Cong., 1st Sess." March 11, 1850.
——. "32d Cong., 2d Sess." 1853.
——. "Pacific Railroad." 1590, April 9, 1862.
US Continental Congress. "The Committee, Consisting of Mr. Duane, Mr. Peters, Mr.
Carrol I. E. Carroll, Mr. Hawkins and Mr. Lee, to Whom Were Referred a Report
on Indian Affairs, Read in Congress on the 21st of April Last, a Letter from General
Schuyler . . . With Messages to and from Certain Hostile Indians on the Subject
of Peace . . . Submit the Following Detail of Facts and Resolutions." Philadelphia:
David C. Claypoole, 1783. https://www.loc.gov/item/90898080/.
US Department of Commerce. "Balance of Payments and Direct Investment Position
Data: US-China." Edited by Bureau of Economic Analysis, 2020. https://apps.bea
.gov/iTable/iTable.cfm?ReqID=2&step=1#reqid=2&step=10&isuri=1&202=1&203
=30&204=10&205=1,2&200=1&201=1&207=56,55,52,49,48,43,42,41,40,39,38,37,36,35
,34,33,32,31&208=2&209=1.
US Department of Defense. *Air-Sea Battle: Service Collaboration to Address Anti-Access
& Area Denial Challenges.* Air-Sea Battle Office, 2013.
——. "Base Structure Report—Fiscal Year 2018 Baseline Summary." 2018. https://www
.acq.osd.mil/eie/Downloads/BSI/Base%20Structure%20Report%20FY18.pdf.
——. "Indo-Pacific Strategy Report: Preparedness, Partnership, and Promoting a Net-
worked Region." Washington, DC: US Department of Defense, 2019.
——. "Military and Security Developments Involving the People's Republic of China
2011." Washington DC: US Department of Defense, 2011.
——. "Report to Congress: Rare Earth Materials in Defense Applications." March 2012.
https://www.hsdl.org/?abstract&did=704803.
US Department of Energy. "Critical Materials Strategy." Appendix A, 111. Washington,
DC, 2010. http://energy.gov/sites/prod/files/piprod/documents/ cms_dec_17_full
_web.pdf.
US Department of State, ed. "Executive Documents Printed by Order of the House of
Representatives, during the Third Session of the Fortieth Congress, 1868–69."
US Department of the Interior. "Final List of Critical Minerals." Washington, DC: Fed-
eral Register, May 18, 2018.
US Geological Survey. "Mineral Commodities Summary: Rare Earths." 132–133. 2020.
https://pubs.er.usgs.gov/publication/mcs2020.
——. "Mineral Commodity Summaries." 2019. https://doi.org/10.3133/70202434.
US House Congressional Record. April 25, 1939.
——. "China and Japan." 1618. March 9, 1878.
——. "Chinese Immigration." March 15, 1882.
——. "Congressional Debate on the Construction of Naval Vessels." March 12, 1940.
US Joint Chiefs of Staff. "Joint Vision 2010." Washington, DC: US Government Printing
Office, June 1996.
US National Security Council. "Two Versions of a Draft on US National Strategy Sug-
gest: US Needs to Counter Soviet Influence over the Oil Producing States in the
Persian Gulf Region; and Communist Persuasion Could Undermine the Viability of

NATO and Cause Economic Disruptions in Europe, Japan and the US." US Declassified Documents Online, December 20, 1980. Memo. https://tinyurl.com/2p8v2knx.

——. "U.S. Plan of Action to Curb the Threat of Chinese Communist Infiltration in Southeast Asia." US Declassified Documents Online. September 25, 1959. http://tinyurl.galegroup.com/tinyurl/6nFpZ3.

——. "United States Objectives and Programs for National Security." April 14, 1950.

US Senate. *Trade Agreements Extension: Hearings before the Committee on Finance, United States Senate, Eighty-Fourth Congress, First Session, on H. R. 1.* 1955.

US Senate Congressional Record. "Chinese Immigration." February 14, 1879.

——. "Legislative Proposals Relating to the War in Southeast Asia." 92nd Congress, First Session. April 21, 1971.

Utley, Robert M. *The Indian Frontier 1846–1890.* University of New Mexico Press, 2003.

Van Apeldoorn, Bastiaan, and Naná De Graaff. *American Grand Strategy and Corporate Elite Networks: The Open Door since the End of the Cold War.* Routledge, 2015.

van Tol, Jan, Mark Gunzinger, Andrew Krepinevich, and Jim Thomas. "Airsea Battle: A Point-of-Departure Operational Concept." Washington, DC: Center for Strategic and Budgetary Assessments, 2010.

Vine, David. *Base Nation: How US Military Bases Abroad Harm America and the World.* Metropolitan Books, 2015.

Vogl, Joseph. *The Ascendancy of Finance.* John Wiley & Sons, 2017.

Washington Post. "Transcript: President Bush Addresses the Nation." September 20, 2001. https://www.washingtonpost.com/wp-srv/nation/specials/attacked/transcripts/bushaddress_092001.html.

Weber, Max. *Economy and Society: An Outline of Interpretive Sociology.* Vol. 1. University of California Press, 1978.

Weber, Max, David S. Owen, and Tracy B. Strong. *The Vocation Lectures.* Hackett Publishing, 2004.

Weigley, Russell Frank. *The American Way of War: A History of United States Military Strategy and Policy.* Indiana University Press, 1977.

Weinberg, Albert Katz. *Manifest Destiny a Study of Nationalist Expansionism in American History.* Chicago: Quadrangle Books, 1935.

White House. "David Aaron and Michel Oksenberg Provide Vice President Walter Mondale with a List of U.S. Objectives for Mondale's Trip to China." US Declassified Documents Online, August 18, 1979. Memo. https://tinyurl.com/4ca8t3zd.

——. Building Resilient Supply Chains, Revitalizing American Manufacturing, and Fostering Broad-Based Growth: 100-Day Reviews under Executive Order 14017. June 2021. 117th Congress, First Session, Supply Chain Security and Resilience Act, H. R. 5505 (2021).

——. "Fact Sheet: CHIPS and Science Act Will Lower Costs, Create Jobs, Strengthen Supply Chains, and Counter China." August 9, 2022. https://www.whitehouse.gov/briefing-room/statements-releases/2022/08/09/fact-sheet-chips-and-science-act-will-lower-costs-create-jobs-strengthen-supply-chains-and-counter-china/.

——. "Joint Statement from President Donald J. Trump and Prime Minister Shinzo Abe." Washington, DC, February 10, 2017.

——. "President Biden and G7 Leaders Launch Build Back Better World (B3W) Partnership." June 12, 2021. https://www.whitehouse.gov/briefing-room/statements

-releases/2021/06/12/fact-sheet-president-biden-and-g7-leaders-launch-build
-back-better-world-b3w-partnership/.

Williams, Alfred. *The Inter-Oceanic Canal and the Monroe Doctrine*. GP Putnam's Sons,
1880.

Williams, William Appleman. *Empire as a Way of Life: An Essay on the Causes and
Character of America's Present Predicament, along with a Few Thoughts about an
Alternative*. New York: Oxford Unviersity Press, 1980.

———. "The Legend of Isolationism in the 1920's." *Science & Society* (1954): 1–20.

———. *The Roots of the Modern American Empire: A Study of the Growth and Shaping of
Social Consciousness in a Marketplace Society*. Random House, 1969.

———. *The Tragedy of American Diplomacy*. Norton, 1988.

Williams, Zachary. "The Plan's Renhai-Class Cruiser and the Future of Anti-Access
and Area Denial." *The Diplomat*, April 29, 2020. https://thediplomat.com/2020/04
/the-plans-renhai-class-cruiser-and-the-future-of-anti-access-and-area-denial/.

Wilson, Woodrow. "Message Regarding Tariff Duties." April 8, 1913. https://millercenter
.org/the-presidency/presidential-speeches/april-8-1913-message-regarding-tariff
-duties.

Wilson, Woodrow, and Ollie M. James. *Speech of Governor Wilson Accepting the Democratic Nomination for President of the United States*. 62nd Congress, Second Session,
Senate. Doc. 903. Washington, DC: Government Printing Office, 1912.

Winters, Jeffrey A. *Oligarchy*. Cambridge University Press, 2011.

Woetzel, Jonathan. "China and the World: Inside the Dynamics of a Changing Relationship." McKinsey Global Institute, July 1, 2019, 2. https://www.mckinsey.com
/featured-insights/china/china-and-the-world-inside-the-dynamics-of-a-changing
-relationship.

Wolfowitz, Paul. "Defense Planning Guidance, FY 1994–1999 (Declassified 2008)."
Washington, DC: National Security Council, April 16, 1992.

Woo, Wing Thye. "China Meets the Middle-Income Trap: The Large Potholes in the
Road to Catching-Up." *Journal of Chinese Economic and Business Studies* 10, no. 4
(2012): 313–336.

Woodrow Wilson Foundation, and William Yandell Elliot. *The Political Economy of
American Foreign Policy*. Holt, 1955.

World Bank. "China at a Glance." https://www.worldbank.org/en/country/china/test
pagecheck#:~:text=China%20At%2DA%2DGlance&text=GDP%20growth%20has
%20averaged%20nearly,MDGs)%20by%20201... (page discontinued).

———. "China Trade Statistics: Exports, Imports, Products, Tariffs, GDP and Related
Development Indicator." https://wits.worldbank.org/CountryProfile/en/CHN.

Wuthnow, Joel. "US 'Minilateralism' in Asia and China's Responses: A New Security
Dilemma?" *Journal of Contemporary China* 28, no. 115 (2019): 133–150.

Xuetong, Yan. "Bipolar Rivalry in the Early Digital Age." *The Chinese Journal of International Politics* 13, no. 3 (2020): 313–41.

Zepf, Volker. "An Overview of the Usefulness and Strategic Value of Rare Earth Metals."
In *Rare Earths Industry*, 3–17. Elsevier, 2016.

Zoellick, Robert B. "Whither China: From Membership to Responsibility?" Remarks to
National Committee on U.S.-China Relations. New York City, September 21, 2005.
https://2001-2009.state.gov/s/d/former/zoellick/rem/53682.htm.